What In The World Is Real?

Challenging the superficial in today's world

Communication Institute
P.O. Box 612
Champaign, IL 61820

Communication Institute is a non-profit Christian organization committed to communicating God's truth through a variety of ministries. Communication Institute is responsible for organizing the 1982 L'Abri Seminars.

The publisher would like to express appreciation for permission to quote from the following:

"Creed" and "Exclusive Pictures" from *Nice and Nasty* by Steve Turner. Copyright 1980 from Razor Books/Marshall, Morgan & Scott, LTD., by permission from Steve Turner.

Excerpt from *A World Split Apart*, Aleksander I. Solzhenitzyn © Copyright 1978 by Aleksander I. Solzhenitzyn. English language translation copyright © 1979 by Harper and Row, Publishers, Inc., by permission of the publisher.

Daniel J. Boorstin, from *The Image*. Copyright © 1961 Daniel J. Boorstin. Reprinted with the permission of Atheneum Publishers. All rights reserved.

Excerpt from "Cambodia: An Experiment in Genocide," TIME, July 31, 1978. Copyright © 1978 Time, Inc. All rights reserved. Used by permission.

To Tim, Betsy, and Robin
who have answered the question
"What in the world is real?"
with their lives

Acknowledgements

Where to begin? It's a frustrating request, in one sense, to be asked to write an "acknowledgements" page knowing that it calls for brevity. We, at the Communication Institute realize that a lot of names of special people will go unmentioned. People's names that, working together as a staff, we've come to recognize as having been influential in each of our lives through their unconditional love, support, and commitment to us. It is these people who will not be recognized in written form. Regardless, we trust you know who you are and that you know we appreciate you. Thanks!

We will, however, attempt to say "Thanks" in written form to a small handful of people who have played a large part in the actual mechanics of this book:

To Becky Roe, who has given her time, talent and creativity as a graphic designer to the cover of this workbook, as well as other seminar material;

To Brian Heller, our "legal-ist," whose professional help allowed us to meet the requirements of the IRS and Federal and State Governments (in triplicate).

To Steve Hawk, who helped with thoughtful discussion questions;

To Mark Fackler, who, along with helping with the discussion questions, spent a lot of hours editing, outlining, and providing much needed expertise in the area of communication;

To Jennifer Follis, who did an excellent job in proofing final copy; and Joyce Mast-Boldrey, who, despite a very busy schedule, also found time to do some editing;

To Helen Kauffman, who has proved to be instrumental in refining the workbook down to its final form;

To Lisa Sussmann, Bruce Boyd, Sharon Monday, and Megan Kelly — our office staff — who not only put in a lot of extra time and energy into making these seminars possible, but most meaningful of all, gave of themselves to us.

And also to our Board of Directors: Tom Drake, Rob Masters, Scott Brizius, and Dave Bryne, who believed in us, prayed with and for us, and encouraged us;

Lastly, a warm thank you and recognition go to Ranald Macaulay and Jerram Barrs. Two and a half years ago they provided the catalyst for this project through their interaction with a young man who is now a member of Communication Institute. It was through many intense discussions that this individual came to see in their lives and understand through their words God's truth more fully.

We hope through this book and this seminar series that Jesus Christ will be glorified.

Contents

Introduction

Imagine an old mystery movie set in a thick, London fog. The hero is slowly walking down the cobblestone street peering ahead. He moves cautiously and fearfully for the fog is resting so heavily on the streets that both clarity and direction are lost. He is not sure where he is or where he should go. This is an accurate picture of today's society.

As we look back we see the causes of our present situation. The political idealism of the 60's has blurred into Vietnam and Watergate. A deep sense of cynicism rests in people's minds eliminating past values and standards. Individuals have seen the poverty of political idealism, the lack of integrity in individuals and have a greater understanding of world wide crises and problems. This greater awareness brings with it a lack of hope for the world or even concern for others. In the aftermath of eliminating our common value system, built on duty, integrity and compassion, a new system has not been cultivated. Individuals are left drifting by themselves in that misty fog, not knowing where they're going or even where they are.

Even so, this very problem of cloudiness and lostness is held up as the solution. In today's language it is called freedom. Freedom provides opportunity to move yet gives no direction. Individuals lose the sense of clearness and distinction of purpose while at the same time they become lost and insecure in a world of whirling value systems.

We live in a society where opinion reigns supreme, conviction as to

Truth is silent or, if present, is seen with the relevance of a chanting Hare Krishna follower. Our society has cultivated a vacuum of cynicism, mediocrity and apathy. As we have already mentioned, the empty Me-ism our culture advocates has proved to be bankrupt in terms of providing satisfactory answers and direction. Some individuals realize the inadequacy and ineffectiveness of their view of the world and hunt for a new answer. Yet in their search for an answer, many individuals often are more concerned with justifying their lifestyle than sincerely seeking what is true. We live in a smorgasbord of world view options each promising greater pleasure and satisfaction. But the question of TRUTH is disregarded as individuals choose the path of least resistance in their search, pursuing fulfillment over truth.

Thus, rarely is God considered as the solution to man's dilemma, more commonly as a part of the problem. There is a certain attitude of familiarity which surfaces when Christianity is mentioned. It is that same familiarity of the second cousin we saw two years ago at Christmas. This sense of familiarity in reality brings with it a veil of ignorance.

Sadly the Christian world has been deeply affected and influenced by our society. The superficial orientation of our culture has penetrated our Christian community. This is clearly seen in an over-emphasis on techniques, pat answers, interest in appearances and a lack of depth in individual's lives. We are losing the ability to distinguish between the light and the dark, leaving a dull muddled gray. With Christianity's popularity there has come a corresponding lack of power. We have made room for complacency in the Christian life by defining it in such a limited way, with so few responsibilities attached that few individuals feel uncomfortable with it. Christianity has become America's most popular spectator sport.

To our situation, we hear the repeating cry or muttered sigh, *What in the World is Real?* It is this pointed question which led to a series of L'Abri Seminars being planned for the fall of 1982 along with the production of this book. Our responsibility as Christians is to challenge what is not real and true in our society with what is true. It is our hope that this book can further this outreach of God's Truth. Each of these articles ask *What in the World is Real?* to a new topic exposing falsehoods and clarifying truths.

I encourage you to read, study, and discuss the ideas that are within this book with one admonition: TRUTH DEMANDS A RESPONSE! You cannot leave these pages uncommitted, for in being complacent you declare your position. There is a vast difference between the individual who seeks to know and the individual who seeks to know so that he might do and be. One is a collector of facts, the other a searcher of truth. Sincerity is the difference. In contrast to today's fog, a clarity needs to be seen and a call to action needs to be heard. Christian, come before the living God and pray, then get up and roll up your sleeves!

Greg Pritchard
Director
Communication Institute

L'Abri, L'Abri Seminars and this Workbook

L'Abri

L'Abri is a french word meaning "shelter." The first L'Abri community was established in Switzerland by Francis and Edith Schaeffer. A Christian theologian/philosopher, Francis Schaeffer has authored, along with his wife, Edith, a number of books about the reality of God and His involvement in the lives of individuals. Each of the four L'Abri communities (England, Switzerland, U.S., and Netherlands) serves as a study center whereby individuals can seek honest answers to honest questions.

L'Abri's desire is to provide a greater understanding of Truth, and therefore, a deeper trust in God. This desire is based on the conviction that the truth of the Bible is 1) authored by God, 2) relevant, and 3) objectively true for all people. In other words, true for the business of everyday life itself.

L'Abri Seminars

As a continuation of L'Abri's ministry, a series of L'Abri Seminars have been planned in 20 cities throughout the United States for Fall, 1982.

When asked in a recent interview how he viewed the relationship between the L'Abri seminars and the original L'Abri community ministry, Francis Schaeffer answered, ". . . because everyone cannot come to the L'Abri branches . . . conferences of this kind are an opportunity for people to share in what L'Abri is saying and how the Lord is using it in their locality . . ., so as I see it, they are not two things, but one in an extension of the other." He went on to say that, "It is our hope and prayer that these seminars will at least attempt to present Christianity in all its richness."

As a staff at Communication Institute, it is our hope that these speeches will not be seen only as ideas, but rather, as catalysts of truth for individuals' lives. As a result, it is our intent that individuals will come to a greater clarity in their understanding of and trust in the living God. This will be accomplished through the growth of deeper convictions based on Biblical truths, and lived out in day-to-day situations.

The Workbook as an Effective Tool

Seminars and conferences can be invaluable as times of refreshment, enlightenment and, as mentioned earlier, catalysts of new life. Yet at the same time, seminars and conferences can have a negative effect unless they are clearly relevant to one's everyday life.

The speeches enclosed are a compilation of most of the talks presented at the seminars by the participating L'Abri staff. This "workbook" has been provided as a tool to help you "work" through the material presented at each site. We trust you will mark these pages, take notes, meditate on and grapple with what is being discussed and what relevance God's truth has for all our lives.

Questions have been provided at the end of each speech to allow for further discussion as to how to initiate and integrate these truths. These can be used through a variety of avenues such as discussion groups, Sunday School classes, personal study, small groups, Christian colleges, seminaries, and study centers.

Additional Copies

Additional copies can be ordered through Communication Institute, P.O. Box 612, Champaign, IL 61820, for $5.95 each. If you desire to study this book but cannot afford to purchase a copy, write us and a copy will be sent to you free. A leader's guide for the workbook is also available at minimal cost upon request. Most of the talks appearing in this workbook are available on cassette tape. These cassettes may be purchased from Communication Institute at $4.25 each. However as with the workbook, if you cannot afford to purchase them, please write us and (specified) tapes will be sent to you free of charge.

Jerram Barrs

Jerram Barrs was born in England. He studied English literature and language at the University of Manchester. While there, Jerram came in contact with Christianity in a way he had never before experienced. The Christians he met were loving people offering answers to life's basic questions. These individuals gave Jerram his first exposure to the Schaeffers and their L'Abri ministry. Jerram became a Christian in his final year at college. After graduating with honors, he traveled to Switzerland to visit L'Abri where he became a worker. During his stay, he married Vicki, who was also working at L'Abri.

After a year there, Jerram moved to the U.S. and entered Covenant Seminary in St. Louis. He graduated magna cum laude with a Masters of Divinity in 1971. Returning to England, Jerram and Vicki joined Ranald and Susan Macaulay on staff at the Greatham L'Abri where they have continued to serve to the present time.

Jerram co-authored *Being Human* with Ranald Macaulay and he has recently finished a book on authority and freedom in the church. He is currently doing some writing on why one should be a Christian and on a Christian's attitude to government.

In addition to his involvement with L'Abri, Jerram serves as an elder, preaching and teaching regularly, in a Presbyterian church which he helped found. He and Vicki have three sons.

"Christianity declares . . . that the order, diversity, the intricate interdependence and beauty of the natural world have been created by the living and self-existent God . . ."

Christianity True to the Way Things Are

Jerram Barrs

Christianity claims that the Bible explains the world in which we live, tells us of the origin and meaning of man's existence, gives us a basis for knowledge and for understanding the difference between good and evil, shows us how to live in this world, provides answers to the problems we face as humans, and offers us a hope for the future which lends a purpose to our life now. Before such claims can be examined, there is an important objection that must be considered.

Some feel that it is unnecessary and unhelpful for the Christian to think about questions concerning the nature and meaning of the world, of knowledge, of man, of good and evil, et cetera. They would say, "Surely these are the questions that philosophy deals with, and Christianity has nothing to do with philosophy." They might continue: "Philosophy is abstract — for intellectuals only. Philosophers ask questions, in language that cannot be understood by the majority of people, concerning issues about which no ordinary human being thinks. Equally, they give unintelligible answers." "No," they might say, "Christianity is not like philosophy. Christianity is an affair of the heart, like marriage. The questions it deals with are practical questions: "Do I love God or don't I?"; "Will I humble myself before God and acknowledge I am a sinner or not?"; "Will I accept the gospel of Christ's death and resurrection or not?".

Some would go even further and argue that it is dangerous and unspiritual for Christians to get involved in such issues and would quote Paul: "See to it that no one takes you captive through hollow and deceptive philosophy, which depends on human tradition and the basic principles of this world rather than on Christ." (Colossians 2:8, NIV); and: "For it is written: 'I will destroy the wisdom of the wise; the intelligence of the intelligent I will frustrate. Where is the wise man? Where is the scholar? Where is the philosopher of this age? Has not God made foolish the wisdom of the world? For since in the wisdom of God the world through its wisdom did not know him, God was pleased through the foolishness of what was preached to save those who believe.'" (1 Corinthians 1:19-21, NIV) "Paul," they would argue, "says that for the Christian to discuss questions about existence and meaning is to abandon the gospel and resort to the methods of the world, of philosophy. Further, the simplicity of the gospel is lost and there is a failure to depend upon the power of the Holy Spirit to convert men's hearts."

These are very serious criticisms, and it is important to answer them. First, Paul is not saying that the gospel is literally foolish, but that this world, the world in rebellion against God, thinks that the gospel is foolish and that, in contrast, its own philosophy is wise. Second, Paul goes on to say that the gospel that men think is folly is, in fact, wiser than the wisdom of men. In other words, it is the non-Christian thinking or philosophy which is, in truth, foolish, and the Christian message which is the only true wisdom.

It is helpful to compare the statements in 1 Corinthians 1 with Romans 1:18-25, where Paul says something very similar. There Paul argues that the universe around us clearly declares God's existence and power and that men are without excuse if they do not acknowledge this. However, men refuse to have God in their knowledge and think that this refusal to acknowledge God is wisdom. In reality, their thinking is foolish, because they worship some part of the creation rather than God, and point to it rather than to God as the cause of life and the means of understanding man's place and purpose in the world.

The thinking of the non-Christian, no matter how wise and sophisticated it may appear at points, is foolish at base. For only the Biblical message makes sense of the way things are in the world. If men refuse to acknowledge God, they can no longer make sense of the world. They have exchanged truth for a lie and worship and serve creation rather than the Creator. Therefore, the Christian ought to be prepared to answer the questions that philosophy asks, that all men and women everywhere ask, because the Christian is not making up answers to the questions; rather, the Bible itself gives the answers to the questions. "We destroy arguments and every proud obstacle to the knowledge of God, and take every thought captive to obey Christ." (2 Corinthians 10:5, RSV) The Biblical answers fit like a glove on the hand of the way things are, whereas, to change the metaphor, the answers of non-Christian philosophy fit like a square peg in a round hole.

The basic questions concern: 1. the nature of knowledge; 2. the nature and origin of life; 3. the nature of human life; 4. the issue of morality; 5. the problem of suffering and evil; 6. the purpose of existence and the meaning of history; and 7. how man should live.

As we examine each of these questions and see the Biblical answer, we will compare it with the problems of the 20th Century western society's basic views.

1. *The question of knowledge.* How do we know? How can we be sure that what we think we know is accurate? Our society's pervading philosophy is humanism. Humanism answers this question by appealing to human reason: man starting from himself has to work out all the answers. David Hume, Scottish philosopher and historian, stated: "Reason appears in possession of the throne, prescribing laws and imposing maxims, with an absolute sway and authority."[1] This belief in the power of reason is basic to our whole modern western society. However Hume himself acknowledged that, beginning from man alone, the value of reason could never be demonstrated, nor the accuracy of one's sense perceptions, nor sure knowledge even of one's own physical existence, nor of the objective existence of the material world around us, nor of cause and effect. In a famous passage Hume acknowledged, however, that, though his reliance on reason as the basis for all knowledge could not be shown to be adequate, yet he would not despair:

Should it be asked me whether I sincerely assent to this argument which I have been to such pains to inculcate, whether I be really one of those skeptics who hold that all is uncertain, I should reply . . . that neither I nor any other person was ever sincerely and constantly of that opinion . . . I dine, I play backgammon, I converse and am merry with my friends, and when, after three or four hours' amusement, I would return to these speculations, they appear so cold and strained and ridiculous that I cannot find in my heart to enter into them any further. Thus, the skeptic still continues to reason and believe, though he asserts that he cannot defend his reason by reason, and by the same rule, he must assent to the principle concerning the existence of body, though he cannot pretend by any argument of philosophy to maintain its veracity.[2]

In the 20th Century this problem that arises from trusting in reason has led many thinkers to a position of complete despair. Man's reason was made into his god — but it has become a corpse around his neck reminding him constantly of the decay of meaning, of the death of value in human existence.

The problem has arisen because man is finite; he is small; he cannot from his own very little and limited grasps of reality generate sufficient knowledge to answer all the questions, or understand the whole of reality. Everything seems so big and yet man is so little; how can he be sure that any of his knowledge is accurate?

For the Christian, man's finiteness is not a problem, We can freely acknowledge that we are small and that our understanding is limited. But God exists, and His knowledge is complete; everything in the universe is known to Him. God has revealed Himself to us in his word, the Bible, and this word, though it does not tell us everything, tells us truly. We have a sure foundation for knowledge in God's word, and further God assures us that He has created us in His image to understand the world in which we live; so that our perception of the world is accurate. Reason, when it stands under God's revelation, becomes a servant of great value, which can be used to explore and reflect on the world in which we live. However, when reason is made master, it is a tyrant that leads man into the blackest night of ignorance and confusion.

2. *The nature and origin of life.* Modern humanist and secular thought in our society is tied up in a single parcel with the theory of evolution. At its crudest, this can be stated as the belief that all of the things we see in the world around us have developed by chance over enormous periods of time; that there is no God who created the world, no first cause that has brought into being the extraordinary diversity of the natural world. This belief requires us to accept that order has developed from disorder, that chance processes have given rise to the immensely complex and interdependent web of life, that matter has given rise to living things, inanimate life to thinking life, thinking life to self conscious life in man.

The irrationality of a system that requries man to believe $2 + 2 = 5$ not just once but thousands of times in the history of the universe is obvious. Christianity declares, in contrast, that the order, diversity, the intricate interdependence and beauty of the natural world have been created by the living and self-existent God whom the Bible reveals to us. Order, diversity and beauty are thus the result of God's creative activity, not chance processes and natural selection. Scripture sees this truth as self-evident, that it is simply a matter of common sense to look at the world and realize that it is the product of a Creator. David wrote: "The heavens declare the glory of God; the skies proclaim the work of his hands," (Psalm 19:1, NIV) and Paul "since the creation of the world God's invisible qualities — his eternal power and divine nature — have been clearly seen, being understood from what has been made, so that men are without excuse." (Romans 1:20, NIV)

When we look at a beautiful painting, we ask, "Who painted that?" and we praise its creator; in the same way, when we look at the universe, we ought to seek to know and praise its maker. "O Lord, our Lord, how majestic is your name in all the earth!" (Psalm 8:1, NIV)

3. *The nature of human life.* Bertrand Russell sums up the dilemma that non-Christian thought is confronted with as it applies evolutionary dogma to man:

> Man is the product of causes which had no prevision of the end they were achieving; . . . his origin, his growth, his hopes and fears, his loves and his beliefs, are but the outcome of accidental collocations of atoms . . . no fire, no heroism, no intensity of thought and feeling, can preserve an individual life beyond the grave; . . . all the labors of the ages, all the devotion, all the inspiration, all the noonday brightness of human genius, are destined to extinction in the vast death of the solar system, and the whole temple of man's achievement must inevitably be buried beneath the debris of a universe in ruins.[3]

Russell has to acknowledge that man is different, that he is unique in this world; that his moral character, creativity, love, heroism, thought and devotion to other men set him apart from all else that he sees; but Russell, like all modern secular philosophy, has no explanation for this uniqueness. Some thinkers like Russell acknowledge the difference in man, but cannot explain it. Others try to deny the uniqueness of man and insist that man's only difference is his complexity. Man, for them, is a piece of complicated chemistry, a physical organism like the mosquito and the mouse, but so complex that he can be compared to a digital analysis computer. Perry London, an American psychotherapist, appeals to this model for man, and then acknowledges that this means that, like a computer, man is completely insignificant, for, if he is only mechanics, he has no responsibility whatsoever for anything he does. In the end man's difference is illusory; the things that we experience every day — love, commitment, choice, creativity, rationality, et cetera, have no meaning at all: they are fleeting shadows on the wall, tricks of sunlight, thrown up by the complicated nature of the brain.[4]

The Christian faith, however, gives an explanation for the uniqueness of man. Man, male and female, is made in the image of God. The infinite person, God, has made other beings, men and women, who are finite and yet are persons like Himself. We are reflections of God's nature. "God is love," says the Apostle John. We are made to love God and to love one another. God is righteous. We are made to distinguish between good and evil, to judge what is right and to choose the good and live it. God is the Creator.

We are like Him, made responsible for every choice we make, made to create life, relationships, beauty, order. God is a communicator: Scripture speaks of communication between the Father, Son and Spirit both in this age and before the world was made. We are made to communicate in language with one another and with God. God is a God of order and not chaos, sense and not nonsense, reason not absurdity. We are made as rational persons, called to reflect on our life, and the world in which we live. All the aspects of our experience which set us apart are the characteristics of personality. Rather than lamenting that our experience of personality is an illusion in an impersonal universe, we can rejoice in it because, as little persons, we are at home in a universe made by the three personal God.

4. *Morality.* How can we know what is good and evil? Perry London, mentioned above, admits that if man is a machine, it is meaningless to speak of good and evil or moral responsibility. We do not accuse computers of criminal behavior, nor do we bring the animals (from which we are said to have evolved) to stand trial for breaking the law. If man is simply a mechanism, a complex physical organism, a relative of the tree rat and the whale, why do we hold him responsible for his actions and regard him as a moral agent? London agrees that good and evil and moral responsibility are imaginary; though men, he recognizes, seem to need them to live meaningfully. He goes on to suggest ways of programming people to create a better society, forgetting that the term *better* is, on his own admission, quite meaningless. We find a theory about reality and man's behavior which cannot explain the common factor in all human societies that good and evil are seen to be distinct, and people are regarded as moral agents. In our own day, however, we see the terrible fruit of a philosophy which denies any final distinction between good and evil. We see it in the West, where the slaughter of unborn babies and handicapped newborns is called compassionate medical care. We see it in the communist world, most strikingly in Cambodia, where between a third and a half of the population were killed in the name of a pure Marxist revolution. *Time* magazine commented on this turning of a whole nation into a concentration camp:

> Where the insane reversal of value lies is in the belief that notions like "purity" or "corruption" can have any meaning outside an absolute system of values: one that is resistant to the tinkering at will by governments or revolutionary groups. The Cambodian revolution, in its own degraded "purity," has demonstrated what happens when the Marxian denial of moral absolutes is taken with total seriousness by its adherents. Pol Pot and his friends decide what good is, what bad is, and how many corpses must pile up before this rapacious demon of "purity" is appeased.
>
> In the West today, there is a pervasive consent to the notion of moral relativism, a re-

luctance to admit that absolute evil can and does exit. This makes it especially difficult for some to accept the fact that the Cambodian experience is something far worse than a revolutionary aberration. Rather, it is the deadly logical consequence of an atheistic, man-centered system of values, enforced by fallible human beings with total power, who believe, with Marx, that morality is whatever the powerful define it to be and, with Mao, that power grows from gun barrels. By no coincidence the most humane Marxist societies in Europe today are those that, like Poland and Hungary, permit the dilution of their doctrine by what Solzhenitsyn has called "the great reserves of mercy and sacrifice" from a Christian tradition.[5]

Christianity does not have this problem of being uncertain of what is good and evil, nor a reluctance to admit that real evil can and does exist. No, God's own character is one of perfect goodness, justice and holiness. His character defines for us what is good and right, and all behavior must be measured against His character and in the light of the final judgment, when all the actions, words and thoughts of men will be seen for what they are.

God's law in Scripture expresses God's righteousness, and man, made to reflect that righteousness, is called to obey God's law and judge his life against it. All men are created with a moral conscience, the law of God written on the heart, but this can become confused or hardened, either by cultural tradition or by the individual's sinful choices. Beyond this, however, we have an absolute basis for knowing what is good and what is evil, for we can check all man's ideas against God's character and law. This means, too, that the Christian has a firm ground to stand on when confronted with the immorality of those in power, either in a democracy or in a dictatorship, or with the will of the 51 percent in a western society where morality changes with the consensus of the day.

In addition, rather than being embarrased by the doctrine of judgment, we should rejoice in it as one of the glories of the Christian faith. All men feel in their hearts that some things are right and others wrong, though unable to explain ultimately why this is so or even give final significance to the notions of good and evil and moral responsibility. The Christian can say with confidence that there is a difference and that in the end, at the judgment, all evil will be exposed and found wanting.

5. *The problem of suffering and evil.* Further, because modern philosophy has no final means of discerning between good and evil or of granting moral significance to man, then, equally, it has a hard time understanding suffering, sickness and death. In the end our culture has to say that suffering is normal, a part of reality. There is good and evil, light and darkness, life and death, kindness and cruelty — all are aspects of the whole.

Some would go further and argue that suffering is a necessary part of the evolutionary process — natural selection means that the strong survive and the weak get crushed. Development and improvement on the earth have only come about by this mechanism of change. Suffering becomes a good, a necessary sacrifice of some for the benefit of all. Teilhard de Chardin sees the evolutionary process this way, and Jacques Monod is wistful at the loss of natural selection in the human race. Modern medicine makes it possible for the weak to survive and pass on their genes to future generations. This stops the process of evolutionary improvement of the human race. This is why some lament and demand that handicapped babies, the mentally retarded, the unwanted and fragile elderly be eliminated: they would no longer be able to breed, nor would they be a drain on society.

The vision thus opened up should be horrifying to the Christian, who must see suffering and death as abnormal and unnatural, as, in fact, all human beings feel in their hearts in some situation or moment. Until they become hardened, little children are appalled at death and see it as horribly unnatural rather than as simply an aspect of life. The Christian knows that this feeling is true to the way things are, for the Bible tells us that we are living in a fallen world, that sin entered the world through man's rebellion against God, and that suffering, sickness, pain and death come in its train. This means that suffering and death are abnormal, that the world was originally good, but now it is marred and broken. Christ could be sorrowful, compassionate and angry when faced with pain and death, even though He is God. He could be angry and sad because He did not create them; rather, they resulted from man's rejection of Him and His law. The Christian, too, must follow Christ in seeing all suffering as abnormality, and rather than consenting to the brutality of the age toward the weak and needy, should reflect God's character of concern for the widow, the orphan, the broken in body and mind, the unborn, the old, the dying.

6. *The purpose of existence and the meaning of history.* Every man feels that his life has some purpose and that history must be going somewhere. However, the question arises, Does he know why his life ought to have purpose or what that purpose should be? Can he be sure history is going somewhere, and where it is going? People, of course, invent all kinds of meanings for themselves and for the human race as a whole; a better lot for all, personal affluence, gods and religions of various sorts, peace for the world . . . Many of these are refuges from facing up to what Bertrand Russell sees as the ultimate reality of history: the death of the individual and the death of the solar system. How can one avoid the consequence that all is meaningless if Russell is right? Neither the individual life nor the history of the human race has any final value on such a view, and Russell is honest enough to acknowledge this. The earlier quotation from Russell goes on: "Only within the scaffolding of these truths, only on the firm

foundation of unyielding despair, can the soul's habitation henceforth be safely built. . . . How, in such an alien and inhuman world, can so powerless a creature as man preserve his aspirations untarnished?"[6] Russell has no real answer to this question, and, of course, cannot have, once he has denied the existence of the God who has revealed Himself to us in the Bible.

The Bible tells us that our longing for purpose and for meaning to history has been placed within us by God, and that this longing can only be satisfied by our turning to God. We have been made to love God, to reflect His character, and enjoy Him forever; to love, enjoy and serve one another; to enjoy and have dominion over the creation as God's vice regents. We are living in a fallen and twisted world where sin has brought enmity and brokenness between ourselves and God, within our own hearts, between ourselves and others, between us and the creation, within creation itself. Everything is touched by sin and death. Yet God in His love has sent His own Son into the world to redeem us and the whole creation from sin and death. Through the work of Christ, by faith in Him, we are restored to fellowship with God, we begin to be made whole within, and we are called to exercise our dominion under God over the whole of life and over all the brokenness which sin has produced in ourselves and in the world. We are called, in fact, to be the firstfruits of the new creation which will transform everything at Christ's return. Christ Himself has already been raised physically from the dead. God promises us that the goal of history is the physical resurrection of all who believe in Christ and the making of a new heaven and a new earth in which there is only righteousness. The brokenness of every aspect of life will be removed and everything made new. At the same time the devil and all evildoers will be judged forever. Our own individual lives are given eternal significance and history is coming to a glorious conclusion.

7. *How man should live.* Our age confronts us with several alternatives, none of them satisfactory. The government decides what is right for man; the majority decides what is right; or the individual decides on the basis of his or her own feeling of what is good for him or her. Again, there are no absolutes, and we see on every side the resultant confusion and sorrow in people's lives and homes.

God promises us liberty if we obey his law. The law of God, as we saw in an earlier section, is a reflection of God's character. Man is made to be like God. The law, then, describes how man should live. It is not a set of arbitrary rules imposed by an angry God; rather, it is fitted to human life. James writes: "the man who looks intently into the perfect law that gives freedom, and continues to do this, not forgetting what he has heard, but doing it — he will be blessed in what he does." (James 1:25, NIV) Similarly, the Psalms describe God's law as being a lamp to our feet to stop us falling into dangerous pits and bogs. If we obey God's law, we shall enjoy life. God's truth sets us free to live. We can see this in any area of life: If we obey God's commandments about marriage, for example, then we will enjoy marriage. If we do not obey his commandments, then the resulting chaos and unhappiness in our society are only too obvious. Again, Christianity fits.

Coming back to our starting point, the Christian need not be afraid of philosophy or the questions that philosophy raises. No, the Christian faith, because it is the true wisdom revealed by God, is wiser than man's wisdom, If we look into Scripture, it answers the questions that are raised by our life in this world. Christianity is true to the way things are.

DISCUSSION QUESTIONS

1. On what basis have some people argued that Christians should not study philosophy, or should not get interested in "humanistic traditions"?

2. What is the true meaning of Paul's idea of "the foolishness of the cross"?

3. How does humanism answer the question: How do I know what is true? Can reason alone provide answer to the big questions?

4. How has the theory of evolution affected modern ideas of man, morals, and even God?

5. What was Bertrand Russell's view of man? Is it possible to live out such a philosophy?

6. How does a Christian explain man's uniqueness? man's universal moral sense?

7. Why should we push the promotors of humanistic views to their logical outcome? In what ways are people inevitably inconsistent with their world view?

8. Why is the explanation of morals and morality a thorny problem for secular humanists? Why must morals be based on absolutes?

9. Why is the doctrine of judgment so important to understand things as they really are?

10. Why is it so necessary to know the full and pervasive effect of the Fall on everything created?

11. If God's law is a reflection of God, what is our proper relation to it?

"We can't talk about humanity or our nation
if we are not prepared to start practicing righteousness
on the individual level of really giving ourselves
to other people."

The Christian
and Society

Jerram Barrs

I am going to be speaking about the Christian's responsibility in society
and the importance of our development of a Christian mind in this regard.

Jesus called us to be the salt of the earth — the salt to preserve society
from decay. In Romans 12 Paul calls us not to be conformed to the world
in which we live, but to be transformed by the renewing of our mind. As
we think about this question of our responsibility to society as a whole and
the place of government and the Christian's responsibility in it, I want to
begin with three quotations which should be a challenge to us as Christians. The first I think is very helpful in describing where we are today. To
repeat what an Australian, Manning Clark said:

> We are entering an era where a great dullness, so deep that no one can fathom it, is going
> to descend on us like a cloud.[1]

This is just to remind ourselves and challenge ourselves as we begin to
think about the Christian's responsibility in society as a whole, that Christians above all others have a responsibility not to be caught in that dullness
of apathy and self-fulfillment which characterizes our society.

Secondly, a quotation from John Stewart Mill:

> No great improvement in the lot of mankind is possible until a great change takes place in
> the fundamental constitution of their modes of thought.[2]

In other words, he is saying quite simply that we need to be prepared to really think through what our responsibility is, and what our calling is, and what the society is in which we live, and why it needs to change where there aren't going to be any changes. As Christians, that's a challenge to us from a non-Christian in an era of apathy and emphasis on the pursuit of pleasure. We have a tremendous responsibility before God to provide that challenge in the modes of thought of our culture — to be a challenge, to be a light and to provide an alternative.

Thirdly, I want to read some quotations from Solzhenitsyn from a speech he gave in 1978 which was extremely critical of the West. Some of you have probably read it before (or some like it), because he gave a whole series of speeches over the last two or three years in which he was very, very critical of the West. It was at that point that people stopped really listening to what he had to say. Everybody was delighted when he came from Russia and was very critical of Russian society, but when he started criticizing the West, people didn't like it very much. His criticisms were very, very profound. Just listen very carefully to his criticisms; they are worth reading, because he had some very helpful things to say.

The first was that he criticized our system of legalistic righteousness. He pointed out that, in the West, people are much more concerned for the letter of the law than the spirit of the law, and that's the way that our whole legal system works. Everybody is pressing the law to its very limit to get his rights and to avoid getting into trouble. Now let's read what he says here.

> "If one is right from a legal point of view, nothing more is required, nobody may mention that one could still not be entirely right, and urge self restraint or a renunciation of these rights, call for sacrifice and selfless risk; this would simply sound absurd. Voluntary self-restraint is almost unheard of: everybody strives toward further expansion to the extreme limit of the legal frames. (An oil company is legally blameless when it buys up an invention of a new type of energy in order to prevent its use. A food product manufacturer is legally blameless when he poisons his produce to make it last longer: after all, people are free to purchase it.)"[3]

That's his first criticism. The kind of legalistic righteousness we have developed in the West. A dependence upon the letter of the law, rather than its spirit. And secondly, he criticized very powerfully the excessive emphasis on individualistic freedom in the West.

> "The defense of individual rights has reached such extremes as to make society as a whole defenseless against certain individuals. It is time, in the West, to defend not so much human rights as human obligations.
>
> On the other hand, destructive and irresponsible freedom has been granted boundless space. Society has turned out to have scarce defense against the abyss of human deca-

dence, for example against the misuse of liberty for moral violence against young people, such as motion pictures full of pornography, crime, and horror. This is all considered to be part of freedom and to be counter-balanced, in theory, by the young people's right not to look and not to accept. Life organized legalistically has thus shown its inability to defend itself against the corrosion of evil."[4]

That is a very profound statement. And again, here:

"Mere freedom per se does not in the least solve all the problems of human life and even adds a number of new ones."[5]

And then he comments on an earlier time. He says:

"And yet in early democracies, as in American democracy at the time of its birth, all individual human rights were granted on the ground that man is God's creature. That is, freedom was given to the individual conditionally, in the assumption of his constant religious responsibility. Such was the heritage of the preceding one thousand years. Two hundred or even fifty years ago, it would have seemed quite impossible, in America, that an individual be granted boundless freedom with no purpose, simply for the satisfaction of his whims. Subsequently, however, all such limitations were eroded everywhere in the West; a total emancipation occurred from the moral heritage of Christian centuries with their great reserves of mercy and sacrifice. State systems were becoming ever more materialistic. The West has finally achieved the rights of man, and even to excess, but man's sense of responsibility to God and society has grown dimmer and dimmer. In the past decades, the legalistic selfishness of the Western approach to the world has reached its peak and the world has found itself in a harsh spiritual crisis and a political impasse. All the celebrated technological achievements of progress, including the conquest of outer space, do not redeem the twentieth century's moral poverty, which no one could have imagined even as late as the nineteenth century."[6]

I have included these quotations at length becaue I think what he says is a tremendously profound and quite accurate indictment of our culture and its moral poverty.

Now as Christians we have a responsibility to do something about this — a responsibility before God to the society in which we live. What I want to do now is to look at the Christian's response, what our calling is, and at some of the issues which we ought to be concerned to fight for in the society. But I don't think that we can really take anything for granted in terms of where we stand, so I want to start with something very basic, and that is to look at the importance of government; secondly, we will look at the purpose of government, then at some Biblical principles of the Christian, and then at the place of Biblical law.

So first of all, the importance of government. I think a Biblical attitude and understanding of the importance of government is very important, because today all around us everybody talks about peace, and hardly any-

body talks about justice. Rather, like Solzhenitsyn said, we all want freedom to have peace, and we are afraid our lives might be disrupted, so we
demand peace. But rather, like Jeremiah said in his day, people were crying, "Peace, peace," when there was no peace, and there is no peace in the
world today. Biblically, peace is only a product of justice. While injustice
and tyranny reign in societies, peace is impossible. Just as for us on the individual level, peace with God was impossible without the death of Christ
bearing the just judgment for our sins, so in any other area of life, peace is
impossible without justice. So I want to start by looking at the place and
importance of government.

The Place and Importance of Government

In the Old Testament, it is absolutely clear that God appointed human
governments within the nation of Israel to be his representatives on earth
to maintain justice. In Deuteronomy 1:13-17, Moses commands the people
to choose some wise and respected men from each of their tribes to be set
over them, and they say, "Yes, this is good." Hear Moses in verses 15-17:

> I took the leading men of your tribes, wise and respected men, and appointed them to
> have authority over you . . . And I charged your judges at that time: Hear the disputes be-
> tween your brothers and judge fairly, whether the case is between brother Israelites or be-
> tween one of them and an alien. Do not show partiality in judging; hear both small and
> great alike. Do not be afraid of any man, for judgment belongs to God. Bring me any case
> too hard for you, and I will hear it. (NIV)

And there — just a simple statement — judgment belongs to God. God is
the one who is judge of all the earth and he has appointed human government (the government, here, of Israel) for the purpose of maintaining
justice on the earth.

In Deuteronomy 16:18-20:

> Appoint judges and officials for each of your tribes in every town the Lord your God is
> giving you, and they shall judge the people fairly. Do not pervert justice or show partial-
> ity. Do not accept a bribe, for a bribe blinds the eyes of the wise and twists the words of
> the righteous. Follow justice and justice alone, so that you may live and possess the land
> the Lord your God is giving you. (NIV)

And over in Chapter 17: 18-20 it speaks about a future time when Israel
will have a king, and it has the same emphasis there. The king is to have
before him a copy of the law of God, which he is to read all the days of his
life and apply in the society and not consider himself better than his
brothers and turn from the law to the right or to the left. He is to rule by
the law of God in Israel.

So the first point I want to make is simply this: That God instituted human government himself. Human government is not simply an idea which human beings have developed and said, "This will help us." Obviously, particular governments are chosen by men in all sorts of different circumstances and ways, but the very institution of government is something which is given by God for a specific purpose.

We could look at a later passage in Psalm 82, which says:

God presides in the great assembly. He gives judgment among the gods. (NIV)

This is a passage which causes people all sorts of confusion. Why does the psalmist use the word *gods* here? The word *gods* is used for human rulers, and it's quite clear as we read down the Psalm that that's who it's talking about. It's used for human rulers with this reason — that all human authorities have the purpose of being God's representatives on Earth to carry out his justice. That is why they are given such a high title in the Psalm. So that is the first thing in the Old Testament — we have a very high view of human government.

But what about when we come to the New Testament? Many people would want to argue that this view changes, that the importance of government, and the place of government, and the Christian's responsibility where government is concernerd, are no longer the same. Many people would point to pacificism and the Sermon on the Mount (like "Don't resist evil"; "Overcome evil with good") to support such a view. But if we look at the New Testament, I think it's quite clear that the same view is continued. In John 10:34, 35, Jesus actually quotes from Psalm 82. Now in the passage Jesus isn't talking primarily about human government — he is defending himself against the accusation of blasphemy. The Jews say to him, "We're going to stone you because you, a man, make yourself equal with God," and Jesus responds by saying, "Does it not say in your law that the Scripture cannot be broken?" In other words, this statement, which he then quotes, is absolutely binding and authoritative, and Jesus regards it as such. He commends such a view. "I said, 'you are gods,'" is the passage that he quotes. In other words, Jesus has the same view of the importance of human government. He sees human government as being God's representatives, God's vice regents on the earth. So Jesus approves of the statement of the Psalm.

When we come to Romans 13, we find Paul with precisely the same attitude towards government and its purpose as the Old Testament has. In this passage in Romans 13, Paul speaks of governments as being God's ministers:

> Everyone must submit himself to the governing authorities, for there is no authority
> except that which God has established. (Romans 13:1, NIV)

The authorities which exist have been established by God; consequently, he who rebels against the authorities is rebelling against what God has instituted. Verse 4 says, "he is God's servant to do you good," and again, "He is God's servant, an agent of wrath to bring punishment on the wrong-doer." So Paul here has precisely the same view as the Old Testament in terms of the importance of government.

Now again, many Christians will appeal to passages in the Sermon on the Mount like "love your enemy,"; and "do good to those who hate you," but we notice that the two ideas about loving your enemies and the place of government and the Christian's responsibility are not opposed to each other. If we look at Romans 12, Paul virtually quotes there from the Sermon on the Mount,

> Do not repay anyone evil for evil. Be careful to do what is right in the eyes of everybody.
> (Romans 12:17, NIV)

> Do not take revenge, my friends, but leave room for God's wrath, for it is written: "It is
> mine to avenge; I will repay," says the Lord. (Romans 12:19, NIV)

Now, you will find many people quoting that passage and saying this means that Paul, just like Jesus, is completely against the Christian ever being involved in any situation of administering justice or the use of force, and that what Paul is saying is that all judgment should be left to God at the end of the age, because it is God's job to take vengeance on evil. But that is not Paul's point, and that is why immediately afterwards in Chapter 13 (which is obscured for most people by the chapter division), Paul goes on to say that governments are God's instruments of wrath to punish the evil-doer. In other words, God has not left it simply to the end of the age for himself to judge, but he has appointed government for this very purpose of judging evil in the present age.

Now there are many situations, of course, in our personal relationships with one another, where we should not resist evil, where we have to return evil with good, where we're not to take vengeance on the personal level. We should be quite clear that the Old Testament law said precisely the same thing. If we were to read Leviticus 19, for example, that chapter says precisely the same thing — that it's wrong to bear grudges against your neighbor, it's wrong to return evil for evil, you must love your enemy, including the alien.

But at the same time, the law of Moses upholds the principle of justice and the punishment of evil. It does not just uphold it, but God requires it as a necessity. So there are many occasions everyday where we are required to forgive each other, not to return evil for evil, not to take vengeance ourselves against one another. But this argument does not apply when it comes to the responsibility of government to punish the evil-doer, which it is required to do by God. So Paul repeats himself there. "Do not take vengeance, my friends, but leave room for God's wrath." Then, the ruler is God's servant, an agent of wrath to bring punishment on the wrong-doer. So again, Paul clearly has the same view of the institution of government as the Old Testament.

The Purpose of Government in Scripture

Now secondly, we want to ask, "What is the purpose of government in Scripture?" What is the purpose of government? We have already seen that:

a. The purpose of government is to rule justly by the law of God and by his wisdom, and there are many statements in Proverbs which talk about that — about the king ruling according to the wisdom of God. So that's the first thing, the first purpose of government — to rule justly according to the law of God, to maintain justice in the land in obedience to God's law. Later, I want to look in detail at God's law in the Old Testament and its place today, to try and give us a program for Christian political action.

b. The purpose of government as appointed by God was to defend the cause of the poor and needy who have no advocate, and there are many, many passages like that which speak of this in the Old Testament. It's one of the central purposes of human government — to defend the cause of the poor and needy who have no other advocate in society. Proverbs 31:8, 9 speaks about the duty of the king. He is to

Speak up for those who cannot speak for themselves, for the rights of all who are destitute. Speak up and judge fairly; defend the rights of the poor and needy. (NIV)

That is the theme that is repeated over and over again in the Scripture. There are many passages in the Psalms which speak like that. Psalm 82, for example, says this:

How long will you defend the unjust and show partiality to the wicked? Defend the cause of the weak and the fatherless; maintain the rights of the poor and oppressed. Rescue the weak and the needy; deliver them from the hand of the wicked. (NIV)

I think today, very often, we have forgotten, or governments have forgotten, that that's one of their fundamental responsibilities — to be the advocate of those who have no other advocate in society. We can all look around and think of those who have no other advocate in society. We can all look around and think of those who are in our own cultures. Who has no advocate? We would have to say that at least some of those who have no advocate are the unborn, the infants who are handicapped and the very old.

c. Another fundamental calling of government (and in a way we have mentioned it already) is to punish those who do wrong and, included in that, those who oppress the weak and the needy. Over and over again, the book of Deuteronomy speaks of the necessity of the punishment of the wicked when it's speaking in the context of selling people into slavery or of murder. Over and over again it says quite simply, "You shall not pity the murderer. You shall rid the land of the blood of the one who has died." And God says, "If you don't, I will require justice for the blood of the one who has been killed of the whole land." In other words, God is simply saying there must be justice and punishment in this age. That is the calling of government.

Often, as Christians we don't think of that as a good thing (the punishment of those who do wrong), but over and over again in Scripture, kings who punish the wicked are commended by God. Kings who fail to punish the wicked are rebuked by God very severely. Over and over again in the Old Testament, the severest condemnations are given for those in authority who do not rule justly, who do not protect the poor and needy, who do not punish the wicked. God's character has not changed from the Old Testament to today. He is still concerned for the poor and needy, and he still requires governments to be concerned for them too and to punish wickedness. The whole idea that we are living in a different moment of history where the idea of justice is one that is no longer important, is one that cannot possibly be maintained on reading of Scripture. God's character has not changed. It always remains the same. That is why the Scripture looks forward to the time with great joy when Christ will come back and finally remove all wickedness from the earth and bring righteousness and justice for the first time in fullness.

God requires that some attempt be made in the present. Rather than saying that the Christian should not be involved in such things, our attitude should be very different. The more Christians who really understand what justice is, who are involved in government, the better. The less likely there is to be corruption, the more likely there is to be some justice in the land. I think I should say here, the issue is not one of violence. Christians often speak about the use of punishment on any level as if it was use of violence, and how can I, as a Christian, use violence? But, in the Bible, the use of force, the just use of force to restrain evil, is pleasing to God. He has established government for that very purpose. If we start using the word "violence" with all the implications it has of injustice, we have lost the battle before we begin.

The Christian's Responsibility in Society

To look at some areas of the Christian's responsibility in society, I want to start with some very fundamental things.

a. The proclamation of the gospel. If we want to know what we're doing, what we ought to be doing as Christians, in our desire to change the society in which we live, we have to begin with proclaiming the gospel for the salvation of individuals who will be salt in the society. The fundamental problem that we face always is the human heart, and that can only be basically changed by the power of the gospel.

b. The gospel must not be proclaimed narrowly. We must teach and practice ourselves the authority of Christ, the Lordship of Christ over the whole of our life, so that we encourage ourselves and one another to be lights in the world. So that Christians who are soldiers, businessmen, workers or judges, or jurymen, or politicians or policemen are taught to be righteous in all that they do and in all their relationships. We don't reduce Christian morality to a very narrow area, but we really see it (our life as Christians) as embracing everything we do. It has to stand under the commandments of God and the practice of righteousness.

c. Obviously related to this, there must be in our own lives the example of righteousness in all our dealings with one another. In every sphere of life, we must love our neighbor as ourself. Starting with ourselves, we are caring for the people around us in need. We are not just concerned with the issues of society as a whole, but we, ourselves, are those who care for the poor and needy, who are prepared to open our homes to them, who are prepared to spend ourselves for others in the same way that Christ did. Our whole life as Christians is like a series of concentric circles. We have to start with ourselves and our own obedience to God, to be sure that our own lives are pure, and then we look out and practice righteousness in terms of caring for other people and giving ourselves to them. We can't talk about humanity or our nation if we are not prepared to start practicing righteousness on the individual level of really giving ourselves to other people. There's a tremendous responsibility in every individual Christian and in every church that we offer a light to our society, like a city set on a hill (to use another of Jesus' images), that we offer an alternative to the kind of self-indulgence that exists around us in our society. But we don't see that as our calling as believers. We don't see ourselves in a time of great need where our calling is to give ourselves to serve other people.

d. Prayer for those in authority over us in government. Paul speaks of this in 1 Timothy 2:2. There are several things we can pray for. I will mention just a few.

1) that they may seek and know God's truth themselves

2) that they may rule justly and wisely in the fear of God and recognize that they are ruling as his vice regents. How many people in government really think of themselves as those whose responsibility it is to apply the commandments of God and to rule under God, and realize they are going to have to answer to him one day for every decision they make in their office of government? That is what the scripture says. So we pray that they may rule justly and wisely and in the fear of God. That, as Christians, therefore (as Paul says), we may be able to live a quiet and peaceful life, instead of being persecuted.

3) that the gospel may be freely preached and that our rulers may not be followers of false ideologies which bring injustice and tyranny against the weak and persecution on the church.

e. We must be prepared to honor and obey governments, and that is rather a difficult idea for us, because we have got accustomed to being completely cynical about governments and the whole office of government, the whole institution of government. We must be prepared to obey and honor governments as God commands us in his word.

f. We must, however, always obey God rather than men, including governments, when there is a disagreement, a conflict, a tension between the two. We must always obey God rather than men.

There are a couple of examples in Acts 4:19 and 5:29, and they are about the preaching of the gospel. But this applies not only to the preaching of the gospel, but also to refusing to do evil which is commanded by the laws of our land. You can think of examples from Scripture: the Hebrew midwives in Exodus 1 who refused to kill the children when they were commanded by Pharaoh; Joseph disobeying Potiphar's wife; Rahab hiding the Israeli spies from her own rulers; or, in our day, in our own generation we can think of Corrie Ten Boom in Holland disobeying the government there and hiding Jews, (rather like Rahab in her house) against the commands of the state. So we must always obey God rather than men.

g. Related to this, we must not think that because we live in a democracy where we have had religious toleration Romans 13 means that all governments are good and must always be obeyed, so that a conservatism quite foreign to the spirit of the gospel is fostered among Christians. We must be very clear at that point. Revelation 13 in the New Testament (also see Romans 13) speaks of a government which is "the beast." We must recognize that the world is against the truth, and that therefore, the Christian must be prepared to expect the hostility of the state against both the gospel message and the practice of justice, both of which the Christian longs to see prevail.

h. We must be prepared to count the cost of being part of the people of Christ, who have no abiding city here, and be ready therefore to suffer, both for the sake of the gospel and for the practice of righteousness, as Jesus says in the Sermon on the Mount in Matthew 5:10, knowing that this may involve suffering for ourselves and also for our families. Again, we live in a society where we all want to protect ourselves, our own rights and our own freedoms, and to create space for ourselves. As Solzhenitsyn said in that very profound article, we are not accustomed to people making any kind of self-sacrifice. But that is what the Christian is called to. There will be many occasions where we may have to count the cost. It's quite obvious when you look at Christians in a situation like the USSR, where they have to count the cost all the time, both of believing the gospel and practicing righteousness. We must have the same attitude.

i. We must be prepared out of love for our neighbors and out of recognition of the high and honorable calling which it is, to be involved in government ourselves — in the work of civil justice, of law enforcements, et cetera. As I said before, the more Christians there are who are involved, the better. The more likely (we would hope) that there is to be some justice, less bribery and corruption, less partiality, and so on.

j. Some of you will find this a rather difficult point, so I will spend a little bit more time on it. What we uphold as believers is not simply government itself, but the rule of law — not the status quo. In other words, in the end, neither a king nor a president nor a prime minister nor a parliament nor the majority in a democracy at 51%, is the standard by which we judge what is right and what we honor ultimately. What we honor ultimately is what is right — the rule of law. The law is king rather than the other way round. The Christian has an absolute standard by which to judge government, and that standard is God's character and word, and that means that even those in government must be subject to the law themselves. Just like it says in Deuteronomy, the king wasn't to consider himself better than the other members of the people of Israel, but he was to do what was right himself. In other words, the law is not made by rulers; rather, the job of rulers is to apply the law. If they break it, they must be subject to the law's reprisals. You can think of President Nixon for example. It was quite right that he was brought before the courts and removed from being President because of his breaking the law.

This raises the problem: What if a government breaks the law, not just here and there, which all governments do, but becomes a tyranny and uses violence to uphold its position? This raises the possibility of civil disobedience by the Christian, and I recommend to you Dr. Schaeffer's book, *The Christian Manifesto*[7], which goes into this question at length — of Christians' practicing civil disobedience. It also raises the possibility of revolution.

Contrary to popular opinion, Christians have not always been on the side of the status quo. Rather, there is a very long and respectable tradition of Christians' upholding the necessity of revolution which goes right back to the Middle Ages and includes figures after the Reformation, for instance Calvin. Calvin held that it was the responsibility of those in the lower offices of government to remove the king if he was a tyrant, because they must bring him before the standard of the law. Or you could think of Cromwell and the Civil War in England, where Parliament resisted the tyranny of Charles I and had to take up arms to do so, to bring him to justice. Or in Holland, the overthrowing of the power of Spain, or the American revolution (which many Christians were involved in). In the Bible itself, wicked rulers are removed from power by God's command and by the use of the sword (Jezebel and Athaliah). We should notice here that what is upheld is not a kind of Marxist ideal of revolution, but the replacement of a tyranny which is breaking the law (in other words, which becomes lawless), by a government which upholds the law. It is a very different understanding of revolution from that which the Marxist puts forward. We are measuring something against an objective and absolute standard; the replacement of a tyranny which is lawless by a government which upholds law.

Of course, we have to say that there is no perfection in any government, just as there is no perfection in any other human institution in this world. As I said before, this is all the more reason for Christians to get involved and to try to improve the situation.

I just want to make a couple of qualifications here. I am not saying that the legitimate use of force to restrain evil is the only way to deal with situations of terrible injustice and confusion. I want to give just a couple of examples. I think you could use Uganda and Idi Amin as a very good example of where revolution was the right and only response. It would have been much better if it had happened earlier. If we had lived there, I hope that we would have been prepared to take part in it because, if revolution is delayed (the replacement of a lawless government by a lawful one), then the land becomes so desolated that it takes many many years for it to recover and for the institutions of law to be set back into place. And that, of course, is what happened in Uganda because the tyranny went on so long.

I want to give a couple of other examples. First of all, in Latin America and in many other parts of the world, there are very unjust dictatorships and the question obviously arises, "Should the Christian join with the Marxist in such a situation in a revolution against tyranny?" My own feeling is that we ought, perhaps, to find a third way and not side in such a situation with either the extreme right or the extreme left. For such a revolution would most likely replace one lawless government with another lawless government.

Now, of course, to find a third way is not an easy solution because it involves the way of the cross and being prepared to be rejected and persecuted by both sides. What must happen in such a situation is that the Christian must be prepared to be the advocate of the oppressed.

The second example, where I would suggest a different kind of solution, would be that of Northern Ireland, where I personally feel that the only solution to the problem lies, not in the use of force, in army occupation, or some government imposed solution to satisfy the Protestant majority, but rather the Protestant majority voluntarily giving up all power to the Catholic minority — the voluntary surrender of their status as British, of their rights and privileges that they may have maintained for themselves for so long. I really suggest that as a serious alternative, and there are Christians in Northern Ireland who are certainly working in that direction. I don't think there is any other human solution to that situation. So don't go away just thinking I am advocating a kind of mindless use of force in any and every situation.

Coming back to where we were, we are responsible as Christians to be active in society. We are responsible before God to be the first fruits in the coming Kingdom of God by being involved in the establishment of some justice on the earth.

DISCUSSION QUESTIONS

1. Why is it crucial to affect societal change by changing *modes of thought* and not mere externals? What are some ungodly societal trends that can be traced to unbiblical modes of thought?

2. How has "destructive and irresponsible freedom" been granted "boundless space", as Solzhenitsyn claims?

3. Why does Solzhenitsyn stress that freedom was given conditionally in the assumption of his constant *religious* responsibility? What does he mean by "religious responsibility"? What bearing does this have on the question of separation of church and state?

4. What should government accomplish for us? What should it *not* try to do?

5. What are some Biblically responsible ways we are to "submit to the governing authorities" today?

6. What are priority responsibilities for the Christian who wants to serve today's society? What are your personal priorities?

7. Practically speaking, how can the analogy of salt as a preservative be related to our involvement in society? What is there to be preserved, and what is to be opposed as being part of an ungodly status quo?

8. Why is voluntary self-restraint and sacrifice so fundamentally important for Christian action and response in the West? In what ways do these notions conflict with the spirit of the age?

9. What are the dangers of allowing human law to determine moral values? Can you cite examples of human law being changed because of a moral crusade?

10. When is force a legitimate Christian response to evil?

11. How is justice and the establishment of it essential to all Biblically mandated structures? How primary is the establishment of justice in the gospel?

"God's existence and character provide a final
and absolute difference between good and evil, . . . we
have an absolute basis for morality against
which we may judge society."

A Biblical Ethic
Jerram Barrs

I want to start by asking a question: "How do we know what is right for
ourselves and our society?" and to simply contrast the Biblical position
with those around us. What is the answer of our culture to this question?
How do we know what is right for ourselves, for our individual lives and
good for the society in which we live? Our culture answers that first of all,
by saying simply, personal freedom. Whatever feels good to me, that is
what I will do. We can think of all the changing attitudes in our society,
towards the family, towards sexual morality, and in so many, many other
areas which show the way our culture really thinks. I have quoted what
Solzhenitsyn says about freedom (see *The Christian and Society*, Jerram
Barrs). How, when we have this kind of freedom for the individuals to
simply define for themselves what to do, that we end up with freedom for
good and freedom for evil. It's not just freedom, but it's freedom to do evil
as well as to do good. He comments on this and says,

"There was a view of man that became the basis for government and social science in the
West and could be defined as rationalistic humanism or humanistic autonomy, the proclaimed and enforced autonomy for freedom of man from any higher force above him."[1]

It could also be called anthropocentricity. In other words, man centeredness with man seen as the center of everything that exists. This new way of thinking which imposed on us its guidance did not admit the existence of intrinsic evil in man, nor did it see any higher task than the attainment of happiness on earth. It based modern, western civilization on the dangerous trend to worship man and his material needs. Everything beyond physical well-being and accumulation of material goods, all other human requirements and characteristics of a subtler and higher nature were left outside the area of attention of state and social systems, as if human life did not have any superior sense. This provided access for evil, of which, in our days, there is a free and constant flow.

Paul says quite simply in Galatians 5:13 that freedom can become a basis for indulging one's sinful nature, and that's what we see in our society, when people insist on defining for themselves what is good for themselves and for the society as a whole.

An alternative would be simply the idea of the majority vote. Whatever 51% of society think, that is right, that is good. When, as in our case, a democracy has lost its commitment to others, its respect for law and its commitment to the basic institutions of human society, then we have the idea again of no real freedom, no true freedom being upheld, and democracy becomes not something good, but something bad. It merely acts as a break on the slide to moral poverty. Plato commented on democracy saying, "The democracy is the best of bad governments." What he meant by that was simply that in a democracy the slide to moral poverty and wickedness just comes a little more slowly than it does in the tyranny of one or a few. So democracy, the rule of the majority, does not defend us from the access of evil into our society when a democratic culture loses its whole basis of law and sense of obligation.

The other alternative would be "might is right." Whatever those in power say is right for the culture, for the society, that is the way it will be, and, of course, this rules a large part of the world. It becomes a terrible incident of oppression. There's no way anybody can appeal against anything, and that is, of course, the problem of the dissident in the USSR. He has no objective standard of law to appeal to. He can be imprisoned or put in a psychiatric hospital for anything whatsoever, because the state has the right to define what is good and evil, what is normal and abnormal, what is sane and what is insane.

How do we know what is right and wrong for ourselves as individuals and for our society?

God's Character is the Basis
The Christian answer is simply that God's existence and character pro-

vide a final and absolute difference between good and evil, that we are at home ultimately in a moral universe, so we have an absolute basis for morality against which we may judge society.

The Law of God in Scripture

I feel there are many misunderstandings about God's law which we need to clear away before we begin to think about its application to us today and the way we can use it as a help to our society.

Many Christians think that, in the Old Testament, the law was given as a means of self-justification for Israel, a means of helping people to earn a relationship with God. This is quite clearly not so.

1. In the Old Testament law, *grace came before law*. The beginning of the Ten Commandments, Exodus 20:1-2, reads:

> I am the Lord your God who brought you out of the land of Egypt, out of the house of bondage. (RSV)

Then the commandments follow:

> You shall have no other gods before me.

This is so all the way through the Mosaic law. Grace comes before law. There is a statement of God's delivering his people and then the requirement that they obey him. Grace followed by law with the motivation of love and gratitude. Look at Deuteronomy 6:5, which speaks in this way:

> Hear, O Israel: the Lord our God, the Lord is one. Love the Lord your God with all your heart and with all your soul and with all your strength. (NIV)

Central to the law is, first of all, grace, and second, the motivation of love in response to God's grace. This, of course, is precisely the same pattern that we find in the New Testament. Again, in Romans 12:1-2, Paul just starts off by saying:

> I urge you, brothers, in view of God's mercy, to offer your bodies as living sacrifices, holy and pleasing to God — which is your spiritual worship. (NIV)

So again, grace is followed by law. We are redeemed by what God has done in Christ, and he calls us in gratitude to give ourselves to him, to obey his commandments.

In the Old Testament, the commandments were not given to God's people that they might earn fellowship with him. They were given to a people al-

ready delivered by God and who were now to be set apart by their obedience to him.

2. *The law taught humility before God.* All law convicts of sin. When
we see the commandments, they expose our failings. Whether it's a commandment like, "You shall not covet," or a commandment like, "You shall
love the Lord your God, with all your heart and soul and mind and
strength" that we just saw in Deuteronomy, all commandments expose our
failings. This was true for the Old Testament believer just as it is true for
us. Central to the Old Testament law was that it made provision for sin in
the sacrificial system. Far from expecting the Israelites to earn fellowship
with God by their perfect righteousness, the law itself presumed that Israel
would fail and made provision for such failures in the sacrificial system.
We can all think of Psalm 51, the cry of a believer who has broken the law,
which we are all quite happy to use as an expression of our own attitude
before God.

3. *The law expressed the character of God* — his holiness, justice, mercy
and love. Leviticus 19 says this over and over again. It gives a commandment, and then it says, "Why are you to do this? Because I am the Lord
your God. Why are you to care for the needy? Why are you not to cut
your fields to their corners? Why are you not to go over them a second
time? Because I am the Lord your God who has compassion." In other
words, the law is based on God's character. It expresses his character of
holiness and justice and mercy and love.

The Old Testament was internal and not only external. Very often people
look at the law of Moses and think that it just was a matter of externals and
that when it comes to the New Testament the law is made internal. This is
not at all true. It's absolutely clear in the law of Moses that it was internal.
We have looked at the passage in Deuteronomy 6:5 about loving the Lord
your God with all your heart and soul and mind and strength, which, of
course, Jesus quotes in the New Testament as the summary of the law and
the prophets. It speaks in the same way about loving our neighbor as
ourself; about not bearing grudges in our hearts; about not hating our
enemies; about helping them. So the Old Testament law was not only external, it was internal, and it was applied to the heart. Jesus' summary of
the law was not a new revelation, it was simply a summary in repetition of
what was already given in the law of Moses.

4. *The law expressed how men should live as persons made in God's image to reflect His character*, and that therefore, the law is for man's good.
Over and over again, as we look at Leviticus 19 and Deuteronomy 24, it
says, "Do this, because I am the Lord." In other words, God requires us to
be like Himself, to be His image, to be His reflections in the world. Deu-

teronomy 10:13 just says quite simply that the law is for our good. Deuteronomy 4:5-8:

> See, I have taught you decrees and laws as the Lord my God commanded me, so that you may follow them in the land you are entering to take possession of it. Observe them carefully, for this will show your wisdom and understanding to the nations, who will hear about all these decrees and say, "Surely this great nation is a wise and understanding people." What other nation is so great as to have their gods near them the way the Lord our God is near to us whenever we pray to him? And what other nation is so great as to have such righteous decrees and laws as this body of laws I am setting before you today? (NIV)

The whole emphasis of the law of Moses is that the law is for man's good. It's not to be seen as a kind of hedge of restrictions around the life of Israel or around the individual believer. It must not be so for us either, but rather as a way of life. If we turn to the Psalms we see this attitude very, very clearly. For example, Psalm 1:2. You are all familiar with these things, because you will have sung them or read them many, many times. But I think we don't really think very often about what it means, because we've been taught to have such a negative attitude towards the law, both because of our tradition within the church, and also because of the negative attitude towards law in our culture. Psalm 1:2, 3 talks about the man who doesn't walk in the counsel of the wicked. It says:

> His delight is in the law of the Lord, and on his law he meditates day and night. He is like a tree planted by streams of water, which yields its fruit in season and whose leaf does not wither. Whatever he does prospers. (NIV)

Now, we mustn't understand this as being some kind of statement that by righteousness, man is earning fellowship with God. That is not the point at all of this Psalm. What it is speaking about is the beauty of the law of God and how obedience to it really gives us life, really gives us freedom and fulfillment as human beings. Psalm 19:7:

> The law of the Lord is perfect, reviving the soul. The statutes of the Lord are trustworthy, making wise the simple. (NIV)

and so on, down through the passage. Then it says,

> They are more precious than gold, than much pure gold; they are sweeter than honey, than honey from the comb. By them is your servant warned; in keeping them there is great reward. (Verses 10, 11. NIV)

This is the attitude all the way through the Old Testament. That law is a good thing. The same idea is repeated in the New Testament in James 1:25. He says:

> He who looks into the perfect law, the law of liberty, and perseveres . . . he shall be blessed in his doing. (RSV)

So this same idea we find in the New Testament too, and it is a very profound idea, because in our culture, law is hated. Freedom from law is considered to be the ideal. Law is considered to restrict a person, to hedge him in from the pleasure of freedom outside the boundaries of law. But the Biblical attitude towards law is precisely the opposite. Freedom from law brings destruction and misery. If we look at a person who does what is right in his own eyes, we see a person who is unhappy and unfulfilled and who brings destruction to every relationship that he has. But if we obey God's commandments in any area of life, then life follows — a harvest of righteousness. Just think about marriage. If we obey God's commandments in marriage, if I take care of my children in the way God commands me in his word, then we will have a good relationship which we can enjoy. We can have fellowship together and a happy home.

We must see God's law as something positive. It expresses how we are to live as those made in the image of God. We should see law as good.

Again, just on this point too. Very often, Christians oppose the Spirit and the law. They say that the new life of the Spirit after the coming of Christ is opposed to the observance of the law. Again, that's not the attitude of the New Testament. I just quoted to you what James says about persevering in the law and Paul says in Romans 7:

> The law is spiritual and the law is holy and just and good.

It is not the law which is the problem, it is me. But the Spirit desires that we obey the law; after all, He gave it, and He empowers us to do so. We are to pray for His strengthening internally so that the just requirements of the law might be fulfilled in us as we walk, not according to the sinful nature, but according to the Spirit. This is how Paul expresses it in Romans 8:4:

> that the just requirements of the law might be fulfilled in us who walk not according to the flesh but according to the Spirit. (RSV)

So effort to obey the law and the work of the Spirit must never be opposed. Everywhere, the New Testament urges us to make an effort to do what is right, to strive for holiness (says Hebrews 12). "Put to death what is earthly in you," says Paul in Colossians. So effort is required on our part to obey God's commandments.

How Much of the Old Testament Law Applies Today?

There are various different views that have been put forward which I want to look at just briefly before I suggest what I think is a better alternative.

1. None of the Old Testament law applies today *because Christians are not under the law in any sense*. But this is a confusion of the Phaarisees' view of the law and the right view. Jesus, of course, condemned the Pharisees for their view, and Paul condemned the Judaisers for what we might call *legalistic righteousness*, in the sense of trying to earn fellowship with God by obedience to the law. Now in that sense, certainly, the Christian is not under the law. But Jesus commended the law of Moses, and we are thinking about the other sense as something which is right and true and a spiritual expression of the character of God and how we, as God's children are to live. Jesus condemned the Pharisees' use of the law, but he commended the law itself. In Matthew 5:17-20, in the very heart of the Sermon on the Mount where Jesus calls us to righteousness he says:

> Do not think that I have come to abolish the Law or the Prophets. I have not come to abolish them but to fulfill them. I tell you the truth, until heaven and earth disappear, not the smallest letter, not the least stroke of a pen, will by any means disappear from the Law until everything is accomplished. Anyone who breaks one of the least of these commandments and teaches others to do the same will be called least in the kingdom of heaven, but whoever practices and teaches these commands will be called great in the kingdom of heaven. For I tell you that unless your righteousness surpasses that of the Pharisees and the teachers of the law, you will certainly not enter the kingdom of heaven. (NIV)

A very strong statement by Jesus there about the persistence of the law. So, then, this first view that none of the law applies today just won't do. It involves a misunderstanding of law.

2. Another view which is very popular is that *only the Ten Commandments apply today*. But as you look into the law of Moses there is no reason to extract the Ten Commandments from the rest of the law as if they were fundamentally any different. The Ten Commandments are, in a sense, simply a summary of the whole of the law, and it is interesting the way Calvin dealt with the Old Testament law. He dealt with the whole law under the Ten Commandments. Each of the other laws, the punishments and so on, he deals with under one of the commandments,

and I think his understanding is quite right, because they were a summary of the law rather like Jesus' summary in "love the Lord your God with all your heart and love your neighbor as yourself." It's an even more concise summary of the whole law. So, again, I don't think this will do either.

3. This is the view which hasn't been around for a while. It's a view that was very popular among Christians after the Reformation and in the 17th and 18th centuries, particularly in America among the Puritans, but it's a view which has raised its head again and it has grown quite strongly among many Christians, particularly in the States. It is this: *the whole law still applies directly and literally to us apart from the ceremonial laws which were fulfilled in Christ.* For example, one group, who took this view in their journal published a couple of years ago, quoted John Cotton's laws of New England in the USA and commended this as the kind of law we ought to bear in our society today.[2] Those laws contained the death penalty for idolatry, for false prophecy, for witchcraft, for adultery, for homosexuality and so on. They are taken straight from the Mosaic law and applied to modern society today. I don't think this view is right, and I want now to turn from that and suggest an alternative, because I think this view fundamentally fails to see the distinction between the calling of Israel within a particular geographical boundary and the calling of the church as a people of God scattered through all the world.

4. I suggest an alternative that *the whole law is to be applied in principle and as a guide to the Christian today.* Paul gives us a key when he says that the law was given to be in charge of the Jews to lead them to Christ (in Galatians 3:24). He gives us, I think, a key there, when he says that the law was given to be in charge of the Jews to lead them to Christ. In other words, the whole law must be seen as having a very particular purpose of leading the Jews to Christ. Or we can think of the other statement, the letter kills, but the Spirit gives life. The law was preparing Israel for Christ's coming, and that purpose of the law which was preparing Israel has been fulfilled as Christ has come. We are no longer subject to the law in the same literal way (as the Jews were), but rather we are subject to the principles embodied in it. Now I want to look at this in some detail.

Subject to the Law

1. *The ceremonial law.* The ceremonial law pointed to Christ and is fulfilled in his coming. It is quite clear as you look at the New Testament that it sees all the ceremonies, all the sacrifices, as pointing to Christ. Think of John the Baptist's statement in John 1:29 when he says:

> Behold, the Lamb of God, who takes away the sin of the world. (RSV)

or of Peter speaking of Christ as the Lamb without blemish and without spot, 1 Peter 1:19. Or Paul, in 1 Corinthians 5:7, says:

> Christ, our Passover lamb, has been sacrificed. (NIV)

So the whole of the sacrificial system, the New Testament sees as pointing to and picturing the work of Christ.

The same with the priesthood. The book of Hebrews makes it quite clear that the Old Testament priesthood was a picture, a type beforehand, of Christ's priesthood. Hebrews 3:5-6, and 7:23-28: that with Christ as our priesthood, there no longer needs to be a human priesthood, either to make sacrifices for us or to seek the will of God for us. All believers now are priests who stand directly before God. So the whole priesthood pointed to Christ too. And, of course, this was already understood in the Old Testament, that the sacrifices and the priesthood were pointing towards the coming of the Messiah. Isaiah 53 and Psalm 110 speak in this way and see the sacrifices and the priesthood as finding their fulfillment in God's Son.

The same with the tabernacle and the temple. The New Testament speaks of Christ as being the fulfillment of what the tabernacle and the temple pictured to Israel. Remember how Jesus spoke about himself as the temple? (John 2:19 and 21, Hebrews 8:1-5)

The same with the Sabbath and the religious festivals of Israel. Paul says explicitly in Colossians 2:16-17 not to judge anybody about how they keep the Sabbath or a new moon, or a feast day, because these were a shadow, the substance is Christ. Paul is saying quite simply that Christ is the fulfillment of the Sabbath and the religious festival days. The whole ceremonial law has been fulfilled in Christ. The pictures have been replaced by the reality, so that we need no temples, no priesthood, no sacrifice and, I would say from Paul's statements in Colossians 2, that we should not require a rigid Sabbath observance in the same way it was required of Israel.

Then we ask the question: Does this mean that there is no application to us at all of these aspects of the law? I would answer that by saying, no, it does not. There are two senses in which the ceremonial law is still applied to us, still two ways in which, in a sense, we can fulfill it.

First of all, the whole ceremonial law, as I said, was a picture of Christ. Even now, after his coming, those pictures can help us understand the completeness of his work. Just as, for example, while I am away, I may

look at a photograph of my children and examine carefully the features of
their faces, so, in the same way, as we look at this sacrificial system, it
gives us the most beautiful picture of Christ's work. I think this is a very
important thing, because over and over again in the history of the church,
views of the meaning of Christ's death have arisen which could not possibly have arisen if people had kept the Old Testament sacrifices and their
purpose in mind. They remind us continually that what was absolutely
fundamental and essential to the death of Christ was substitution, propitiation for sins and the bearing of judgment in His death on the cross.

Secondly, the language of the sacrifices and ceremonies and priesthood
and temple is applied to believers in the New Testament. In other words,
the principles embodied in the ceremonial law are to be fulfilled in our
lives. Romans 12:1 again:

> Present yourselves as a living sacrifice to God

or 2 Timothy 4:6

> I am being poured out as a drink offering

or Hebrews 13:15 or 1 Peter 2:5, which speaks about the priesthood. We
are a new priesthood, we are a living temple. We are a priesthood (1 Peter
2:5-10) and we are a living temple (1 Corinthians 6:19), speaking of the believers as the temple of the Holy Spirit. So then, the whole ceremonial law
teaches us how we are to see our lives, giving the sacrifice of ourselves. Just
as the priests offered the burnt offering, the whole burnt offering on the
altar, so we are to sacrifice our whole selves, and, of course, this is what it
pictured to Israel. As well as being a picture of the sacrifice of Christ, it
was also a picture of purity. In this sense, the ceremonial law still applies
to us in principle and still should be fulfilled in our lives. There are many,
many passages in the New Testament where ceremonial laws applied to
the believer's life are to be expressed internally as we offer ourselves to the
service of God.

2. *The laws of the state setting Israel apart from the other nations as a
people.* Israel, as a nation, in a particular geographical location, was to be
set apart from the nations round about. The nation as a nation was to be
seen as the people of God. Consequently, there were ritual laws which set
Israel apart, the laws about clean and unclean food, for example, and there
were many other laws like this.

It is quite clear in the New Testament that we do not have to observe the
food laws and the ritual laws literally. Paul says in Colossians 2:16, "Don't
let people say to you, don't touch and taste and so on." In Mark 7:19, Jesus

declares all food clean and in Acts 10:1-15 and 28, 29, you have Peter's vision of a sheet being lowered from heaven with unclean animals in it, and he is told to arise and kill and eat. That vision tells us what the purpose of those food laws were, those ritual laws. They were setting apart Israel from the Gentiles, and the vision makes clear to Peter that that time is finished, it is fulfilled, and now there is to be the one people of God made up of people from all over the earth, from all the nations, so that the wall of partition which those laws set up between Israel and the nations is now set aside (as Paul expresses it elsewhere in Ephesians).

Today, as I said, the people of God are no longer to be identified with one geographical situation. We are a pilgrim people, Hebrews says (Hebrews 13:14), who are scattered all over the face of the earth, and we have no abiding city here. Our citizenship is in the kingdom of Christ which will one day be established in fullness on the whole earth when he will reign. But now the church must not be identified with a particular nation, so there is a change with regard to these laws, but again they speak to us about the purity of life. That is what Jesus does when he is talking about them in Mark 7. He speaks about the necessity of the purity of the heart. So what the ritual laws pointed to, which was the set-apartness of Israel, has again to be fulfilled in principle in our lives. In other words, unlike Israel, which was set apart, we are to be in the world now, Jesus says, but not of it. Our lives in purity are to be set apart from those round about us in our culture. Not by the ritual laws themselves, but what they pointed to: internal purity of the heart and of the life.

Also, in Israel, because of this set-apartness of them as a nation, there were particular punishments, serious punishments. The punishment of death for idolatry, false prophecy, false teaching, for sins of doctrine and belief. Within the boundary of Israel, these things were to be punished by the death penalty. Now this may strike us as odd today, and many Christians see it as quite barbaric and primitive, but we ought not to see it that way. When Elijah put the prophets of Baal to death on Mount Carmel, it was pleasing to God, and God's character does not change. We mustn't see it as barbaric. The question is, should we do the same thing today? Now within the boundary of Israel, God wanted to show with His temporal punishment the importance of the purity of doctrine and of true belief in the living God. We should notice that these laws were not applied outside the boundary of Israel. Think of Daniel in Babylon, or Jonah in Nineveh. Jonah wanted them to be applied directly but God commanded him to bring repentance instead.

Now the New Testament does not have a less serious attitude to false teaching. You can think of Jesus' statements in the whole Bible about false teaching — one can't imagine anything more powerful — where He says:

> If anybody causes one of these little ones . . . to sin, it would be better for him to have a
> large mill-stone hung around his neck and to be drowned in the depths of the sea. (NIV)

The New Testament still has this very strong attitude towards teaching falsehood. But the punishment changes because of the nature of the people of God as a pilgrim church scattered through the world, proclaiming the gospel in all nations to those who worship false gods. Our calling is to call people out from the worship of other gods: whether it is Allah, or materialism or the self, or whatever it is, not to put them to the sword.

Again, in the New Testament, even within the church, the punishment changes. Church discipline is spoken of in the New Testament for idolatry and so on. Think of Revelation, the letters to the churches there. (Revelation 2:14, 15, 20 and 1 John 4) The church is rebuked for tolerating false teaching, and it is quite striking when you look at the ministry of Jesus and the apostles that they did not demand the death penalty for those who opposed their teaching. The change in Paul is dramatic. Before his conversion, as a righteous Jew who seeks to observe the law of the Old Testament, he seeks to have those he sees as blaspheming God (*i.e.* the Christians) put to death. After his conversion, his attitude changes dramatically. He speaks about treating one's opponents with gentleness (in 2 Timothy 2:25-26) with a desire that they may return with a full commitment to the truth. Sometimes we get the most terrible vindictiveness and judgmental attitude among evangelicals towards others. Paul calls us to speak the truth with love and to refute our opponents with gentleness. If we are vindictive and negative and judgmental, we make it very, very hard for someone to return to the truth.

Again, the idea that we should punish idolatry and so on today ignores the parable of the wheat and the tares in Matthew 13. So we have to say that the Reformers and the Puritans were wrong when they sought to maintain true faith with the sword and have heretics put to death, that they confused the state of Israel with the calling of the church. In our own day, we would have to say that, if in practice this is what we did, then the gospel would be denied access to every other country in the world. What country would possibly let missionaries in if it knew that as soon as they gained any control at all, they would have all the false teachers put to death? It undermines the calling of the church to proclaim the gospel to all nations.

Now again, there is an application today, in the sense that these laws are to be fulfilled in principle within us. We are to hold fast to the word of God that is delivered to us and make sure that we teach it faithfully, and hold onto the absolute seriousness of the truth, and these penalties in Israel should remind us of the seriousness of teaching God's word and how God regards it, that we are to teach His word and not our own. Think of James' words in James 3:1 where he warns:

Let not many of you become teachers . . . for you shall be judged with greater strictness. (RSV)

and again, of Jesus' words to the Pharisees. Tremendously powerful words. These laws, again, have to be fulfilled in principle in us, so that anybody who teaches the word of God should teach it with fear and trembling. I mean that seriously: to teach us to have a sober attitude to God's word.

Also, in Israel, you have the death penalty for adultery and various other practices. Again, God was showing within the boundaries of Israel, by the penalties of the law, those things which are fundamental to the well being of any human society. But in the New Testament it is clear that the punishment changes from the death penalty to church discipline. So, whereas in the Old Testament the penalty for adultery was death, in the New Testament Jesus allows divorce for adultery and church discipline is required in the case of incest in 1 Corinthians 5 (and we can think of other examples). So the punishment changes, but again there is something which can be applied to us in the sense of seeing what is important to God, what He regards as fundamental to human life and to the sanctity of any society, when we see those areas in the Old Testament law where the death penalty was given for disobedience. But they cannot be applied directly.

The Principles Embodied in the Law

It should be clear from this that the law cannot be applied literally and absolutely in a kind of wholesale way, so that we take the Old Testament laws and write them down and say these should be the laws of the land, which is in a sense what the third suggestion I gave really says, that, apart from the ceremonial law, we can just take the Old Testament law and set it down wholesale as the law for our country today.

If we regard the law as a guide to us, both for our lives as individuals and for things that are important to our society, what are some of the principles which are embodied in the law? That's what I want to look at now. What are some of the principes which are embodied in the law, which the Christian ought to be working at to see put into practice in our society to-day? Remember, again, the statement from Deuteronomy 4:5-8, how God said no other nation had such just laws and that all the other nations would look and say, "Who are these people and who is their God, that they have such righteous laws?"[2]

1. *We can speak of the laws about the sanctity of human life, the sacredness of human life.* That is something which should be fundamental to us as Christians in terms of what we see as important to hold within our society. I just want to deal with one objection here. There are those Christians who argue that abortion involves the compassionate killing of unborn babies and handicapped newborns, infanticide, and that it is necessary, because it is the lesser of two evils. That is the argument of many: that it is compassionate. They appeal to the principle of the lesser of two evils, that not to abort or not to kill a handicapped newborn baby, not to sedate them so that they don't ask for food, is compassionate and is the lesser of two evils. Appeal is made to Biblical examples which they say show us the lesser of two evils. One example often appealed to is the death penalty, how God gave the death penalty for various things. They say, "You see, God regarded human life as sacred, and, in certain cases, He allowed human life to be taken." Another example I have come across is the appeal for divorce. God says divorce is wrong, but in the case of adultery, He allows it as the lesser of two evils. Or Rahab's lying, when she sheltered the Israeli spies. All of these are put forward as the example of the lesser of two evils, to undermine the sanctity of life.

I just want to respond to that before going on to the next point. These examples of the death penalty, of divorce and lying cannot possibly be compared to the instance of an unborn child or of a handicapped newborn baby. They are not examples of the lesser of two evils, I don't think. Rather, they are examples of the application of justice, which is a very different thing. It is the application of justice against somebody who has done something wrong, and certainly a handicapped newborn baby and an unborn child are not in that position. It is the murderer who forfeits his life as God's just penalty for murder. It is the adulterer who loses the right to marriage as the penalty for his adultery. It is the tyrant who loses the right to the truth as in the case of Jericho or Corrie Ten Boom in Holland sheltering Jews from the Nazis. The unborn and handicapped are innocent and not guilty and these kinds of examples cannot possibly be used to support the loss of sanctity of life. We have an absolute principle there which, it seems to me, is seen most clearly in the person of Christ, in the womb of Mary, that from the moment of His conception in Mary's womb, that that little child developing there was the Son of God and the Son of Man. This will be the first area, the sanctity of human life.

2. *The importance of family life.* Again, we see this as something fundamental to the Old Testament law. Now law cannot make people righteous,

it cannot force them to be righteous, but it can prevent some evil, and it can protect people from themselves and from one another. The Bible sees the family as the foundational unit of all society, and our laws ought to protect it and help give it respect; if they don't, if there is no respect for the family in society, there will be no respect for any other human institution. God has given the family from creation as something fundamental and foundational to all human society, and if we don't respect that, we will respect no other institution of society, and, of course, that is what we see. If we can't respect our wives or our husbands or our children or our parents, why should we respect somebody else, anybody else?

3. *Economic justice.* As Christians, we must be prepared both to give personally and to require just wages for people, as the Old Testament law does. Not the minimum that can be given at this moment because of the state of the market, but *just* wages. And on the other side, a just day's work, not, again, the minimum one can get away with at this moment in history.

4. *Impartiality in justice.* There are many, many times in the Old Testament law where those who judge are commanded to rule impartially, not to take bribes, not to be corrupt, and told that if they do, the whole institution of justice and government is undermined. We should notice here that the Old Testament law commands no partiality to the rich and that is its primary emphasis. It also commands no partiality to the poor, because God recognizes the moral responsibility of all human beings, so that all, no matter what their circumstances, are brought before the same standard of law, rather than their behavior simply being explained away by their circumstances. We come before a standard which God has given, no matter who we are. If we deny that, we end up denying the responsibility and significance of the person altogether. I can always remember a rather striking example from Truman Capote's book, *In Cold Blood*, where he was talking about that appalling murder that was done in Kansas, near a Kansas farm house. The lawyer for the defense appealed that these two men had really no responsibility for what they did because of their environment, because of their appalling upbringing (and they had an appalling upbringing). But, in the end, one of the men himself said: "This is ridiculous. You're making me into nothing, as if I had no control whatsoever over any of my life," because he recognized that fundamentally his human significance was being removed.[3]

5. *The importance for each generation to have a new beginning, and for each individual to have work.* I recommend you to look at the Sabbath and Jubilee year laws in Deuteronomy 15 and Leviticus 25. As you do, what you see are several things: that the failures of a previous generation

were not held against somebody; the law required the return of the land to the family, to the son, if his father had been either misfortunate or if he had been foolish or lazy in his handling of it, and so had lost it; it was required to be returned to the next generation so that there was the possibility for each new generation making a living. We have to say that an economic system which encourages unemployment and regards the economic machine as more important than people cannot be considered right. Essentially, the modern system of economics, this kind of thing we have in Britain at the moment, comes not from something Biblical, but from a Deistic understanding of a mechanical universe where, if you apply certain laws, everything will turn out right for as many people as possible. Neither understands the complexity of the world nor the sinfulness of human beings and institutions. As Christians, under the law of God, we have to put people before mechanisms.

6. *In the Old Testament law you see appropriate punishment.* In the West, our legal system, our punishment system, is breaking down because of the lack of appropriate punishments. There was no imprisonment for stealing, but rather repayment plus extra, and if there was no repayment, there had to be work until it was made up.

7. *Care for the poor.* Again, the Sabbath laws speak of this. The Sabbath year laws. The food of the land is there for the poor. The law required interest-free loans for the poor and the widow and the needy. (Exodus 22:25) The corners of the field were not cut, the fields wer not to be gone over a second time because they were to be left for the poor. I know Christians who practice that. My father-in-law does that in California. It's a wonderful thing, because there are many people still who do not have enough to eat. At the Sabbath year there was canceling of the debts for the poor, and the tithes were to be distributed to the priests and the Levites and the poor and the alien and the widow. (Deuteronomy 14:29, 26:12, 13) So that there is a requirement under the law. The government is the advocate for the poor and needy who have no other advocate both to make sure justice is done for them, and also to make sure that their needs are met.

8. *A high standard of evidence is required for conviction.* (Deuteronomy 19:15-21)

9. *The recognition of the hardness of men's hearts.* We have to accept as Christians that change in the law can only come gradually and involves very hard work. You can think of Jesus' comment on Moses' divorce law where He says it was allowed for the hardness of their hearts. But we, as Christians, have to recognize this. If we really want to affect our culture, we have to recognize the hardness of men's hearts and the difficulty of

bringing change, particularly to law. We can think of Wilberforce in the last century and slavery. It is a good example. It took him more than forty years before the law was changed, forty years of hard work. So if we are going to say that it's important to affect our society and to make sure that it has just laws, we have got to be prepared for hard work, and we ought to all be concerned for this. But we ought to pray, too, that some of us will see it a particular calling to be involved in this, just as Wilberforce was.

10. *The protection of the dignity of all human beings, regardless of race, or class, or color or culture.* There are always those in our society who are underprivileged and discriminated against, and, as Christians, we ought to be in the forefront of making sure they have an advocate.

These are some suggestions for Christian involvement in society on the basis of the teaching of the Old Testament law. I am sure you could add many, many others but these are a beginning. What is central must be our commitment to practice justice and mercy ourselves. In the whole of Scripture, we are to see our lives as consisting of a series of concentric circles or ripples going out from the center, and we have to start first of all with ourselves. Do I practice justice in my economic relationships? Do I pay people just wages or the minimum I can give them? Do I do a hard day's work? Do I consider what is right in my relationships? Do I care personally for those in need, for the widow and the orphan? How much of my time is devoted to them? That is where we must begin. Then, the next stage out, the next circle out, is, as Christians, we ought to be working to provide alternatives, creative alternatives in these areas, so that we're providing pilot lights, sign posts of the coming kingdom of God and setting up situations which take care of the need, which are a practice of justice which people in the culture round about us can see. The practice of justice and mercy on the individual level, and then corporately as believers, so that we are really finding good alternatives to care for people, whether it's unmarried mothers who are pregnant, or handicapped people, or whoever it is. That we as Christians are really providing a constructive alternative. That we are thinking and praying for God's wisdom to find creative alternatives.

The third circle is our responsibility to the society as a whole to change its laws. We must get them in that order and not the other way round. We cannot say we are concerned for mankind if we are not concerned for man, on an individual level. We become hypocrites.

DISCUSSION QUESTIONS

1. How does modern culture answer the question "What is right?"

2. Why is a society's value system so important in how that society operates?

3. Grace and law are often portrayed as opposites. Which appears first in Biblical revelation? Does either supersede or overrule the other?

4. How does the law reflect God's character? What effect does this have on how we should live?

5. What have been some of the misconceptions of the law in the believer's life? Explain.

6. How are we to grasp and integrate principles from God's truth into everyday life?

7. Why is it dangerous to consider any one political or legal system as the truly Biblical system?

8. In our modern era, should people be held responsible for their actions even though the actions may have psychological or environmental causes?

9. Should Christians work for political parties, trade unions, political action committees, or other lobby or legislative efforts? What assumptions of the major parties (from Libertarian to Marxism) flatly contradict God's truth?

10. The vast majority of humans have lived under the "might is right" approach. What forms of advocacy can you undertake to represent the powerless in other countries, in this country, and in your city or county?

"A fundamental part of our calling is to demolish
arguments and every pretention that sets itself up against
the true knowledge of God, and to take captive
every thought to make it obedient to Christ."

The Christian Mind
Jerram Barrs

Many of you have probably heard statements like, "Don't ask questions,
just believe"; "People don't need to think about God, they just need to respond to him"; "Ignore the mind and strike for the heart." Now this kind
of statements, which unfortunately we often hear among Christians,
point to the tradition which we have of a neglect of the mind, a tradition
which is particularly obvious among evangelical Christians, unfortunately. Christianity has been seen by many of us as an affair of the
heart only — something like marriage. Do I love God or don't I? Will I
humble myself before him and acknowledge I am a sinner or won't I?
Will I accept the good news of Christ's death and resurrection or not?
Now, of course, these questions are very important, and a personal
response to the gospel is absolutely essential, for there is nothing more
ugly than a dead orthodoxy, a mouthing of the right answers without
any reality of life, without any humility of heart, without a life of prayer
and personal commitment to Christ. But what I want to speak about is
this other problem — the neglect of the mind: the refusal and inability of
Christians, very often, to answer the questions that people give to them
about their Christian faith; the failure that we have to acknowledge as
Christians, the failure to really think as Christians about our lives and
about the societies in which we live; and the failure to really think as
Christians about our work, our study and our play. Now I want to ap-

proach this issue by asking a series of questions and attempting to answer
them.

1. Why the Neglect of the Mind Among Christians?
This is the first question:
>   Why is this? Why has there been this neglect of the
>   mind among Christians?

and I want to suggest the following reasons.

a. *The Influence of our Culture*
First of all, the influence of our culture — it's an obvious thing to say
that we live in a society which is materialistic, which is devoted to the pursuit of pleasure. In every hoarding we see, every advertisement that we see
on television and that we hear on the radio, we are encouraged to pursue
our own needs and our wants, and not just our needs and our wants, but
to become aware all the time of more and more ideas of need and want
that aren't really areas of need and want at all. We are encouraged by our
society to get more money and things, to get more space for ourselves,
more freedom for leisure and more pleasure.

The consequence of this pursuit of self-satisfaction in our society is a
great apathy. An apathy about issues which confront our culture, an
apathy about ideas, an apathy which says nothing is really important
enough to get worked up about except my own fulfillment, my own pay,
my working hours, my play time, my home. Manning Clark said in 1978:

> We are entering an era where a great dullness, so deep that no one can fathom it, is go-
> ing to descend on us like a cloud.[1]

I'm afraid that's a very true description of the culture in which we all live.
Now as Christians we can't fail to be influenced by this pervasive attitude.
Nothing can seem so important to us as our own welfare. As Christians we
may include our spiritual welfare along with our material welfare, but we
can become deeply self-centered, deeply materialistic, contemplating our
own well-being, if you like, contemplating our spiritual and material
navel.

Now this is one reason why I think there has been a neglect of real thinking about our Christian faith.

b. *The Move of Our Culture from a Biblical Understanding of Reality*
Our whole culture over the last 130 years or so has been moving further
and further away from a Biblical understanding of reality. Whether we

think of Darwin in the middle of the 19th century and the rise of evolutionary thought in our society — the way science is said over and over again in
our culture to completely contradict the Christian faith — whether we
think of the criticisms that have been made of the Bible historically, we are
living in a culture which largely dismisses Christianity as irrelevant and irrational. Christianity is considered by many in our society to be the refuge
of the weak who can't cope with the problems of life — they believe that
you have to commit intellectual suicide if you are going to become a
Christian.

Now the fact that we have this attitude toward Christianity in our culture
has caused many Christians to develop a kind of defensive response. The
enemy seems so big. Wherever we look in our culture, there are people who
say that Christianity is unnecessary and you really can't believe what the
Bible says. It's just a load of fairy tales. And for many Christians, their
response to this has been simply: well don't bother with all those questions, just believe. They don't really matter anyway, Christianity is just an
affair of the heart, and all these things are just red herrings. We can just get
on, and we can believe, we can pray and we can read our Bibles. The
society can go to the dogs with its ideas. So there's been this very defensive
attitude, and that's led all of us as Christians into a kind of ghetto where
we have become separated from the culture in which we live. We have
very little to say to it and very little comment to make about it. We have
adopted a defensive position — we've dug our trenches and we've got into
them.

c. A Non-Christian Can't Think about the Christian Faith?

A third reason is that some people have understood or have felt that the
fact that all human beings are sinners means that a non-Christian can't
really think about the Christian faith, that just because he isn't a Christian,
his eyes are so blinded to the truth of the gospel, that it's pointless to discuss whether Christianity is true. To get involved in apologetics (the defense of Christianity) is considered a waste of time because people say,
"Well, the non-Christian can't really think about it anyway. How can he
respond, his mind is darkened?"

d. Conversion — A Matter for the Spirit Only?

Fourth, and related to that, people have said that conversion is a matter
for the Holy Spirit only. Our task is simply to present the gospel to people
and pray, but to get involved in discussion and answering the questions is
a red herring. As I said at the beginning, ignore the mind and strike for the
heart. That's a very widespread attitude — "Who do you think you are,"

people say, "to think that you can persuade somebody that Christianity is true? That is the Holy Spirit's work." Could I remind you of a quotation from an American theologian earlier this century, when he said:

It is the Holy Spirit's work to open the heart,
it is ours to present the evidence.[2]

e. *The Use of Paul to Support this Teaching*

Fifth, some people have even used Paul's teaching in the New Testament to support this kind of approach to Christianity, to support the approach to saying, "Well, it's pointless discussing with people, it's pointless reasoning with them because, in fact, Paul says the gospel is literally foolish." They quote Paul's statements in 1 Corinthians and Colossians and use these passages to say that Christianity really is folly and it's pointless talking to somebody and trying to prove that it's true because the natural mind is folly

1 Corinthians 1:18:

For the message of the cross is foolishness to those who are perishing, but to us who have been saved it is the power of God. For it is written: "I will destroy the wisdom of the wise; the intelligence of the intelligent I will frustrate." Where is the wise man? Where is the scholar? Where is the philosopher of this age? Has not God made foolish the wisdom of the world? For since in the wisdom of God, the world through its wisdom did not know Him, God was pleased through the foolishness of what was preached to save those who believed. (NIV)

Now many Christians have looked at that passage, and they have drawn the conclusion that the Christian faith really is intellectual folly, foolishness, and that to get involved in discussion is a waste of time. Or Paul's statement in Colossians 2:8:

See to it that no one takes you captive through hollow and deceptive philosophy, which depends on human tradition and the basic principles of this world, rather than on Christ. (NIV)

So this kind of Scripture is quoted to support a neglect of the Christian mind.

2. What are the Unfortunate Effects of this Teaching?

Now I want to ask another question, and that is this: What are the unfortunate effects? What are the effects of this teaching which says that Christian thinking is unimportant? These, I suggest are some of the effects:

a. *A Loss of Emphasis on the Fact of the Truth of Christianity*
First of all, because we have not used our minds to think about the Christian faith, there has consequently been a loss of emphasis on the fact that Christianity really is true, that it really is the truth about the world in which we live, that God actually exists, that He has made the world, that He has made us, that these statements are actually true. As Christians we have retreated into holding onto our Christian faith as a religion which we believe, but we don't really think in our heart of hearts that it is the truth about reality that can actually stand up against the world in which we live. Because we have neglected a Christian mind, we have developed increasingly a view that Christianity is simply a refuge when we're in trouble. And, of course, Christianity is a refuge when we're in trouble, but it's a refuge when we're in trouble because it's true.

b. *A Failure to Answer the Questions of Non-Christians*
Secondly, because of this failure to think as Christians, we have failed to answer adequately the questions of non-Christians. Even though Peter says in 1 Peter 3:15 — "Always be ready to give an answer for the hope that is in you," many non-Christians have gone away from us thinking that our attitude means that you have to lose your mind to come to Christ.

I remember the first Christians I met at university were like that. When I tried to ask them questions, they didn't want to know. They just said, "Well, put those aside, don't think about those kinds of things. Just listen to the gospel." This is a very serious failure, and we're disobedient to the Word of God if that is what we have done.

c. *A Failure to Answer our Own Children's Questions*
This is something which is very sad, because we have neglected a Christian mind, we have failed to answer the questions of our own children adequately. So often we have said to our children, "Don't ask these questions, just believe," that when they get out into the world, (when they get to college or university, or even into high school, when they get to work, when they read the magazines and watch television), they have no means whatsoever of resisting the pressure of a culture whose ideas are totally opposed to a Biblical understanding. A point I want to make here is this: some of you may think that what I am talking about is something which applies only to intellectuals. Nothing could be further from the truth. My own children, who are 5, 8 and 9, ask me the most difficult questions that anyone ever asks me. All small children ask questions. They ask questions about death, about suffering and about evil in the world, they ask ques-

tions about the Trinity ("How can Jesus be God and man?"). They ask questions like, "If God knew it was going to be so awful, why did he create the world?" They ask questions about evolution and Adam and Eve because they get taught evolution at school, even in primary school. When you read the Bible to them, they say, "Did that really happen?" when you read an account of a miracle. It is not at all an issue of being an intellectual. These are the questions that all people ask.

Now what do we say when our children ask us these questions? Do we say if they ask us about suffering and death, "You're only five, you're much too young to worry about such things. You must leave this big things to God. He'll take care of them."? Or, when they get a bit older, do we say, "Well, what you need to do is read your Bible some more, and to pray some more, and then these things will fall into place, and they won't seem so pressing"? Now if we do that to our children, we build up an unconscious attitude in them and later a conscious attitude, that it isn't worth asking questions, because there aren't any answers to the questions, and they grow up thinking Christianity really can't deal with the questions at all, and it's no wonder when they go out and leave home, that they just turn away from the Christian faith in droves. They grow up with an enormous divide between what they're taught to think in school and from the television, and what we teach them to believe. It's no wonder that a split comes at some point, and what they often give up is their Christian faith.

d. *Application of our Christian Life to Ever Smaller Areas of Life and Thought*

If we neglect to think as Christians, what happens is simply that our Christian faith becomes applied to smaller and ever smaller areas of life and thought. For many of us, our Christian faith applies only to areas like reading the Bible and praying (which of course, are fundamentally important), going to church and some narrow aspects of personal morality. Our thinking hasn't gone beyond that in terms of what attitude we really ought to have toward the society in which we live. Why do we hold this particular morality? When our children say to us, "Well, why shouldn't I sleep around like everybody else?," do we just say, "You don't, because God says so?" Or do we explain why? It's a very profound thing because our Christian thinking gets applied to smaller and smaller areas if we neglect a Christian mind.

e. *Copying the Thought of the World*

In fact, of course, we can't avoid thinking, and we think all the time. But if we don't think as Christians about the affairs of our life and the affairs of the society in which we live, we just copy the thought of the world. We really have no alternative: either develop a Christian mind or simply think the way the world thinks. (God has made us with minds, whether we like it or not.) What happens is, as we copy the ideas of the world, of the culture in which we live, we end up with a great division between our Christian thinking or our Christian faith and what we actually think about — the things that make up the greater part of our life.

I am not exaggerating when I say this. When I speak at universities in England (to Christian Unions), it's very rare to find any students who have thought at all from a Christian perspective about the subjects which they are studying. They may be in psychology or politics or sociology, learning ideas which are completely opposed to a Biblical understanding of man and of human life and of the Christian's calling. They may simply accept these, because nobody has ever suggested that they think as a Christian about what they're hearing.

I went to a university in South Wales a couple of months ago, and the Student Union leader stood up at the beginning of the meeting and said, "I've just read something which says that 90% of Christian students, when they leave the university, either give up being Christians altogether or they just become pew warmers." And he said, "Now, what's the solution to that? The solution is that we might help each other to have better devotional times." But that is not the solution to the problem. It may be a partial solution, but the fundamental solution is giving people a really solid foundation for their Christian faith, and a really clear understanding of what they believe and why they believe it, so that when they go into the world they can stand up. They needn't be ashamed as Christians, and they needn't have this terrible division between their Christian faith and everything else that they think.

So what we're talking about is something which is a real tragedy — a tragedy which causes us to lose our children, to not present the gospel faithfully to people and to be a very poor witness in the world, because Jesus has called us to be the salt of the earth, and that means, among other things, to — in the area of thought in our culture — offer alternatives to the terrible ideas that exist in the society around us.

3. What is Paul Saying in 1 Corinthians 1 and 2?

What is Paul saying, in fact, in 1 Corinthians 1 and 2? He's talking in verses 18 and 19 about the message of the cross being foolishness to those who are perishing, and then he says in verse 20:

Where is the wise man? Where is the scholar? Where is the philosopher of this age? Has

not God made foolish the wisdom of the world? For since in the wisdom of God the world
through its wisdon did not know Him, God was pleased through the foolishness of what
was preached to save those who believed. (NIV)

Now what is Paul saying here? Is Paul saying that the gospel is literally
foolish? That to present it to the mind is a waste of time, that the mind
must be bypassed? No, he's not saying that, and it's quite clear in the
passage. What Paul is saying is this: That the world in its rebellion against
God thinks that the gospel is foolish in contrast to its own ideas and
philosophy. That the world, the society in which we live, thinks that its
own ideas are wisdom and that the gospel is folly.

a. *Men Who Reject God think the Gospel is Folly*
So, first of all, it is not that the gospel is folly but that men who reject
God think that it is folly. The reason they think it is folly is because it says
the very opposite of what they think, the very opposite of the philosophies
that our society or Paul's society developed. But the Bible's ideas about the
nature of the world and about the nature of man, are completely opposed
to the ideas of our culture. Therefore our culture thinks that the gospel is
folly.
But what does Paul say in verse 20? He says, "God has made foolish the
wisdom of the world." And verse 25? "The foolishness of God is wiser than
man's wisdom." So what is Paul saying then? He's saying this: That, in
fact, it is the non-Christian thinking which is foolishness; the gospel is not
actually folly, but it is the thinking of the world which is in fact foolish.
God has made it foolish, for the gospel is the only true wisdom. That is
Paul's point in this passage — that the gospel is the power and wisdom of
God as opposed to the foolishness of the thinking of the world.
Now it's very helpful to compare this passage with Romans 1:18-25 because, there, Paul says something very similar. You will notice in this passage how Paul uses some of the same language about foolishness and wis-
dom that he uses in 1 Corinthians 1.

The wrath of God is being revealed from heaven against all the godlessness and wickedness of men who suppress the truth by their wickedness, since what may be known about
God is plain to them, because God has made it plain to them. For since the creation of the
world God's invisible qualities — his eternal power and divine nature — have been clearly
seen, being understood from what has been made, so that men are without excuse.
For although they know God, they neither glorified him as God nor gave thanks to him,
but their thinking became futile and their foolish hearts were darkened. Although they
claimed to be wise, they became fools and exchanged the glory of the immortal God for
images made to look like mortal man and birds and animals and reptiles.
Therefore God gave them over in the sinful desires of their hearts to sexual impurity for

the degrading of their bodies with one another. They exchanged the truth of God for a lie, and worshipped and served created things rather than the Creator — who is forever praised. Amen. (NIV)

There, again. Is Paul saying in these two passages that the gospel is folly, is foolish, and any attempt to approach the mind with it is doomed to failure? No! Paul's contrast is between the wisdom of the world (which is truly folly because it has rejected God's truth) and the truth of the gospel — which is the only true wisdom, but which men in their foolishness say is folly.

And again, is Paul describing as simple a presentation of the gospel as possible, regardless of questions? No! He isn't! Paul insists here that we should persuade people, we should be involved in discussion, in showing them Christianity is really the truth, that it is the only true wisdom about the world in which we live. What Paul insists is this: when we proclaim the gospel, what we proclaim is the truth of God's Word. What we proclaim is God's wisdom rather than human ideas. That is the problem, of course, because it's very easy for us to think, "Well, I can make the gospel acceptable to people in the 20th century by making a synthesis of Christian ideas with the ideas of the society in which we live." So we have a mixture of Christianity and Marxism, or we have a mixture of Christianity and eastern religions, or we have a mixture of Christianity and materialism (or whatever it happens to be). But it's this that Paul is absolutely rejecting, because he says that the ideas of our culture (of the world) are folly. They are folly because they reject God and in rejecting God, they reject what is true. He says the whole universe declares that God exists, that Christianity is true, that it's clearly to be seen by people. When they reject that, they are being foolish.

Now, if we try to present the gospel in the wisdom of the world, — that is, to mix it with the world's ideas — then we're doing something which is very dishonoring to God, because we're mixing his wisdom with the foolishness of man. So Paul again, here, as he does in Corinthians, contrasts the wisdom of God's truth with the folly of human ideas.

But it's clear from elsewhere in the New Testament also, that Paul never simply made what is called "a simple presentation of the gospel". Of course, he said it as simply as he could and as clearly as he could, but he says in Acts 20:27, "I didn't hesitate to proclaim to you the whole counsel of God." In other words, this is what I proclaim to you: God who exists and His creation of the world; the fall of man and the redemption of man from sin; and the second coming. In other words, he proclaimed the whole Christian faith as the truth.

As we look through the book of Acts we see Paul's own practice. How did he speak to people? Read Acts 17-19 in light of what I have said here. In that passage we see two different kinds of situations. When Paul went to a Jewish situation, to a synagogue — what does it say? It says Paul reasoned with them, he argued with them, and he sought to persuade them that Jesus was the Messiah. It says he stayed there three months, seeking to convince them that Jesus is the Christ. He reasoned and argued and persuaded. It says it over and over again in the book of Acts. Paul didn't hesitate to use his mind to appeal to the evidence to present the Christian faith. Those were the Jews who already believed in God! When he went to a Gentile situation (Acts 17), what did Paul do there? He started talking about the fact that God made the world, that it's foolish to worship idols when human beings are so much more than idols. In other words, Paul went to where the people were and he started from there to proclaim Christianity as the truth. He presented it and the evidence for it to the minds of his hearers, and he sought to convince them, to persuade them that it was true. And Paul wasn't working against the Holy Spirit — of course not! He prayed for the work of the Holy Spirit. But he saw as his calling to insure that there should be no stumbling block in the way of people believing.

b. Our Response

So then our response has to be — if we have neglected the development of a Christian mind — a confession that this is wrong, that it's displeasing to God, that the effects it's had have been disastrous on ourselves, on our children and on the people whom we have tried to speak to. We must be prepared, first of all, to really try to answer the questions that people ask us. In the end, it's not a matter of being intellectual, it's simply a matter of compassion. If somebody comes to me and says, "Why is there so much evil in the world? Why do you believe in God?" and I refuse to answer that question, it shows a terrible lack of compassion. So out of compassion, we must be prepared to answer the questions that people bring to us. And if we can't answer them right away, because we haven't thought about them, then we must say to the person, "Well, I shall go away and think about it, and then I will try to answer your questions." We must be prepared to do some hard work to try to answer the questions that people have, because the answers to those questions are here in Scripture. It's God's truth, and it's laziness in the end not to answer either our children's questions or the questions of others.

And second, we must be prepared to develop a Christian mind, to really understand the society in which we live and to make a positive Christian contribution to it.

I want to finish by just looking at a couple of passages in the New Testament which speak about this necessity of getting to work where our minds are concerned. Remember, Jesus said, "Man does not live by bread alone, but by every word that proceeds from the mouth of God." Now, for us as Christians in this materialistic culture, it's very easy just to live by bread alone. But Jesus calls us to live by every word that proceeds from the mouth of God, to really think about what His word says to us and to understand it and apply it in our lives and present it to others.

There are three short passages which I will quote:

First, Romans 12:2

> Do not conform any longer to the pattern of this world, but be transformed by the renewing of your mind. (NIV)

That's what Paul calls us to. Not to conform to the society in which we live. But how can we not conform? He says we will only be transformed, we will only be changed when we renew our minds. Then we will be able to test and approve what God's will is, his good, pleasing and perfect will.

And then, in 1 Peter, Peter says this:

> Prepare your minds for action. (1 Peter 1:13, NIV)

That should be our desire every day of our lives — to prepare our minds for action because we are surrounded by ideas which are hostile to our faith and which undermine our commitment to be obedient to God in our lives, practically. So we have to prepare our minds for action.

And third, in 2 Corinthians 10:3-5:

> For though we live in the world, we do not wage war as the world does. The weapons we fight with are not the weapons of the world. [Again, they're not the wisdom of the world.] On the contrary, they have divine power to demolish strongholds. We demolish arguments and every pretention that sets itself up against the knowledge of God, and we take captive every thought to make it obedient to Christ. (NIV)

And that is our calling as Christians. A fundamental part of our calling is to demolish arguments and every pretention that sets itself up against the true knowledge of God, and to take captive every thought to make it obedient to Christ.

DISCUSSION QUESTIONS

1. Why is thinking important as Christians? Is an accurate understanding enough?

2. Why is there a neglect of the mind among Christians? How has our culture, our evangelism, our modern Bible study, supported this view?

3. What is the effect of a "neglect of mind" in our convictions? our evangelism? our lives?

4. If we don't think with a Biblical mind what are we left with?

5. How does a lack of thinking divide our Christian lives from our daily lives?

6. What is "the foolishness" Paul speaks of in I Corinthians?

7. How are we to develop a Christian mind?

". . . all human beings, whether male or female, are made to reflect God's personhood of love and moral righteousness, of rationality and creativity."

Male/Female Relationships

Jerram Barrs

Let's try to think through a Biblical understanding of what our attitude ought to be towards our relationships together, between men and women in marriage and as single people. I want to start by speaking a little bit about the background in our culture; then, second, say something about unhelpful Christian responses to the background in our culture; and third, suggest a way to a Biblical response.

The Background in our Culture

I want to divide this into two parts — first to talk about male chauvinism, just very briefly, and then about the feminist movement.

1. *Male Chauvinism*

Whenever we think about this issue of what the relationships ought to be between men and women, we have to understand that we are living in a culture which is very chauvinistic, that in the past — and to a great extent, still in the present — our society understands the role of men and women in a very strict way. The role of most men is seen to be strictly outside the home as providers. Many women in our society are treated as servants by their husbands, servants whose only calling in life is to keep home and raise children. Now, obviously, keeping home and raising children is in itself a good thing, but in our culture — in a male chauvinist society — these tasks have been considered as menial tasks, below men to do. In such a society single women are regarded as unfulfilled: people to joke about and to be amused by. We are accustomed in our culture, in a male chauvinist society, to a double standard of morality where for many people it's all right for men — for husbands — to be unfaithful or to sleep around before marriage, but for women it's considered unforgivable.

We have a history of a lack of equal opportunity for women and a lack of equal pay for equal work. To a greater degree still, there are many people in our culture who think that women ought to have no part to play in wider society. Sometimes, in some cultures, it's been even worse (as in the Islamic society — basically women have been hidden away). This male chauvinism in our culture has led to the fact that even when women do things outside the home, they are usually still expected to do all the housework. I always remember a couple who lived opposite my parents who were like this. They worked together in a university department in Southampton. When they came home at the weekend, after having very full days all week (both of them), the husband went off to drink with his friends and to sports and things, and the wife had to stay at home and do all the week's housework. That's the kind of background that we have to consider as we think about this issue.

2. *The Feminist Movement*

Next, I want to say just a little bit about the family's response to this. Quite understandably, there's been a rebellion against many of the ideas of our chauvinist society, a longing by women to break out of a stereotyped role that chauvinism has put upon them, a longing to break away from the view of women as a kind of piece of goods, a chattel servant and an emotional weakling. A right demand for equal opportunity and equal pay and recognition of their gifts and talents in society at large.

But along with this quite understandable and quite right reaction, there has gone also, largely in the feminist movement, a longing to break completely out of the role of the woman as the child bearer and the child rearer and home maker, and to see career as the only real fulfillment for a woman — a career out in society. In England, the paper I read is *The Guardian*, and over and over again in the women's pages in *The Guardian* the great majority of the articles are encouraging women to see any kind of role in the home as a home maker or child raiser as something which is completely unfulfilling and that the only way to be fulfilled is to go out to have one's own space, to create a career in the culture at large. I think this has had a very damaging effect and I want to come back to it later.

Along with this has gone a rejection of any authority structure in marriage at all, because, to the feminist, any kind of authority structure is seen simply as male dominance. Sadly, the feminist movement has been influenced by the general demand of our culture for total freedom — not just simply freedom from male chauvinism and freedom from male dominance, but complete freedom. Our society defines freedom simply as the freedom to do what one desires. So, they have argued for sexual freedom for women. Rather than freedom to do what is right, they want to have freedom sexually like they see men having, and even freedom over their own bodies in the campaign for abortion.

Unhelpful Christian Responses

Second, I want to look at some Christian responses to this which I consider unhelpful to this social background.

1. *Re-emphasis of Strict Roles in Marriage*

First of all, many Christians, in alarm at what they see happening in our culture, have re-emphasized very strict roles in marriage. There are many books which have been published on a Christian view of marriage which have emphasized these strict roles. These have said that we look at the society and see marriages falling apart, we see the home crumbling. What is needed to solve this problem is a re-emphasis on authority. So you have the teaching of the chain of command — God, man, woman — that all authority resides in the man and that a woman's role is to submit and to serve, to raise children and to keep home. This is often very narrowly defined. If one asked a series of questions of many of these books, they would answer the questions: who should make the decisions in the home? who should control the money? who should be the aggressive leader? It should be the man. Who should follow? Who should care for the children? Who should be passive? The woman.

I always remember reading in one book, and it's not one of the most extreme by any means (a book on the Christian family), where the author actually said that it was wrong for men to ever change diapers because this would damage their role in front of any older children. There is an enormous amount of absurd teaching like this in reaction to some of the ideas in our culture.

Along with this has gone the idea which I also think is very unhelpful (and I want to come back to it later when we look at a Biblical response), of the chain of priesthood in the home. That is, that the man is the priest in the home and that any decision that the wife makes has to be covered by her husband. Some of you have probably heard of this idea of covering. It's sometimes taught that if the husband is away, the wife is subject to attacks of Satan, that she always needs her husband's covering before she makes any decisions. So basically, again, when we are thinking about spirituality, in this kind of response to our society which some Christians have put forward, we have a kind of chain — a chain of priesthood of man and woman, with one below the other.

2. *The Evangelical Feminist Movement*

Another response which I think is unhelpful (by some other Christians), has been what I might call the evangelical feminist movement. These have insisted that we should be prepared to abandon different roles for men and women completely. They have argued that Paul's teaching on marriage structures in Ephesians 5 and Colossians 3, where Paul speaks quite clearly about the husband as the head of the home, is reversible — that we can just turn it around at will. We can say that both the husband is the head of the wife and the wife must obey her husband, and that if the wife is the head of the husband, then the husband must obey the wife. They have just turned them straight around.

Others, like Paul Drewitt in his book, *Man is Male and Female*, (which is tremendously influential), have argued that Paul's teaching on structure in marriage is simply wrong. The reason Paul had such a view of structure in marriage and authority in marriage is that Paul had a pharisaical training and that even though Paul Drewitt says Paul was the greatest apostle of Christ, yet Paul couldn't escape from his pharisaical training. In this area of marriage and male/female relationships, what Paul teaches is essentially pharisaical. He goes on to say that in the 20th Century, we have a greater spiritual insight at this point, that we can recognize that Paul was caught in his culture, and we can simply abandon those roles. Drewitt insists that it is impossible to have both the quality and the structure in marriage.[1]

3. *Pre-marital Relationships*

A third unhelpful Christian response, but in a slightly different area, is that many Christians have simply copied the culture in terms of their understanding of pre-marital relationships. We are living in a culture where sleeping around is taken for granted and seen as a right — an essential freedom. An increasing number of young Christians in our society have copied this pattern. There are many still who are not prepared to actually sleep together, but at every other level of their relationship, they just live in the way that the rest of the society does. There is the same basic mentality towards the necessity for sexual fulfillment, for human fulfillment; the same basic mentality towards the way we dress, towards the way we present ourselves sexually to others and the way we view others sexually (as sexual objects); the same basic mentality our culture has towards being single — that is, as a time of self-fulfillment without responsibility.

A Biblical Response

Third, to come to a Biblical response.

1. *The Importance of Personhood*

First of all, Biblically, we must say in this area that our central emphasis has to be placed on the importance of personhood, not on sex or on different roles. Genesis 1:26, 27 makes it quite clear that we are made male and female in the image of God; that all human beings, whether male or female, are made to reflect God's personhood of love and moral righteousness, of rationality and creativity. It is very striking that the Bible says very little about roles and differences in roles and very little about the difference between the sexes. The fundamental emphasis of the whole of Scripture is on personhood, on being human, on being made in the image of God and being restored to the image of God through the work of Christ and the power of the Holy Spirit.

The central emphasis of Scripture is not (like many Christian books today), on the difference between the sexes in terms of different kinds of roles. The central Biblical emphasis is on the fact that we are all humans, so that almost all the commands of Scripture are directed to both male and female, without any differentiation. Now this means, among other things, that a home must be a place where the fundamental characteristics of the image of God are lived out and practiced and passed on to the children. This is the responsibility of both parents, of father and mother.

a. A home must first of all provide the experience of love, acceptance and forgiveness, because God is love and we, as his children, are made to love one another.

b. A home must provide the experience and teaching of judgment for wrong doing, of discipline according to God's law; and this applies to both parents simply because we are human.

c. A home must provide a positive example in the teaching of holiness and righteousness, or relationships that are good, that have integrity, of sexual faithfulness and hard work.

d. A home must provide the teaching of the truth — how to think and discern truth from falsehood so that our children may grow up no longer infants tossed to and fro by every wind of doctrine, but really understand the truth. This is the responsibility of both parents.

e. A home must provide the experience and the teaching of creativity and significance, of responsibility: that fundamental to our humanity is that we are made to be creative, we are made responsible that both we ourselves as parents and our children will have to give an account to the Lord for the way we have built our lives.

Then, of course, one could spell out many, many other things. Fundamental things which involve our human existence are the responsibility of both parents in a marriage and in a home — not of one or the other;

they can't be divided up.

2. *The Priesthood of all Believers*

In considering a Biblical response we have to say that the New Testament teaches very clearly the priesthood of all believers — male and female. It does not teach a chain of priesthood as if a man had a greater, or more special, access to God in the home than the woman. We can think of Paul's statement in Galatians 3:28-29 where he attacks very strongly any idea that, simply because I am a man, I should be reluctant to learn about Biblical truth or about Christian spirituality from a woman. If I am reluctant to learn from a woman in these areas, the problem is mine — it's a problem of my arrogance rather than any kind of obedience to Scripture.

The question of eldership in the church is quite a different matter because that's clearly seen as a part of the structure that God has given in Scripture.

But on the personal level of being prepared to learn from one another, all of us must be humble before one another and be prepared to learn from another male or female.

3. *Biblical Structures*

There are clearly Biblical structures given. The New Testament teaches in Ephesians 5 and Colossians 3 and elsewhere that there is a headship given in marriage to the man. How do we then respond to Paul Drewitt's charge that it is impossible to have both structure and equality? My response would be this: We can look to the parallel of the Trinity. In the Trinity we see both equality of persons and the structure of relationship. Christians have always affirmed that the Son is fully God, that in His Godhead He is equal to the Father. But at the same time, Christians have always affirmed that there is a structure in the relationship between the Father and the Son, where the Son submits Himself to do the Father's will. So that in that doctrine which is the very heart of the Christian faith, we see both structure and equality. This, I think, is what we are taught about marriage in Scripture, quite clearly.

While we should not be prepared to accept the very rigid understanding of roles that is taught in some Christian books (as I suggested earlier), it is quite clear in Scripture that there is some role difference between men and women.

I think we must say that the feminist criticism is not radical enough. The feminist, in devaluing somewhat motherhood and home making, has in fact not made a radical enough criticism of what is happening in the society. What they have done, in fact, is to accept the male chauvinist evaluation of human worth. The male chauvinist evaluation of human worth says our worth is determined by our income and our job status in society.

As a Christian, I would want to reject that absolutely. There is nothing in Scripture that teaches that my worth as a human being is created by my income and my job status in society. The feminists have made the mistake, I think, in accepting that evaluation and then insisting that the only way for freedom and fulfillment for women is to compete equally in the market place and find fulfillment in careers, and that therefore it's necessary to demean motherhood and home making. As Christians we have to respond to that and say, "No, that is not so." We have value because we are made in the image of God, male and female. It's hard to think of anything which has more value than being a mother, bearing and raising children and creating a home which is a godly home.

To look at the women in the last chapter of Proverbs is very instructive. What we find there is a life that is a home-centered life, but one which is not limited to the home. That woman is going out, she's buying and selling, she's doing all kinds of things out in the wider society. It's a life which is radiating outwards from the home.

4. *Service — the Center of all Relationships*

We must stress that, while there are Biblical structures which are given in marriage (and to some extent there are roles which cannot be just lightly rejected), the Scripture teaches that what is central in all relationships is service. Whatever relationship we are talking about, whether we are talking about the parent/child relationship or the husband/wife relationship — what is central Biblically is love and service. Paul says in Philippians 2 that all of us in all our relationships are to imitate Christ, that we are to look to the interests of others, that we are to think of others and their needs more highly than we think of ourselves. So that headship in marriage for a Christian man does not mean domination, it means commitment to serve. Paul spelled that out very clearly in Ephesians 5 — that we are to love our wives as Christ loved the church. He loved it and gave himself for it.

Contrary to our society, which says that fulfillment comes from freedom: freedom for the individual, the freedom to do one's own thing, the freedom to have one's own space, Biblically, freedom and fulfillment come for us through service, for both the husband and wife. Our whole attitude toward marriage as Christians ought not be: What expectations do I have from this other person? but: What obligations do I have to him/her? Scripture does not encourage us to ask, what are our expectations? It spells out for each of us, whether man or woman, what our obligations to each other are in serving one another under the lordship of Christ.

5. *Singleness and Sexuality*

Just finally to say something briefly about singleness and sexuality.

Contrary to our culture, which insists that fulfillment for single persons comes because they are free from obligation, free from right responsibility, the Scripture has a very different view. Fulfillment for the single person comes through service, just as it does for the married person. I think we ought to say that the gift of singleness which Paul speaks of in 1 Corinthians 7, 8, the charisma of singleness, is one of the most neglected gifts in the church. This is the fault both of the married people who have often felt that single people have little to give and are unfulfilled, and of the single people who have copied the pattern of the culture where singleness is seen as a time of freedom and irresponsibility.

If we look at Christ, he certainly wasn't unfulfilled. We should see singleness in the kingdom of God as something very important. Being single gives one an unequalled opportunity to serve other people in a way that becomes very difficult when one is married and has children, because one's primary responsibility is to them. We should not see singleness as a kind of temporary hole between adolescence and marriage, but rather as a time of unequalled opportunity for serving others.

Also I think we need to make a radical re-examination of our understanding of relationships between the sexes for single people. If we ask what the New Testament says about how we should treat one another outside the context of marriage, we remember Jesus' statement in the Sermon on the Mount (Matthew 5:27-30) where he says that if we even look at people to lust after them, we commit adultery in our hearts. In other words, Jesus is saying it is not good enough just not to sleep with people, but our attitude between the sexes has to be one of purity from the heart outwards. In other words, we can't copy the standards and practices of our society and have a casual attitude towards casual physical and sexual involvement. What we are called to by the New Testament is something radically different. Paul says in 1 Timothy 5:1, 2:

> Treat younger men as brothers, older women as mothers, and younger women as sisters, with absolute purity.

Absolute purity — that has to be the standard by which we treat one another outside of the context of marriage. Now why?

In Scripture, sexuality is seen as a good thing, as a gift from God, but the expression of sexual desire in Scripture is limited to the commitment of one man to one woman on a lifelong basis, and the expression of sexual desire outside of that is contrary to Jesus' command. Basically, it is selfish and self-centered. What we do in our relationships very often is simply to treat one another as objects. We treat one another as objects by separating sexuality from the whole commitment of one person to another person in all of our lives. When we separate sexuality from that whole commitment, what we are doing is ultimately destructive and hurtful. According to God's word, sexual expression brings the consummation of a commitment of a man to a woman in the whole of life. If we want to have sexual expression without that commitment, what we are doing is hurting one another and being selfish, thinking of our own temporary pleasure and fulfillment and not at all of the other person. Sexual expression communicates commitment — it necessarily arouses the expectation of commitment. When there is no intention of that, its effect can only be damaging; it's basically something which is self-indulgent.

What we are saying in casual, physical involvement of our bodies ought to mean "I love you." But in fact we're saying, because we refuse to express commitment in any other way, "I really don't love you," in terms of what love really means. Consequently, we're simply being selfish.

DISCUSSION QUESTIONS

1. What have been the negative consequences of our chauvinistic culture?

2. The Feminist Movement seems ample evidence of the desires of many women to "break out" of society's mold for them. What is good about this? What is damaging?

3. What are the ill-effects of complete personal "freedom"? Why is it a myth to believe in such a concept?

4. How have roles for men and women been traditionally defined? In breaking with traditional roles, men and women have also surrendered valuable responsibilities. What are some?

5. Why is personhood the emphasis of the Bible rather than roles, differences in sexes, etc.? What effect does this have on how we live?

6. In what ways are the home-centered duties of a mother-wife considered menial in our society? Why is this view wrong?

7. To dismiss Paul's teaching concerning women as cultural teaching no longer applicable for today seems fashionable in some "Christian" quarters. How does this undermine the authority of Scripture? How is it overall harmful?

8. How does the Trinity help us understand the relationships and responsibilities of men and women?

9. Why *must service* be the center of *all* relationships? How can one serve and at the same time be a leader?

10. Barrs states that fulfillment comes *not* from self-freedom, but from self-sacrifice and service. Is this true? Is using freedom to serve having any freedom at all?

11. Why is there an authority structure given for marriage in Scripture? Why is it unhelpful to emphasize this in a narrow, restricted sense? Is it bad to disregard this structure altogether? What is the home to provide?

Dick Keyes

Dick Keyes

Born in Massachusetts, Dick studied history at Harvard University. After graduation, Dick traveled in Europe where he had contact with the Swiss L'Abri. These times of study and exposure were critical in his assessment of Christianity. It was at the end of this year of travel and study that Dick became confident in the truth of the Gospel and made clear his commitment.

Returning to the United States, Dick worked in business, served in the Army and then pursued graduate studies. He completed a Masters of Divinity at Westminister Theological Seminary in 1970, specializing in apologetics and counseling. He and his wife, Mardi, visited the Swiss L'Abri and then traveled to London to work at the English L'Abri. At the same time, Dick served as a pastor at a local International Presbyterian Church in the area. In 1979, the Keyes moved back to the States to organize a L'Abri community in Southborough, Mass., a suburb of Boston.

"It is far easier to develop and project a certain image of yourself to others than it is to actually be that sort of person."

Image & Reality in Society — Part I

Dick Keyes

The word 'image' comes from the Latin *'imago'*, meaning imitation or likeness. It is the likeness of reality, not the real thing itself. As image has come to function in modern society, dealing in images has many advantages over dealing in realities. Two of the main advantages are first, that an imitation is quicker and easier to produce than its corresponding reality and second, that it is much more malleable in your hands than the unyielding real world. Let me give you some illustrations.

It is far easier to develop and project a certain image of yourself to others than it is to actually *be* that sort of person. One can wear the clothes and adopt the swagger and vocabulary of John Wayne much more easily than one can live out the kind of life he did in his films. Likewise, one can project the image of an academic with a different sort of wardrobe and vocabulary much more easily than one can actually *be* a learned person.

Or, take the case of a corporation in building its public image. It is more economical to have the advertising department of a lumber company establish an image of ecological sensitivity and long range responsibility than it is to run the company that way. In fact, it is also more effective, because the public would never be in the position to make such a judgment on the basis of what they observe about practices of reforestation. What the public can do, though, is to form a judgment based on good advertising which shows the company protecting the kind of scenery that the public wants protected. In the same way, a university might well do more for its prestige nationwide by buying a good football team than by upgrading its education.

If an image were a lie, then things would be relatively simple. In the words of Daniel Boorstin, an image "has an ambiguous relationship to reality."[1] It is in that ambiguity that its power lies. The above examples do not constitute direct falsehoods, they have real bearing on reality, but exactly what that bearing is, is very hard to say.

We have shown the advantages of an image for the one who sends or projects it. The critical advantage of image over reality, however, is for the one who receives it. That is to say that we can easily prefer image to reality. The main advantage of an image is that it is simple. It is easily understood and by-passes all the complexities of a real person, corporation or university. If I want to feel that I know a person, or understand a corporation or a university, I will find it easy to grasp some kind of an image of them — especially if they have produced one for my consumption. If on the other hand I want to know them as they really are, I have a difficult and complex task ahead of me that may have no end. For most of my decision-making, dealing with the complexity of reality is awkward and unwieldy. This is the seductive side of images, that they enable us to maintain our oversimplified picture of the world and its possibilities for us. Ben Stein wrote in *Saturday Review*:

> A writer sold to a TV producer a concept about a generous owner of a small manufacturing company. It came back completely revised, the hero now a villain. He was advised that in TV, businessmen can never be heroes. Another of his story proposals, about a heroic college professor, was turned down by a couple of Hollywood eminences as a complete impossibility. Everyone knew, they said, that professors are either crazy or fags.[2]

Here we have those who control the media letting out only as much reality as they think conforms to the images in the viewers' minds. The viewers, after all, must not be denied the comfort of believing that they understand what is what in the business and academic worlds.

Daniel Boorstin, in his book *The Image*, attributes the power and the confusion of images ultimately to our extravagant expectations. I will quote him at some length:

> When we pick up our newspaper at breakfast, we expect — we even demand — that it bring us momentous events since the night before. We turn on the car radio as we drive to work and expect "news" to have occurred since the morning newspaper went to press. Returning in the evening, we expect our house not only to shelter us, to keep us warm in winter and cool in summer, but to relax us, to dignify us, to encompass us with soft music and interesting hobbies, to be a playground, a theatre and a bar. We expect our two-week

vacation to be romantic, exotic, cheap, and effortless. We expect a faraway atmosphere if
we go to a nearby place; and we expect everything to be relaxing, sanitary, and American-
ized if we go to a faraway place. . . .

We expect anything and everything. We expect the contradictory and the impossible.
We expect compact cars which are spacious; luxurious cars which are economical. We expect to be rich and charitable, powerful and merciful, active and reflective, kind and competitive. We expect to be inspired by mediocre appeals for excellence, to be made literate
by illiterate appeals for literacy. We expect to eat and stay thin, to be constantly on the
move and ever more neighborly, to go to the "church of our choice" and yet feel its guid-
ing power over us, to revere God and to be God.

Never have people been more the masters of their environment. Yet never has a people
felt more deceived and disappointed. For never has a people expected so much more than
the world could offer.[3]

The argument of the book is that reality cannot measure up to our expectations at many levels, but images can. Because we hold so dearly to
our expectations, the world of image becomes more real to us than reality
itself. The real world becomes gray and bland by comparison. It is our expectations that fuel our image-making; we deceive ourselves and pay
others to deceive us.

Boorstin points to a critical shift with what he calls the Graphics Revolution. By this he means our sudden improved ability to communicate images in the last hundred years. This brief span of time has seen the advent
of telegraph, telephone, radio, TV, the still camera, motion pictures, video
tape, high-speed printing and many other inventions transforming our
public communication. We will look at a number of areas where this impact has been felt: the news industry, the world of commerce, of politics
and of values, but first we will begin with what is in some ways more basic
— our idea of our own image.

The Individual World

There are two ways to speak of "self-image." We have a self-image that
is our own picture of ourselves which is quite a private thing, and then
there is the self-image that is something we try to project to others. The
second is inseparable from the first in the sense that it is never independent
of it, but at the same time it is a different thing. It is the impression you try
to create of yourself in the minds of others. We vary enormously from one
another in the content of this attempted impression, and also in the degree
to which we care what others think about us at all. It is this second sense of
self-image that I will be concerned with here — the impression that we try
to make for others' benefit, whether it corresponds to our inner experience
of ourselves or not.

Erving Goffman in his book, *The Presentation of Self in Everyday Life*,
cites an example from William Sansom's novel, *A Contest of Ladies*,

which highlights the obsessional nature of some attempts to create an image of ourselves. It tells of an Englishman called Preedy on vacation making his debut on a Spanish beach.

> But in any case he took care to avoid catching anyone's eye. First of all, he had to make it clear to those potential companions of his holiday that they were of no concern to him whatsoever. He stared through them, round them, over them — eyes lost in space. The beach might have been empty. If by a chance a ball was thrown his way, he looked surprised; then let a smile of amusement lighten his face (Kindly Preedy), looked round dazed to see that there *were* people on the beach, tossed it back with a smile to himself and not a smile *at* the people, and then resumed carelessly his nonchalant survey of space.
>
> But it was time to institute a little parade, the parade of the Ideal Preedy. By devious handlings he gave any who wanted to look a chance to see the title of his book — a Spanish translation of Homer, classic thus, but not daring, cosmopolitan too — and then gathered together his beachwrap and bag into a neat sand-resistant pile (Methodical and Sensible Preedy), and tossed aside his sandals (Carefree Preedy, after all).
>
> The marriage of Preedy and the sea! There were alternative rituals. The first involved the stroll that turns into a run and a dive straight into the water, thereafter smoothing into a strong splashless crawl towards the horizon. But of course not really to the horizon. Quite suddenly he would turn onto his back and thrash great white splashes with his legs, somehow thus showing that he could have swum further had he wanted to, and then would stand up a quarter out of water for all to see who it was.
>
> The alternative course was simpler; it avoided the cold water shock and it avoided the risk of appearing too high-spirited. The point was to appear to be so used to the sea, the Mediterranean, and this particular beach, that one might as well be in the sea as out of it. It involved a slow stroll down and into the edge of the water — not even noticing his toes were wet, land and water all the same to *him*! — with his eyes up at the sky gravely surveying portents, invisible to others, of the weather (Local Fisherman Preedy).[4]

What you observe is two worlds, one in which Preedy thinks, feels and determines what his strategy will be, and the other the acts that he goes through to create a certain impression. Of course there can be a complete discrepancy between the one and the other. We can be in agony inside and project a happy exterior almost as if we were wearing a mask. Goffman calls this process "impression management."[5]

There has always been a performance aspect to our lives. We cannot help letting the fact that others are observing us influence our actions, and this is not necessarily a bad thing. However, today, with such image-awareness, the usefulness of establishing an image, and the ease of doing it are encouraged and techniques are developed as to how it should be done. Take for example an advertisement for the book *Image Impact* ("Radiate success — America's top experts reveal their secrets"). It is a book designed "to help you upgrade your image and achieve total confidence in your appearance." It is by eighteen "image consultants" who will "transform you into an executive headhunter's dream."[6]

The problem is, of course, that if our impression management takes too great a piece of our conscious time and motivation, we go through a total loss of integrity and of individual identity. Our full attention is spent on the mask without thought for what is behind it. The more we live in this direction, the less, in fact, there is behind it. The focus of life is shifted from who I am and what I do to how I can appear, from reality to image. The seductiveness of this drift is that it seems to be an ingenious shortcut to being a whole person, to success, it promises to make good on our expectations.

The News Industry

As we try to evaluate the functioning of images in our society, a good part of the public arena to start in is journalism. Today, the communication of news is both a large industry and also has profound bearing on the course of history.

Daniel Boorstin pointed out that the first newspaper in this country was published in 1690 and was called *Public Occurrences Both Foreign and Domestic*. It was to be published once a month, more often only if "any glut of occurrences should happen." This is in contrast to a modern paper which may publish up to seven editions a day. In the earlier model, God (and the Devil) made up the news and the reporters simply reported it. If there was little news, or if what there was was not very interesting, it was not the reporter's fault. Today, however, it is the responsibility of the reporter to make news; if he does not, he is fired. News, according to Boorstin, is after all, anything that makes the reader say, "Gee Whiz." He points to this change being more far-reaching than simply the growth of one industry — it shows a shift of the idea of truth and reality in our society.

One of the most important categories of Boorstin's analysis is what he calls a "pseudo-event," now more sympathetically called a "media event" by the media itself. The main characteristic of a pseudo-event is that it is an event that happens primarily to be reported. The question is not so much whether or not it is true, but whether it is newsworthy or believable. Of course much of what goes on in the modern political world falls into this category — the press conferences, news leaks, interviews, public relations banquets, et cetera.

To give you an example from close to home, we had our own pseudo-event recently at the Southborough L'Abri. A local reporter came to do a story on this new L'Abri work. After looking around the place and talking for some time she says she wanted to get a picture of some one working in the garden (it was November and the ground had been frozen for several weeks). The fact that there was no work going on in the garden made no difference, so one of the girls went out to pretend she was pulling up a cabbage and was photographed doing it. Boorstin's analysis would raise the question — was this real? Well, yes and no. What was photographed was a real girl pulling on a real cabbage, and yet the whole event had a staged phoniness about it. Had it not been for the reporter's camera, she would never have been there. A pseudo-event has an ambiguous relationship with reality.

If a statement is a lie, it at least has the possibility of being exposed and therefore discredited as a lie. A pseudo-event is not so clear. If you try to unmask or debunk it, it becomes "news behind the news" and is all the more fascinating and newsworthy. If you know about it, you know how the news was made, and *you* are somehow on the inside. When President Carter appointed Muskie as Secretary of State he openly gave as one of the reasons that he wanted to "improve the image of the administration." Instead of outrage at this (why not, after all, appoint someone on the basis of his qualifications for the job?), there was great interest and speculation. Why does he want to change the image? What did he think the image was in the first place? How will Muskie change it?

A by-product of the growth of pseudo-events has been that the news industry has often become introverted or incestuous, in that the making of the news is more newsworthy and interesting than the news itself. Over a year ago the President was inaugurated, and the Iranian hostages were released on the same day. One almost got the impression that more important than both those events was the way in which NBC, ABC and CBS were able to report them simultaneously. A good deal of the coverage, especially when actual news was scanty, was on *how* the press and TV were accomplishing that coverage. This is the press reporting on how the press reports, or the press generating news. This brings the media into the place increasingly where it does not primarily report the news, but it *is* the news. This seems to be true in the case of the most televisable event of all — an assassination. Despite the fact that there is never very much to be said, the television must sustain one's interest for at least twenty-four hours after the event. In this case, how reports were found and/or bungled makes up the news. *Time* writes this after the attempted assassination of Reagan: "As the afternoon progressed, it became evident that television was becoming not just the story's messenger, but part of the story itself." In the same article, *Time* summarizes TV's performance: "often confused, sometimes wrong, but always breathtaking. For one draining afternoon, TV turned America into a giant newsroom."[7]

The growth of pseudo-events can also take a sinister turn. The press has a direct linkage to public opinion. Public opinion, in turn, has obvious effects on political issues. *Time* writes somewhat self-righteously about the extent to which the guerilla war in El Salvador is a "media event." Both sides, but especially the guerillas, are not just fighting a battle, but their moves are carefully orchestrated for the benefit of the observing press. Rosenthal from the *New York Times* returned from El Salvador to say that he had never seen a place "where journalism was more part of the process..." Shirley Christian from the *Miami Herald* said: "People here will be left with the solution partly or wholly created by us — not just the American Government but the American press. Then we will all leave when the story disappears." *Time* writes with a certain indignation that the war should be so influenced by the press's influence. Here, the press blames the politicians and generals for being so susceptible to their own (the press's) power.[8]

One often hears the complaint from almost any trouble spot in the world that there is "too much press, too little information." There is just not enough news to satisfy our expectations for interesting and exciting news. One notices two directions taken by the media in order to generate news: "human interest" stories and preoccupation with gore. Both take their toll on public consciousness.

The "human interest" story too often involves a voyeurism into the lives of the victims or celebrities. TV cameras went into the home of Billy Gallegos, a hostage in Iran, in order to film his family as they watched his release on their own television. The climax was the point where the announcer observed that tears didn't come until they saw him the second time. This is a voyeurism into human suffering and emotion in which all involved are cheapened. We who watch it are looking peeping-Tom-like into a private affair, and those whom we watch are having something made public and commercial which ought to remain private.

The demand for reporting of violence has got to be considered a collective neurosis. It is articulated in a poem, "Exclusive Pictures," by Steve Turner.

> Give us good pictures
> of the human torch
> which show the skin
> burnt like chicken,
> bursting like grapes.
>
> It will teach us
> to avoid flames.
>
> Give us good film
> of the lady on the ledge
> as she leaps open mouthed
> and hits the streets
> like a suicide.

It will teach us
to use stairways.

Give us sharp colour
coverage of the African
troubles. Show us
interesting wounds,
craters in fat and flesh.

It will teach us
not to point guns.

Give us five page spreads
of the airliner that fell
like a pigeon to the ground.
And make sure you get there
before the victims are pulled out.

It will teach
engines to function.

Don't give us
any of that shaky
hand-held stuff
where the trapped children
are smoke-like shapes
and their screams barely audible
beneath the wailing sirens.
Get in there with your lenses
and your appetite for danger
and your hard new head
and give us what we're after.
Make us informed.
Make us feel we're really there.
Provide us with education.
Broaden our backgrounds.
We live in a democracy
and we need to know.[9]

When we get this kind of reporting we feel as if we are getting the real thing. Having seen it, we know what horror is like. But ironically, this takes us a step farther away from reality. Having seen it on a TV screen or in a newspaper, we feel as if we understand it, but this is misleading, because we have only seen it at an infinite distance. At any moment we can turn off the TV or put the paper down! The horrifying thing about horror is that it is not a temporary titillation of our imagination — it is impossible to turn it off or put it down; we are caught by it and in it. In the

public consciousness this turns real anguish into sentimentality and cal-
loused resignation.

According to Daniel Boorstin's analysis, another result of the growth of
the role of the media is that heroes are transformed into celebrities. Heroes
have fared poorly under the hand of men such as Marx and Freud, their
heroism explained by unconscious ego-centric motivations, but the
graphics revolution has done even more to discredit them.

A hero is one who has done something heroic, for which we should
respect him. A celebrity, on the other hand, is someone who is well-known
for being well-known. The celebrity is not respected, but envied for being
famous. The celebrity is a human pseudo-event, whose main virtue is that
he or she is reported. Some students of human behavior have noticed that
fame has the value to modern man that salvation did to the man of the
Middle Ages. If this is so, then the media is its priesthood. This would explain the almost mystical power of the media, the power to confer celebrity
status on a "nobody" in a matter of minutes. (The most reliable way is to
shoot a celebrity.) Lewis Lapham, editor of *Harper's*, goes a step further:

> Now that God has been pronounced dead, it is conceivable that people would like to
> transfer His powers and dominions to the media. What else do they have to put in His
> place? To a large extent the media have had roles of judge and inquisitor thrust upon them
> because so many other institutions have proved themselves inadequate to the task of
> omniscience. The media disguise their lack of knowledge with the quality of knowingness,
> their weakness with the power to forge the metal of celebrity and transmute a political
> issue into a salable commodity.[10]

It is not that there are no more heroes or heroines today. It is that they
tend to be changed into celebrities and trivialized in the transition. To illustrate his point. Boorstin gives the example of Charles Lindbergh. His trans-
atlantic flight was without question an extraordinary heroic achievement.
But the media, even then in its relatively more primitive form, could only
make just so much of the achievement itself. You could tell and retell the
story only a limited number of times. They then began on the human interest stories. How did he feel now that he had become such big news? Did
he feel different as a famous man? Had he ever dreamt that such a thing
would happen to him? Did his parents ever anticipate that their son would
reach such fame? The stories focused on his leap from obscurity to fame in
a matter of hours. Lindbergh was outraged at the badgering of the press
and at the invasions of his own privacy. He suddenly felt that they had
claimed him as public property, so he took considerable pains to avoid
them. This, then became the next story: his efforts to stay *out* of the news.
His terror of reporters became the most reportable thing of all and sold as

many papers as the news of his flight itself. A real hero became a celebrity, the main focus of interest being no longer what he, in fact, had done, but what the press had made out of him, and human greatness existed only at the level of image.

The music group, The Beatles, experienced this same transfiguration. John Lennon noted with insight that they were just a band who had made it big and the more success they achieved the more unreality they had to face. He saw that what the public wanted was human greatness, but that they were only talented celebrities, unable to fulfill the outsized expectations of their fans. The whole thing became more and more unreal until he, of course, fled.

The Commercial World

The field of advertising is well known for its exploitation, and for this reason I shall be more brief here. However, the specific role that image plays bears mention. Ernest Dichter advised a fellow advertiser on the best technique for selling. He found it is most effective to paint a picture for the customer of the kind of person he would like to be, then convince him that your product is a necessary ingredient of that picture. This advice is fascinating. Notice that there is nothing about persuading the prospective consumer that the product is good, or that it will do the job required. You just create a model of the way he likes to imagine himself or herself, then manage to make the association with the product. For many products it is far more effective to sell by communicating an image that the consumer relates to the product in his or her own imagination, than it is to engage his or her mind with discussions of the practical benefits of the product.

The interesting thing is that about 90% of people polled report that they don't believe what advertisers claim about their products. They feel that many advertisers deliberately misrepresent and cannot be trusted. How can we assess this? Are corporations wasting billions of dollars trying to con a public that is smarter than they think? I doubt it. Through market research they have excellent ways of telling if an advertisement is working or not, and they are working well enough for firms to spend the billions that they do. What, then, is the discrepancy between the facts and figures of the marketing people and the public's profession of "seeing through" advertising? The fact is that the public may well "see through" some advertising and recognize oversized promises, but this has little to do with whether or not they buy the product. The truth or false-hood of any persuasion may be irrelevant to the success of the advertisement. The appeal is rather to your own imagined image of yourself linked to the product, by-passing the question of the virtues of the product. Thus, advertising does not normally lie, it just has an ambiguous relationship to the truth. It is you yourself who contribute the lie as you allow your imagination to act directly on your volition. The advertisement never *claims* in words that you will be like the model if you buy the product. We would laugh at it if it did, and feel very superior. But when you supply the lie yourself, it is not so easy to detect. We are not dealing with false advertising here, but with images which, because of their power and ambiguity, befuddle the mind. The image keys to something desirable in society (*e.g.* freedom or sophistication) and attracts you to it by its bigger-than-life brilliance. This attraction draws you to the product that you are led to associate with it in a completely non-rational way.

Roman and Maas, in their book, *How to Advertise*, write, "Former agency head, Jack Tinker, once estimated that over a billion dollars had been spent advertising each of these six objectives: new, white, cool, power, refreshing, relief."[11] Bear in mind that this was not spent on advertising certain products as much as on communicating these words as images and making associations with products. The process has nothing to do with persuasion and everything to do with non-rational association.

One of the most familiar images is of the Marlboro Man, and he provides a good case in point. He does not make a promise that Marlboros taste better or cause less cancer or any other such transparent hype. He is just there, usually on a horse in the midst of vast scenery, striking the image in our minds of masculinity, the whole tradition of the American West, and freedom. In fact, if you look closely, you will see that in a significant number of the advertisements he is not even smoking a cigarette. I have often wondered if he has perhaps read the Surgeon General's health warning and given them up. Of course, it is because the advertiser feels that the image itself functions so powerfully and that the association is so clearly there in our minds, that the actual cigarette is superfluous. It is important to notice as well that there is never a promise that if you smoke Marlboros, you, too, will end up as a cowboy in the Rocky Mountains, ever free and confident. We would immediately detect this as false advertising and scornfully despise it. However, the image leaves us nothing to reject rationally, only a picture, laden with cultural meaning and associated with the product. I can only judge its effectiveness by its extraordinary longevity.

An example given by Boorstin is of the experience of Schlitz Beer. Their sales were sagging, so they hired a well-known ad man to help out. He looked over their whole operation and noted that their bottles were steam cleaned before the beer was put into them. He hit on the idea of advertising Schlitz and the 'pure beer' because its bottles were steam cleaned. Sales jumped from fifth place to almost first place. There was nothing false about the advertising, but it was a pseudo-event since *all* beers clean their bottles with steam. No promises were made, nor unfair comparisons asserted. An image was conveyed which overshadowed dull reality.

Time writes of the dynamic at work in the world of modeling:

> With lots of blusher but no shame, the peacock profession of modeling gives face and body to our covetous dreams, then mocks us as we press our noses against the window glass. What unimaginable delight made the pretty lady swirl and smile as the photographer snapped her picture? What season of debauchery brought the sulky thrust to this beauty's lower lip? At what groveling serf does the fine young lord in the Ferrari scowl with such contempt? Nothing; none; at no one; these glossy apparitions are moments that never were — yet they tease us because their reality is beyond question, while our own stored moments, caught in snapshots and thrown into a drawer, are obvious and pallid fakes. Fascination sidesteps good sense, and we wonder; How was this lovely bunkum done?[12]

The fuel that powers images like this is our own extravagant expectations. With the ability of images to convey that these expectations will be met without use of rational persuasion, our own mundane lives, where our expectations are so often shattered, tend to seem dull and less real.

The Political World

In the world of politics in this time of TV and newspaper coverage, a politician must be able to create and project the right image of himself. Some critics of our political system claim that if one can project the right image, there is nothing else that one need do to be elected. Although this is a bit too cynical, there is an undoubted shift to the tremendous importance of image. In the last presidential election, for example, there was a conscious de-emphasis on issues by strategists on both sides, with the corresponding attention put on image projection.

Boorstin cites Franklin Roosevelt as the first to take full advantage of the media in communicating his image of understanding the sufferings of the people and having the situation in hand. Joe McCarthy, in a completely different style, was a master of pseudo-events in press conferences, news leaks and innuendos. He was able to create the image of a person dangerous to the nation because of communist connections without ever stating clear facts that could be refuted.

In the world of image, truth is beside the point. Take the example of Nixon's press secretary, Ron Zeigler, when he referred to one of his own earlier statements about the Watergate break-in as "inoperative." Some suggested that this was just a face-saving euphemism for a lie. Others, however, looking a bit more deeply into political communication, say that he meant exactly what he said. He meant that the statement would no longer function as an effective image. It could no longer be passed off as believable. The truth or falsity of the statement was beside the point.

Many of the aspects of image orientation in the political world emerge in a party convention, which is at least half pseudo-event. I will quote a newspaper's evaluation of a pre-convention extravaganza. This was before the Republican convention, but it could well have been either party.

> Like all commercials, the convention is not a reasoned argument, an assessment of strengths and weaknesses. It's an emotional appeal, an attempt to group unrelated themes and feelings, an attempt to mingle the many meanings of good. . . .
>
> It appealed to that nonideological muddle in our subconscious, that sea of dreams and memories that somehow connects stalks of wheat and Thomas Edison and Lindbergh's flight and oil derricks and snow-capped mountains and stiffly posed old photographs in a "past" most of us have never known except as imagery or schoolboy metaphor.[13]

Here we see all the elements of image-making which are more at home in the advertising world. Content is avoided, reasoned argument is by-passed. The imagination is to carry us past the need to think critically. It is to gather together our emotions and drive us to action.

Another side of political events of this sort is the sheer importance of the role of the media itself. This influence is not always sought for, but may come more as a result of the media's own image of omniscience. Here is an example of the same convention:

> Television, with incessant demands upon it to provide instant information and analysis, displays reporting in its rawest form. During conventions, viewers are required to do their own sifting and editing. . . . The network anchormen themselves seemed unhappy over the situation. David Brinkley, on NBC, groused about television having become "something of an intercom" over which rumors and other raw information "fly back and forth."
>
> One of the more telling moments came after midnight when a haggard-looking Mr. Bush, in a polo shirt, told television reporters how "surprised" he was at his selection. Why was he surprised? a reporter asked. His name had been on everyone's list of possibilities for weeks. Mr. Bush then showed that he, too, had determined his reality from TV. "You people were circulating a lot of rumors out there," he said, "and maybe they were based on a lot of fact.[14]

One has the idea as one watches a convention that, despite the inane blowing of horns and waving of hats and banners that take place on the convention floor, there are some men in a smoke-filled room somewhere nearby who know what is going on and who are pulling the strings. There may be a lot of dirty pool, but at least someone knows what is happening amidst the chaos. What this article implies, however, is that although there are men in the back room, they are watching television to *find out* what is happening on the convention floor, and *nobody* is in control! The media do not welcome this role. In fact they are usually irrate when they discover it, but it is a problem partly of their own making, as they have built their industry by feeding people's insatiable expectations for instant news.

Jacques Ellul, in his book *Propaganda*, raises many of these same issues, but, lest we think that as educated people we are free from such rank mindlessness, he points out that educated people can be the most susceptible to it. There are three reasons given. First, it is the educated person who absorbs the greatest amount of secondhand and unverifiable information. Second, it is the educated person who feels the need to have an opinion on every important question of his time. Third, it is the educated person who considers himself capable of reaching a judgment for himself on the basis of his accumulated wisdom. When all is said and done, he needs propaganda more than anyone. Of course he is not arguing against education, but merely saying that coming with education there can be a certain naivete and overestimation of one's grasp on the world.

In bringing this part of our discussion to a close, I will quote Boorstin again at length:

> Until recently we have been justified in believing Abraham Lincoln's familiar maxim: "You may fool all the people some of the time; you can even fool some of the people all the time; but you cannot fool all the people all the time." This has been the foundation-belief of American democracy. Lincoln's appealing slogan rests on two elementary assumptions. First, that there is a clear and visible distinction between sham and reality, between the lies a demagogue would have us believe and the truths which are there all the time. Second, that the people tend to prefer reality to sham, that if offered a choice between a simple truth and a contrived image, they will prefer the truth.
>
> Neither of these any longer fits the facts. Not because people are less intelligent or more dishonest. Rather because great unforeseen changes — the great forward strides of American civilization — have blurred the edges of reality. The pseudo-events which flood our consciousness are neither true nor false in the old familiar senses. The very same advances which have made them possible have also made the images — however planned, contrived, or distorted — more vivid, more attractive, more impressive, and more persuasive than reality itself.[15]

DISCUSSION QUESTIONS

1. What does Dick mean by 'image'? How are images being used today?

2. Do you agree with Daniel Boorstin: "Never has a people felt more deceived and disappointed. For never has a people expected so much more than the world could offer"? Explain.

3. What are some consequences of the prevalence of images over reality in our relationship with other people?

4. Do Christians project images of the Christian life which are not realistic? How?

5. In what ways have you been affected by what Goffman calls "impression management"?

7. How does modern society view the concept of heroes? Celebrities?

8. How does an image appear more real at times than what is real? What effect does this have on us?

9. How are images used in the political world?

10. Why, in Ellul's opinion, is the educated person the most susceptible to propaganda?

11. What happens when churches turn their focus from values to images?

"Our life is not to be governed by
constructing and projecting our own image,
but by living out His likeness."

Image & Reality in Society — Part II

Dick Keyes

Having examined the notion of image in modern society and seen something of its use in various fields, we will look at ways in which images have displaced values or ideals even in the church, where one might have hoped this tendency would have been resisted. We will then turn toward a solution in the Biblical teaching on integrity.

Truth and Values

Values have usually been principles, ideals and norms which were recognized to have worth or be good. Moral values are those things that are right by virtue of some standard of truth, whether it be tradition, reason, or, as the Christian would say, the character of God. They are solid, nonmalleable. We are not able to change them at our whim.

The word "value" is maintained: in fact, the word itself may be getting more use than ever, but there is a difference. Now *values* refers to those acts or customs which are considered favorably by a certain group. It is the approval of the group or even the individual, that invests them with value. The value does not exist as a value independently of our approval of it. We are familiar with "value clarification" in our schools. It is surely a good idea to clarify our values. No one would argue for confused values. However, is this all that we can do? Can we only clarify values that we already have? Can we not challenge our values, demanding that they be rooted in something that is true? Can we not discuss the possibility that some people's values may be wrong?

In the last century Carl Schurz wrote "Ideals are like stars. You will not succeed in touching them with your hands. But like the seafaring man on the desert of waters, you choose them as your guides, and following them, will reach your destiny."[1] His point is that values or ideals are external to us, not man-made. You cannot get your hands on them to monkey with them. If you could move the stars around in the sky, they would no longer be of any value in navigation. The value of values to us is that they are not malleable, but stand independently from our individual or collective whim. They demand to be served, adhered to, they have a claim on us. In a certain sense, whether we believe in the values of love and justice is irrelevant to the values themselves. They are true whether we believe in them or not, fail to live up to them or not — legitimized on a different basis than our favor. We do not make values, we bow to them.

It would be a fruitful study to chart what *values* has come to mean in our society and why the changes have happened. However, that is beyond the scope of this paper. We will look at the ways that image-thinking has replaced value-thinking. If an educational instititution finds itself in a slump and a financial crisis, it is a prodigious task to reaffirm its adherence to high standards of education. Even if the standard of education is raised, it would take several years for that to be noticed by anybody. On the other hand, if they should bring in some consultants who could, through some well-done, well-photographed brochures, change the image of the school in the public eye, then perhaps far more of an impression could be established. As with an individual, if you have a change of face there may seem to be no need for a change of heart. Boorstin calls image the "pseudo-events" of the ethical world. They have the brilliance to give us a sense of direction, but there is nothing more than a mask.

Images have shown themselves to be so effective in so many different fields that it should not surprise us to see the church get on the bandwagon. This the church has done, but in several different ways, none of which have been a credit to it. Today one hears many outcries from the secular world against the church, charging it with secularism. Many of these are quite justified. Think of the existentialist Ernest Becker, who wrote:

> Today religionists wonder why youth has abandoned the churches, not wanting to realize that it is precisely because organized religion openly subscribes to a commercial-industrial hero system that is almost openly defunct. It so obviously denies reality, builds war machines against death, and banishes sacredness with bureaucratic dedication. Men

are treated as things and the world is pulled down to their own size. The churches subscribe to this world empty heroics of possession, display and manipulation.[2]

Isn't there some truth to this? The world looks to the church to see something different, but too often the church has outdone the world at its own game. There are two main ways that this has happened, one a tendency in those churches which we would call theologically liberal, and the other in churches which we would call conservative.

To take the liberal church first, I draw on an article in the *New York Times* concerning the Methodist Church, "Methodists, in Search of a Coherent Identity, Acknowledge Crisis." One could have picked any one of the main American denominations here; I have no intention of making a special critique of Methodism, but it serves as a good illustration of image-orientation in a church context. It is a report of a General Conference in 1980.

Both the left and the right have responded to the oft-spoken anxiety over the apparent loss of a clear image of the church that can stir the enthusiasm of members who have become complacent, the same kind of middle-class Americans that were called "forgotten" by Richard M. Nixon, the same citizens who worry about the nation's moral stability but have little faith that either the church or government will present answers.

"We commissioned a Harris poll recently to test our image," said Dr. Norman Dewire, general secretary of the church's board of ministry, "and we found overwhelmingly that Methodism has no image in the general population any more. Then we asked just Methodists, and we got the full gambit of responses. There is no image left. That worries me because we started out clearly evangelical in the best sense, as circuit riders went from town to town, out front on all the issues."

For the moment, the church appears to prefer a middle course between the liberals and the conservatives. The general confrence, the supreme ruling body of 1,000 delegates that meets every four years, resisted the extremes, heard accounts of the problems and seemed satisfed that the two-week session had passed without further splitting members into factions.

For example, the conference appeased neither the left nor the right on the issue of homosexuality. The delegates reaffirmed a church stance that homosexuality is "incompatible" with Christian teaching but refused explicity to bar avowed, practicing homosexuals from the ministry. The Good News caucus had campaigned for the outright prohibition while liberals opposed the church's general rejection of homosexuality.

The conference also continued the church's strong support for racial justice, the elimination of sexism and the development of churches and services for ethnic minorities. In a departure, the conference took an unusual step in the direction of evangelism by voting to raise $25 million to buy a commercial television station.[3]

I hope that by now a number of aspects of this article will appear familiar to you. Note that there is no more concern with truth than Ron Zeigler had when he said that his earlier statement had become "inoperative." The only question is that of how the image, or lack of it, functions. They are concerned that their image never grips any one, not that they might not be *doing* the truth. Can you imagine the apostles of the first century sitting down and anxiously polling the residents of Jerusalem and Antioch to see what their image was of the church? They had far too much to do in preaching the gospel, and the source of their gospel was not in public opinion, but was in the spoken word of God.

Also, the nature of the image presented was that of advertising and politics. Just as the political convention tried to "mingle the many meanings of good" in order to appeal to that "non-ideological muddle in our subconscious," so this ecclesiastical conference tried to conjure up notions of fearlessly standing for the truth as the old circuit riders had, but also of being liberal, undogmatic, contemporary and ever open to change. It is a play to the world of our expectations where we can still eat and stay thin, have compact cars that are spacious and be constantly on the move and ever more neighborly. It is in our world of expectations that a church can be everything to everybody. As long as this is maintained one must avoid ever dealing with issues such as homosexuality and stick to contradictory politically dictated statements about it. The whole focus is on the mask, not the face behind it; perhaps Boorstin would call it an ecclesiastical "pseudo-event," pointing to a great hollowness behind the mask. The hope is that some of that hollowness might be filled by a new TV station.

Lest those who are theologically more conservative would look judgmentally on this kind of procedure, we see image-orientation in a different form in their ranks. Here the problem is not so much the issue of image to take the place of lost substance or content, but is in the uncritical adoption of many of the methodologies of the commercial world. Image advertising seems to have made a solid foothold in the style of communication used by parts of the church.

For example, Bob Bloom, a Texas ad man whose agency is used by one of the major denominations of this country said, "We are trying to sell a product, and that product is Jesus Christ." Market researchers discovered that the number one problem for Texans was hopelessness. Therefore, they made up a series of 30 second spots with celebrities from sports and entertainment saying how Jesus Christ had changed their lives and given them hope. Featured were Eldridge Cleaver, Ephram Zimbalist Jr. and others. Or, on another occasion, a church held a "double miracle day" to double church attendance. There were revivals led by an assistant coach of the Dallas Cowboys, a millionaire interior designer, Miss Teenage America, and the yo-yo champion of the world. These examples appeared in a book written by a non-Christian who is impressed by the depth and cultural value of Christian teaching (thought not believing it to be true), but despairing of the superficiality in which Christians live and communicate. Virginia Owens, in her book *The Total Image*, sees similar problems:

> . . . as Bruce Cook, the former advertising agent for Coca-Cola who engineered the "I found it" campaign, put it, "Back in Jerusalem when the church started, God performed a miracle there on the Day of Pentecost. They didn't have the benefit of buttons and media, so God had to do a little supernatural work there. But today, with our technology, we have available to us the opportunity to create the same kind of interest in a secular society."[4]

Do we really think that the same kind of interest is raised as on the Day of Pentecost? I doubt it. Perhaps a better Biblical event to use as a paradigm would be Palm Sunday. It was an entirely up-beat occasion. Jesus was widely recognized as the foremost celebrity of the season, and rumors about him were spreading like wildfire. It is hard to imagine greater "interest." Everyone was excited, fascinated — except of course Jesus himself who wept as he looked at Jerusalem. He knew that this acclaim was superficial, skin-deep, and that it would last less than five days. Where were all those people on Good Friday? Perhaps some were even among the multitudes who shouted to Pilate, "Crucify him." Wherever they were, there was something more interesting going on then than defending Jesus against his accusers. What they had responded to on Palm Sunday was their own image of the Messiah. When the Son of God failed to measure up to that image and expectation, they had better things to do with their time.

Virginia Owens continues to evaluate the Christian media blitz:

> The point is to make the picture so appealing that the customer wants to see himself within the frame. Health, wealth, youth (or at least youthful age), sharp clothes, exuberant optimism. Is the product Coca-Cola or Christ? It's hard to tell.
>
> Actually, the product is lifestyle, that loathsome word that has succeeded in trivializing our existence for us. It is a necessary component in the wardrobe of someone with a good self-image. One opens the closet, puts on his life-style, looks in the mirror, and there's his self-image smiling at him.
>
> The product that Mr. Cook and other Christian advertisers are supposedly selling is Christ. Yet Christ is nowhere to be found in the picture. If he were, it would severely limit the marketing potential of the picture. Christ is motivationally equivalent to, say, Geritol. Any ad man knows there is no point in putting out a picture of a bottle of Geritol. Instead, he shows a picture of a youthful, happily married couple who attribute their health and success to Geritol. The same with Jesus. He himself doesn't sell well, any more than a bottle of tonic. So the ad shows pictures of people who can testify to the therapeutic results in their lives. The appeal is the same as in any image advertisement: put yourself in this picture.[5]

There are two problems with this kind of communciation. First, it too often fails to communicate Christ at all — it miniaturizes and trivializes him. It uses his name to titillate our extraordinary expectations of life, and therefore fascinates us. He is no longer the Lord and Maker of heaven and earth who will one day have us all at His feet. The second thing is that the *way* Christ is presented encourages and plays to the very kind of worldliness (success and celebrity) that Christ, in fact, calls us out of and to repent from. Despite certain undeniable results from this kind of communication, at the end of the day, it seems that the preponderant result will be Palm Sunday faith.

Perhaps it is that, in a society which fabricates almost everything else, it should be expected to fabricate God as well. It seems that modern society has done just that. How is God perceived in the media? He is evaluated through polls which report the percentages of people who believe in His existence, pray to Him, go to His churches, read His word, and so forth. There might be graphs in *Time* and *Newsweek* of church attendance over the last decade, with a similar graph charting sales of Plymouths on the next page. Could it be that there is more concern with God's image than His existence? After all, questions of His existence are seldom newsworthy. The discussion becomes too difficult to follow in a media presentation. The newsworthy item still remains God's prestige in a secular society. As Boorstin points out, He is no longer the Alpha and the Omega, the first Fact, the Creator and Sustainer of Heaven and Earth, He is the author of the world's best-selling book, and is therefore, reduced to the status of a celebrity. The relevant question is not whether or not God exists, but whether He is useful for a "God-fearing" society to believe in.

God, therefore, has all the earmarks of being a pseudo-event. His power is in terms of how widely He is reported, His prestige is measured by public opinion, and His relationship to reality is highly ambiguous.

Integrity: Toward the Recovery of Reality

The image-orientation of our culture is not localized in certain ideals or social structures. For many it reaches to their basic tacit assumptions about reality; it is their pair of glasses through which they see the world. As such, it will not do to aim at making adjustments to our style of doing advertising or politics. We must start with God as the final reality.

Remember that one of the main advantages of an image is its malleability in your service. It enables you to maintain extravagant expectations of the world and of your role in it. This attitude is captured by one stanza of the poem "Creed" by Steve Turner.

> We believe that each man must find the truth
> that is right for him.
> Reality will adapt accordingly.
> The universe will readjust. History will alter.
> We believe that there is no absolute truth
> excepting the truth that there is no absolute truth.[*]

By contrast with this attitude, the final ultimate reality, God himself, is in no way moldable by us. Boorstin rightly remarks how different the modern view is from the mind-set of the American past.:

> . . . the God of the American Founding Fathers, whatever other qualities he might have had, was a constitutional monarch. He ruled by laws which he was not free to change at his whim . . . For neither God nor man was the world wholly plastic.[7]

If the world was not wholly plastic to God, how much more is it unplastic to us, and how much further beyond our reach is God himself? In fact, this is one of the clear distinctions between the God of the Bible and idols as the Bible defines them. The Psalmist points out that:

> Our God is in the heavens;
> he does whatever he pleases.
> Their idols are silver and gold,
> the work of men's hands.
> They have mouths, but do not speak;
> eyes but do not see. (Psalm 115:3-5, RSV)

The extraordinary thing is that God should pay any attention to man at all. The ultimate question is surely not the prestige of God in the eyes of man, God's public image in a secular society. That question is dwarfed by a far larger one — namely, what does God think of us? One day He will judge us. Every knee will bow and every tongue confess that Jesus is Lord. This will be the great culmination of history on this planet, but there will not even be any TV coverage. There will be no reporters or observers, there will be only participants.

The real issue is the one raised by Micah, "What does the Lord require of you?" The answer, of course, is "to do justice, and to love kindness, and to walk humbly with your God." (Micah 6:8, RSV) But how do we do this as sinners in the midst of a highly sophisticated social and economic system which would scorn the idea that God might make requirements of us at all? How do we confront the image-orientation that is so powerful and effective?

There is no use trying to avoid the use of images, whether individual or corporate. Life does have a performance side. This is not to say that all of life is a performance or that performance governs all of our actions. It is rather that we are aware of being observed by others at times and that their observation affects our behavior in varying degrees. Corporately also, it is impossible not to project images. Our social institutions do communicate impressions, whether we like it or not, and whether these impressions have been intended or not. In most institutions there is at least some conscious awareness of the impression projected out to those who observe. Thus the idea of projecting images and impressions is unavoidable, and a distinction must be made between legitimate and illegitimate use of images.

Perhaps the place to begin is to say that through all our involvement with performance, God himself must be in the audience. God is not only completely free from our control, the Bible says that He is in control of our world and that He sees absolutely all. God, then, is the final audience; nothing on earth happens apart from His observation. It is a tendency of sinful man to forget or ignore this fact in his pretended autonomy from God. This is a primary characteristic of the fool:

> "Understand, O dullest of people!
> Fools, when will you be wise?
> He who planted the ear, does he not hear?
> He who formed the eye, does he not see? (Psalm 94:8, 9, RSV)

> Woe to those who hide deep from the Lord their counsel,
> whose deeds are in the dark, and who say, "Who sees us?
> Who knows us?"
> You turn things upside down! Shall the potter be regarded as the
> clay; that the thing made should say of its maker,
> "He did not make me"; or the thing formed say of him who
> formed it, "He has no understanding"? (Isaiah 39:15, 16, RSV)

On page after page of the Bible we are assured that "a man's ways are before the eyes of the Lord, and He watches all his paths." (Proverbs 5:21, RSV) This turns out to be either comforting or horrifying depending on which side of God we are on.

If God is part of our audience in any meaningful way, it eliminates hypocrisy. This is simply because He sees through anything and everything — even our thoughts before we think them. If He then is the primary one before whom we act, there is no reason to try to create an artificial image; impression management is utterly useless since reality is right before Him. Before Him we are like clear glass. He knows us far better than we know ourselves.

Have you ever wondered why so many people who are honest in all their other dealings, cheat on their income tax? Part of it is the common notion that stealing is not really stealing when you steal from someone who is big enough. But more than that, the thing that distinguishes income tax evasion is that no one can see you doing it. Who is to know that you did not report that part of your income? Because no one can see, the chances of getting caught are minimal. But, you see, if God is part of the theatre of our awareness, He sees it quite clearly. He sees it as clearly as He sees us if we rob a bank in broad daylight. We are in His theatre whether we know it or not or whether we like it or not. We are never off stage.

Let us look at some examples of how this works out in the lives of some of the characters of the Bible. The contrast between Saul and David is very stark on this point. Saul was very concerned for his image before the people. He saw it as the basis for his legitimacy as king, but it was his downfall. In both incidents that caused God to turn away from him (1 Samuel 13:15) he cared primarily what the people thought. First, it was that he was afraid of losing his following, so he made a sacrifice when it was not lawful for him to do it, and second, he disobeyed God's instructions because he "feared the people and obeyed their voice." (1 Samuel 15:24, RSV) He was living mainly in the theatre of the opinions of men and was aware of God in his audience only when he was confronted with his own sin and its punishment. Then we can see the contrast that David offered as he had the chance to kill Saul, who by that time had become his enemy. He saw Saul not as just his enemy who was out to murder him, but as God's anointed one whom he dare not touch simply because he was *God's* anointed one. (1 Samuel 24:6) God, at this point, was very much within David's theatre. He had the courage to go against the advice of his men, risking losing his following because he knew that what was right before God who could see was more important than what seemed to be expedient.

The New Testament abounds with examples that illustrate the same point. Take the case of Ananias and Sapphira. (Acts 5) Their downfall was caring too much about their image in the eyes of the church, their Christian friends. They cared so much that they lied to establish this image of generosity and general Christian heroism. Perhaps the seriousness of their sin was in using the things of God for their own image-building. Peter's rebuke was to the point, "You have not lied to men but to God." (Verse 4, NIV) God was there in their theatre, but they ignored His presence, living as if the theatre was filled only with men. Perhaps this was the lesson the early church had to learn in this very hard way.

The Sermon on the Mount is another case in point. Take Jesus' teaching on giving and on prayer:

> Thus, when you give alms, sound no trumpet before you, as the hypocrites do in the synagogues and in the streets, that they may be praised by men. Truly, I say to you, they have their reward. But when you give alms, do not let your left hand know what your right hand is doing, so that your alms may be in secret; and your Father who sees in secret will reward you.
>
> And when you pray, you must not be like the hypocrites; for they love to stand and pray in the synagogues and at the street corners, that they may be seen by men. Truly, I say to you, they have their reward. But when you pray, go into your room and shut the door and pray to your Father who is in secret; and your Father who sees in secret will reward you. (Matthew 6:2-6, RSV)

Here the contrast is made sharply between those who live in the visible world, for the effect that they can create within it, and those who are aware of and live in the sight of the invisible world. Jesus highlights the question, which world are you living in? How big is your theatre? Some men stand and make exhibition of themselves and get the reward of establishing a public image of piety which results in praise and prestige. Others disregard what people think and pray and give to God because what He thinks matters. The command to "not let your left hand know what your right hand is doing" counsels a real freedom from impression management when we are dealing with God and the things of God. Surely the height of hypocrisy is when we say we are speaking or giving to God, but in fact are only talking to or giving in front of other people for the sake of the effect on them.

What a profound one sentence comment Jesus made about Nathaniel when He said to him, "Behold, an Israelite indeed, in whom is no guile." Nathaniel was a man about whom there was no deception. His public image was not something he spent a lot of time worrying about. There was a continuity between what was within him and what was perceived by those who knew him. He was a man of integrity.

Having emphasized the way God sees all, I do not want to give the impression that He is like a great interrogator or theatre critic, ever frowning and recording our mistakes in his notebook. If we are in Christ, He is a forgiving, accepting, loving Father who sees all our sins but casts them into the depths of the sea, blots them out. The more we are aware of Him in the audience, the higher will be our level of integrity and also the greater our awareness of His love.

We are made in the image of this God. Our task, then, is to realize that image in our thoughts, words and deeds, it is to become more fully what we were intended to be. Our life is not to be governed by constructing and projecting our own image, but by living out His likeness. Our self-image is not God, God is God.

If we live in awareness of these things, then our image will find its own place. Our image will be where it is meant to be, subservient to the reality of who we are. We will certainly do some things because others are observing us — things that we might not have done otherwise. For example, you will act differently when you are reunited with an old friend than you will at a job interview. In a job interview you must convince the person of your competence to do the job, but this can be done without a highly contrived impression. You should convince the person that you are competent because you *are* competent. If you are not, then you should look for another job. All this can be done with God in our audience, without compromise.

The apostle Paul discussed his own flexibility when he said that he was free to become like one under the law, though he was not under the law himself, or to become like one outside of the law, or like one who is weak. "I have become all things to all men, that I might by all means save some." (1 Corinthians 9:22, RSV) Here Paul is possessed with the overarching determination to spread the gospel. With this end in sight, he feels quite free to change his habits (probably clothes, customs, vocabulary) depending on whom he is with. He is not compromising, he is just trying to make sure that he does not put an unnecessary stumbling block in the way of anyone's seeing the claims of Christ clearly and taking them seriously. In the interest of preaching Christ crucified to them, he had to be sensitive to their hang-ups and traditions that he might let the gospel itself be the thing to cause offense, not some way in which he stepped on their toes. Or, to take a more contemporary example, ᵗhink of a minister coming into a church. His own effectiveness as a minister depends on his being able to establish an image in the minds of his parishioners of one who is trustworthy, caring, wise and so forth. The question is — how will he do this? By telling stories and dropping names to illustrate what a fine minister he is and thus aim directly at creating an impression, or by *being* trustworthy, caring, wise and letting his image take care of itself? Perhaps the latter course will take longer, but in it he can function with a genuineness and integrity which is of infinitely greater value.

When one comes to public institutions, here, again, there is no way that images can be avoided, whether it be with a school, college, church, corporation, product or nation. In all areas, however, we must lean toward the importance of truth and reality over contrived impressions. This matter is much too complex to subject to general rules. I will only give a few illustrations of a more helpful direction.

On the National Public Radio in our part of the country there is a morning program of music preceded by a news broadcast. The announcer is startingly different from the average breathless narrator of the news. He speaks slowly and seems relatively unaffected by the need to emphasize the spectacular. One morning I even heard him say: "Well, there's really not very much news this morning, most of the stories are things that might happen or of things that are going to happen but didn't." He was removed from his responsibility as a newsbroadcaster and replaced by someone more conventional, but there was such a storm of protest from the listeners that he was back in three weeks. Why can't the news industry sometimes admit that on certain days there isn't a lot of news? Why is that so unthinkable? Why not deliberately puncture our foolish expectations from time to time?

For Christians in elected political office, re-election cannot be the highest goal. If it is, then one's hands are tied by expediency, and there is little room to influence the path of government in any direction in which it does not already want to go. Also, the attention to image must be held in check by putting emphasis on the issues themselves. The last presidential election in the United States was a good example of how this was not done. The televised debates were a case in point. It seemed that the main point for both candidates was to establish their image and run their opponent's down, with as little attention spent on the issues themselves as possible. Carter tried to project an image of the one who was the incumbent and, therefore, knew far more about the workings of government than anyone could who had not been President. Therefore, he was always talking about "the oval office" — about when he was in it, what he said in it, what it represented, and so on. He tried to paint the picture of Reagan as an irresponsible war-monger. Reagan, on the other hand, tried to have us identify our feelings of nostalgia with him — he represented the "good old days" before the government was on your backs and when everybody did an honest day's work. He countered with the image of Carter as a fumbling incompetent. There was little light shed on anyone's decision as to who to vote for. It is very hard for anyone in politics to resist its image-orientation, certainly impossible to do it completely, but one must lean against the tide.

Advertising is one of the most difficult fields of all, since it is already built around so much image-making. A Christian working in this field who wants to keep God in his theatre of observers must lean toward persuasion or information advertising instead of sheer image advertising. The approach would be to highlight the real virtues of the product, not to aim so much at getting the consumer to identify with the setting in which the product is being used in the advertisement. Of course, this is not a black and white thing, but there are many gradations between the two poles of information and image. It is impossible to avoid image-making — people make some sort of image out of every ad that they see — but the question is, is that all there is? Also, appeals to greed, snobbery, lust and sheer illusion cannot be justified. They are all very powerful and seductive means of leverage on any human being, simply because they strike such a sympathetic vibration with our tendencies to pride and self-indulgence. If we are in any sense to be salt of the earth in the midst of a corrupt generation, we must be able to resist this kind of direction, not just in our private lives, but in our working life. Some of the best advertisements that I have seen are those that debunk materialism itself. Some of the Volkswagon advertising presented the product effectively and through use of humor pricked pins into the bubble of modern materialism.

A big consideration in all three of the fields that I have mentioned — news, politics and advertising — is that people who would like to change the direction for the better are often found not at the top of the pile but somewhere in the lower ranks. They are, therefore, not free to simply redirect major policies, but if they are to remain in the institution, must be content to lean as much as they can in a helpful direction.

Lastly, we turn to the work of the church and Christian works in general. The church is in a role of primary responsibility here. If the church will not stand for truth, who else can be expected to? Paul referred to the church as the "pillar and bulwark of the truth," (1 Timothy 3:15, RSV) meaning that it is the church's task to maintain, guard and live out the truth of the living God. At its most irreduceable, the task of the church is to worship God, spread the gospel and love each other and the world. If the church or Christian work is doing this God-given task faithfully, its image will take care of itself. In an image-oriented culture, the Christian church must be attuned to the dangers of importing the world's methodologies and means of communication uncritically. The church has at its disposal a deep and rich source of guidance in the Bible itself, not just in the form of lists of rules, but in the form of profound insights and obligations about who people are, how they are to be treated, how the message of God is to be communicated and so on. We are living in a culture which, by contrast, has no coherent view of man and has only one guide to action, which is "Does it work?" The methodologies of the world may be seen to work in a limited way, even in the work of the church, but my impression is that it is more in the direction of Palm Sunday faith.

A helpful passage in the writings of the apostle Paul captures much of what I have been trying to say:

Therefore, knowing the fear of the Lord, we persuade men; but what we are is known to God, and I hope it is known also to your conscience. We are not commending ourselves to you again but giving you *cause* to be proud of us, so that you may be able to answer those who pride themselves on a man's position and not on his heart. For if we are beside ourselves, it is for God; if we are in our right mind, it is for you. (2 Corinthians 5:11-13, RSV)

Paul begins with an over-arching principle of life. It is "knowing the fear of the Lord." That is the attitude with which we persuade men. Because we fear God, there is no room for hypocrisy or manipulation. God is there, he is watching. He is our ultimate audience. There is an appropriateness to the verb *fear* as well. It is not as if we crouch in terror of being stricken by lightening, but on the other hand, as C. S. Lewis wrote, "He is not safe." He is not mocked. Then Paul is able to tell them that what we are is known to God and to you. This is something extraordinary. If God and the Corinthian church were to compare notes on the sort of person Paul was and the kind of ministry he had, Paul is sure that the two sets of notes would be in agreement. God, of course, sees the whole truly, but because Paul was a man of integrity who carried on his ministry with real openness, the Corinthians knew him truly as well. He was like Nathaniel, an "Israelite in whom is no guile." He could say that they were not commending themselves to the Corinthians, but giving them *cause* to be proud of Paul. That is to say, he was not indulging in impression-management for the sake of establishing an image of himself in the church. He, through his life, was giving them real cause for pride. It was a question of real life, not a pseudo-event existing only to be reported. Paul is concerned that they be able to have an answer for those whose view of life is image-oriented in that they pride themselves on a man's position, status or image, rather than on his heart or where he really stands as a person. And lastly, in verse 13 he seems to be answering some who have charged him with being beside himself. He brushes this aside making it clear that it is not an important point with him what they happen to think.

I mention this passage at some length because it is Paul's transparency and integrity that end up being a far more effective witness to those inside and outside the church than all the efforts expressly contrived to be witness, despite all their sophistication. In his life there was an affirmation of reality over pseudo-events which has been a beacon to Christians and non-Christians alike down through the ages. It is a witness that is especially powerful because it flows completely naturally out of the things he believed about himself, God and the world.

In each age Christians are called on to fight worldliness in whatever form that worldliness shows itself. Today, images as they foster illusion, deception and confusion are a part of the world spirit of this age. This spirit we are called on to resist, even though it has titanic force behind it.

The battle must start in our individual walks with God Himself. He must be the primary audience before whom we live. We are never off-stage in His theatre, out of sight of His scrutiny or out of the range of His love. The final reality is God Himself. It is from His character that our values and ideals come. Our priorities must be formed around them and any image-making that we do must be within their boundaries.

A pertinent question is, "What in the world good will it do for the individual Christian to try to combat a vast orientation of our culture?" It is one thing to fear God in the way I have described in our individual lives and another to think of influencing our culture. Most people see what needs to be changed, realize that they cannot bring about those changes in their lifetimes and then don't do anything. But under God, we are not called to be successful (much less to be able to bask in awareness of our success) but to live with integrity before God. No one of us can hope to challenge our society head-on, singlehandedly, but we can do something to influence the little piece of society that we touch, and we can do a great deal to influence the course of our own lives and encourage others. By God's grace we *can* "do justice, love kindness, and walk humbly with our God,"; the visible success in this world then is up to God Himself. Christians, even in a minority, have accomplished extraordinary things.

DISCUSSION QUESTIONS

1. What is a value and how do values effect us? How can an image be considered a mask?

2. What shift has occurred in the concept of "value" in our society? Why is this shift important? Has the Church adopted this in any way?

3. On what basis does assigning values effect all things that we believe and do?

4. Why must the Christian stress that values are eternal to feelings or situations?

5. How has the church subscribed to secular imagery? How can community, sacrifice, accountability and other basic Christian principles combat this imagery?

6. In what ways has God, in much of modern evangelism, been cast in the role of a celebrity? Why is this blasphemous?

7. Why is it important to always remember that God is observing us? How does this eliminate our hypocrisy and bring about integrity?

8. How are lusts for power, prestige, and pleasure used to sell products?

9. Knowing the fear of the Lord is to be an over-arching principle of our lives. Explain why and what this means in everyday life.

10. When does the Bible speak of integrity and why is it important?

". . . our models can tyranize us by
setting up unrealistic standards of heroism, therefore
condemning us to frustrated shame"

The Meaning of Shame and Guilt

Dick Keyes

Shame is often felt but little talked about and little understood. This is in part because it is so often confused with guilt, as if the two words were synonyms. It is also because the Bibilical teaching on shame and its implications has been little developed by Christian theology.

To clarify the meaning of both words, let us look at their opposites. The opposite of guilt is innocence or moral purity. The opposite of shame, though, is not innocence; it is honor and glory. Think of Hosea 4:7, ". . . I will change their glory into shame," or Philippians 3:19, ". . . they glory in their shame." Shame is related to dishonor. Both shame and guilt are falling short of some standard, the subjective experience being the feeling of unacceptability and badness. Guilt is clearly for violating a rule, law or commandment. It is solidly in a moral framework, but from where, then, does shame come? What standard is violated when we experience shame?

If we look at three kinds of relationships between guilt and shame, the definition will become more clear. First of all, guilt and shame can come together for the same act. For example, I can tell a lie and feel guilt because I know it is wrong, but also feel shame because I had thought I was a strong enough person to have told the truth. Secondly, guilt and shame can function independently of each other. This goes both ways. I can know that I have done the wrong thing morally, but I can be quite unashamed about it. This is not to my credit, but it happens. In the same way

I can feel shame for all kinds of things that are morally irrelevant. I can feel shame for being poor, for having been to the wrong kind of college or for having read or not read certain books. One area where most people feel shame is about their bodies. They feel ashamed of what they look like. In no sense are these moral problems or even moral issues. They are morally neutral, and yet we can experience extreme and painful shame over them. The third kind of relationship between guilt and shame is that of opposition: the two can work against each other. In other words, we can feel shame for doing the right thing, or sense a certain glory in doing the wrong thing. For example, in the Bible we are warned against being ashamed of Christ. We usually do not see the psychological implications of this. Believing and being identified with Jesus Christ is the most morally right thing we can do — and yet we can feel ashamed of doing it.

How do we explain these confusing things? The fact that guilt and shame can function independently or in opposition to each other shows that they point to two different systems or standards of self-evaluation. Guilt and innocence deal with morals, rights and wrongs. Shame, however, deals with models, our sense of what is heroic, which is measured in terms of honor and glory on the one side and shame on the other.

Because we are all more familiar with moral categories, I will expand on models. All of us have heroes or heroines, people that we would like to be like. There is some kind of notion in our minds of the person that we would like to be. Psychologists call this our *self-ideal*. It functions as an ideal self-portrait by which we measure ourselves. We feel shame when we (often suddenly) fall short of this model of heroism. Sartre gives a good example of this in his book *Being and Nothingness*.[1] He describes a man eavesdropping on someone else, looking through the keyhole of the person's door. Suddenly he hears a footstep behind him, and there is someone watching *him*. This would be an experience where most of us would feel intense shame, because that sort of behavior is not "me"; I'm not a voyeur or peeping Tom, and yet there I was, doing it! The experience goes beyond the fact of public exposure (that someone saw me doing it) but its impact is that it shows me myself in a new way that is utterly shocking. I am not the person that I thought I was, after all. I had no idea that I was so unheroic. I thought I was a bit closer to my self-ideal. Shame may or may not involve public embarrassment but always involves a painful loss of trust in oneself and with it a feeling of unacceptability.

This means that the kinds of things that cause us shame depend on whatever it is that to us is heroic, the content of our self-portrait. Of course our models can tyrannize us by setting up unrealistic standards of heroism, and therefore condemning us to frustrated shame most of the time because of our failure to live up to them. Even though our heroes and heroines must be utterly unrealistic, they still exert a tremendous level of control over our lives.

An obvious problem that we can get into is to have our morals derived from the Bible and our models defined by Hollywood. This is like having one foot in Jerusalem and the other in Southern California. It is too long a stretch between the two. It leads to a crossfire of self-rejection. We are condemned whichever way we turn. If we do what is morally right, we might feel ashamed of being "goody-goody"; if we do what might seem to us glorious and heroic, we would feel guilty. We inflict great suffering on ourselves by having morals and models that are incompatible or at least out of focus with each other.

The difference between guilt and shame is born out in the solution that the Bible offers to both. God's solution to our moral problem of sin is clear-cut and well known in Christian theology. As we trust in Christ, we are forgiven. The death of Christ legally satisfies the requirements of justice which would otherwise have condemned us. Through receiving the free gift of salvation by faith, we are pronounced justified in the sight of God. It is a legal acquittal that is involved. But when we come to shame, it does not seem to be so clear. It makes no sense to apply a moral and legal solution to a problem that may not be a moral problem. Here we begin to see that what the salvation of Jesus Christ involves is more than forgiveness. There is something more than just legal acquittal — and that is personal acceptance. The fact that salvation is often expressed in legal terms in no way means that it is limited to legal categories. Personal acceptance is more than forgiveness, but includes it. For example, I can forgive you for something you have done to me but I still might not like to spend time with you, I might not want you along on my vacation. Christian salvation goes beyond legal pardon. It is the work of a loving Father who adopts us into his family. He loves us and accepts us as we are. The parable of the prodigal son (Luke 15:11) is a good example. The father ran out to meet the son and welcomed him back with a banquet and great celebration. God's answer to shame is that He accepts us in our acceptability. The writer of Hebrews points out the Jesus "is not ashamed to call them brethren." (Hebrews 2:11) He is not ashamed to have us numbered in his family, even with all of our sin and shame. How easy it is to feel ashamed of those who are in our family — parents of their children's public bad behavior, and vice versa. Yet Jesus is glad to call us His brothers and sisters and be identified with us. So, God's solution is forgiveness for our moral problem, acceptance in the midst of shame, and the promise that one day He will replace our shame with honor and glory.

Another whole question that must be raised is what to do with our heroes. When we are dealing with models, we are touching on the role of the imagination and its function in our psychology. Our imaginations need to be redeemed. They are cluttered with all kinds of heroes that have no business being there. This process has two sides, the negative and the positive.

Negatively, we must get rid of many of our heroes and heroines. Many of them come from Hollywood and Madison Avenue and are heroic for their exploitation of others in every imaginable way. As such, they have a powerful appeal to our pride. The Bible has a great deal of space devoted to exploding empty heroism. God seems to use humor and sarcasm to the fullest in doing this. Isaiah's words bear the sting of scorn, "Woe to those who are heroes at drinking wine, and valiant men in mixing strong drink." (Isaiah 4:22, RSV) On a wider scale, the Biblical doctrine of the fool is a development of the theme of unheroism disguised as if it were glory. The fool is usually the one who thinks he can outwit virtue, but ends up destroying himself. He is the archetypal loser, and the Bible spares nothing in his exposure. Perhaps this is because God knows that He must reach into our imaginations to discredit these heroes.

Positively, the Christian has the hero to end all heroes. Jesus Christ is the "hero and perfecter of our faith." (Hebrews 12:2) The various commands to imitate Christ are commands to make Him our hero. The imitation of Christ is not meant to be the imitation of His every action and circumstance. Some have felt that it meant that being celibate or not owning a house were especially virtuous because Jesus was celibate and did not own a house. God might call any of us to either of these things, but they are not good just because Jesus did them. The focus of the imitation of Christ is the imitation of His quality of life. There are at least six areas of Jesus' life that we are told to imitate, to do things because and in the way that Jesus did them. We are to love one another as Jesus loved His disciples. (John 13:13-15) We are to forgive one another as "God in Christ forgave you." (Ephesians 4:32 ff) We are to be willing to suffer unjustly. (1 Peter 2:20 ff) Since Jesus was rich and became poor that we might become rich, we are to give and be generous with each other. (2 Corinthians 8:9) If Jesus lowered Himself to become a man and die on a cross for us, we can afford to be humble. (Philippians 2:3-8) Finally, our greatness and fulfillment is found in serving, not in being served, because Jesus came not to be served but to serve, to give His life as a ransom for many. (Mark 10:43-45)

The imitation of Christ is not the imitation of one who is far off and irreproachable like a statue on a hill. The one whom we are to imitate is the same one who is not ashamed to call us members of His family. He is beside us, walking arm in arm with us. The imitation of Christ is, therefore, not a moral bludgeon to make us squirm under an awareness of our failure, but is a call to redeem our imaginations, that having understood the radical acceptance and forgiveness of God, we would have our imaginations filled with this powerful model of true heroism.

All of this is not a recipe for getting rid of all feelings of shame. However, if we have Christ as our model, it will eliminate a great deal of unnecessary shame, shame for things that are not really shameful. If Christ is our model, then our models and our morals are in perfect focus because Christ lived out the commandments of God. If this is the case, we will experience shame and guilt together for things that are really wrong and therefore dishonorable before God. It will also mean that we experience the forgiveness and acceptance of God that comes to us through Jesus Christ, "the hero and perfecter of our faith."

DISCUSSION QUESTIONS

1. Explain the differences between guilt and shame.

2. Describe how guilt and shame can work against each other.

3. What is the Bible's solution to shame?

4. How can our imaginations be redeemed?

5. What changes would happen to you if Jesus became more the model of your imagination?

6. If Christ is truly our model, are we still liable to experience guilt? shame?

7. Is guilt or shame a larger burden in your life? Can you identify the source of your guilt and the reason for your shame?

8. Do you have a plan for ridding yourself of these impediments to godly growth?

Ranald Macaulay

Of Scottish heritage, Ranald was born in Natal, South Africa. While growing up, he became persuaded by agnostic arguments that were antagonistic toward Christianity and all that it implied.

After being accepted to study law at Cambridge University in England, a close friend of his became a Christian and brought to light the whole issue of Christianity. However, it wasn't until he was into his first year at Cambridge that he was confronted with a clear presentation of the Gospel, and he believed.

It was during this time at Cambridge that Ranald had his first contact with L'Abri when Dr. Schaeffer visited the university presenting lectures and leading discussions.

After graduation and his marriage to Susan Schaeffer, Ranald spent the next four and a half years as staff at the Swiss L'Abri. The Macaulay's then returned to England to establish the English L'Abri during which time Ranald earned an honors degree in Theology at Kings College with a college prize in Church History.

He co-authored *Being Human* with Jerram Barrs. Ranald and his wife have four children.

"Confrontation is inevitable and the
Christian mind must not
flinch from it."

The Christian Mind
Ranald Macaulay

There are a number of things within our evangelical (or Bible-believing) heritage of the past 150 years about which we can be justly proud. In particular, its faithfulness to the Bible's teaching about itself, that it is God's word written, and therefore, completely reliable and absolutely authoritative. This has been one of the principal features of evangelicalism, and, in a day of almost universal defection from such a view, both in the so-called Christian churches and in the culture as a whole, this has been no small achievement.

However, of one thing evangelicalism can *NOT* be proud: namely *its failure to develop and exercise a Christian mind.* Harry Blamires begins his book, *The Christian Mind:* "There is no longer a Christian mind," and he continues:

> Unfortunately the Christian mind has succumbed to the secular drift with a degree of weakness and nervelessness unmatched in Christian history. It is difficult to do justice in words to the complete loss of intellectual morale in the 20th century church. One cannot characterize it without having recourse to language which will sound hysterical and melodramatic.[1]

These statements were echoed more recently by Charles Malik in an address given at Wheaton College in 1980. He said: "The greatest danger besetting American evangelical Christianity [though the same, we may add, could be said of evangelicalism in the United Kingdom and elsewhere] is the danger of anti-intellectualism . . . The mind as to its greatest and deepest reaches is not cared for enough." Whereupon he outlines the serious consequences of this mistake: "The arena of creative thinking [has been] abdicated and vacated to the enemy."[2]

Such statements may at first sight seem extreme; after all, have there not been determined efforts made by evangelicals during the past four or five decades, especially by those involved in universities, to reverse this tradition? There have. Yet, for whatever reason, these have not as yet been widely enough felt to make any appreciable difference to the tradition, and certainly not to the culture at large.

Evangelicalism has not been sufficiently committed to the development of a Christian mind; therefore, anti-intellectualism has remained endemic within it as Malik says. The purpose of this paper is to try to dislodge the infection.

The Necessity of a Christian Mind

As with all our ideas, we must start with the Bible. What is the Biblical evidence which leads us to conclude that a Christian mind is important?

But first we must clarify what we mean by the term "a Christian mind." Nothing more or less than the proper use of the intellectual faculty which God has given to each of us. Whether we like it or not, we have minds, just as we have eyes and ears. And we are exhorted in God's word to "love . . . God with all your heart, and . . . soul, and mind and strength." (Luke 10:27 quoting Deuteronomy 6:5) So the expression of the Christian mind is a shorthand for this activity, the loving of God with the mind.

The summary of the law is helpful in two ways: first, it shows the importance of the mind. But second, it shows that the mind is only a part of a greater whole. The Christian mind cannot be considered in isolation from the rest of our duty. It is not merely an intellectual concept. The mind is only a part of what it is to be human; therefore, the mind must not be divorced from the rest of our human experience.

This is important, for we need to distinguish at the outset the Christian emphasis on the mind from, say, the Greek. The Greeks elevated the mind, the Ratio, above all else — hence, they were Rationalists. (And they have had many descendants!) But Christianity is not rationalist — it is *rational*, yes: I mean it makes sense (to our minds) of the reality of our experience; but it is not, therefore, the elevation of the human mind above all else, leastwise above God's person and revelation.

All this is already implied within Jesus' summary of the law: that the mind is important but only within its appropriate sphere *i.e.*, as a portion only of the greater whole of human experience, of heart and soul and strength. Following on from this, then, the first reason (Biblically) for an insistence on the importance of the mind is that it is part of the created order within man's experience: the mind is important, because God made it that way — just as beauty is important (and, as a corollary, man's creativity and aesthetic capacity), because God made it that way.

Nor has the Fall destroyed this! Even though our human experience is damaged by sin, it still exists. So when Scripture (Ephesians 2:1) speaks of man being "dead" and hence, of needing to be "born again," et cetera, we must be careful how we understand this. What the Bible is referring to is the absolute need which every person has for a relationship with God to be restored. Man is "dead" in the sense that he lacks what actually constitutes "life," *i.e.* a relationship with God! So, in this sense, he needs to be born again. But "dead" does not mean in the Bible that man is no longer a person, having the faculties described (in Genesis) as "the image of God." Man, even though sinful, remains man (and not a machine, say). Man is not junk. Man can create beauty, and live, and reason, and discern by means of a conscience what is good and bad, et cetera. Calvin's comments on Genesis 9:6:

> Should anyone object that this divine image has been obliterated, the solution is easy. First, there yet exists some remnant of it, so that man is possessed of no small dignity and, second, the celestial creator himself, however corrupted he (man) may be, still keeps in view the end of his original creation; and according to his example, we ought to consider for what end he created men and what excellence he has bestowed upon them, above the rest of living beings.[3]

Hence, we can say that, in this sense only, even though each person *is* dead, when he is born again, there is a *restoration of what already exists.* Take as an illustration a rose bush, or fruit tree, which has been abandoned, which needs pruning to restore it to its original purpose and fruitfulness. So it is with fallen man. "True spirituality is not a super-human religiosity — it is simply true humanity released from bondage to sin and renewed by the Holy Spirit."[4]

Second, the *Bible states the importance of the mind*, of the development of a Christian mind, *both explicitly and implicitly.*
1. *Explicitly.*

We have considered already the implication of Jesus' summary of the law: God himself requires us to use our minds. Nor is it possible to love God if we do not love him *with our minds.*

Furthermore, Paul says, if we are to be sanctified, it must be by means of the *renewing of our minds* . . . "Be transformed by the renewing of your

mind." (Romans 12:2, NIV) We can deduce from this that while sanctification is not only an intellectual activity, it certainly is an intellectual activity
— our minds have to be renewed if our lives are to be restored. And they
are renewed only by a deliberate "setting of them," *i.e.* focusing of them,
upon objective truth (*cf.* Colossians 3:1, 2), which means, obviously, understanding truth.

Hence, the emphasis throughout the Bible upon the need to *understand*
God's word. Paul says, "Let the word of Christ dwell in you richly." (Colossians 3:16, NIV) Joshua is told "do not let this Book of the Law depart
from your mouth; meditate on it day and night, so that you may be careful
to do everything written in it." (Joshua 1:8, NIV) Psalm 19 extols the law
of the Lord because it can revive the soul, it can make wise the simple, it
can give joy to the heart — and so on.

What are these if not exhortations to understand with the mind what
God wants us to know –- not to be "understood" merely, as if the process
were only an intellectual activity, like understanding the statement $2 + 2$
$= 4$. For our response, whether of gratitude or repentance, of joy or con-
trition, is also included in the idea of "understanding." But certainly it
must include the basic element of intellectual comprehension. How else
can the truth of the ideas within God's word begin to have their proper effect upon us?

All this is, of course, obvious. The word of God has to be understood in
the same way that anything in language is understood. It is directed via the
mind to the person. Because it is truth, it can be directed no where else!
The mind is of crucial importance. In fact, there is no greater indication
that our minds are important from *God's* point of view than that he has
given us a written word as the chief means of our sanctification.

2. *Implicitly.*

It is a common misconception amongst evangelicals that (since mankind
is fallen) the mind of unbelievers is not open to reason. This is partly due
to a misreading of Paul's statements in 1 Corinthians 1 and 2 which we
shall come to later. There Paul says, "the man without the spirit does not
accept the things that come from the Spirit of God, for they are foolishness
to him, and he cannot understand them, because they are spiritually dis-
cerned." (2:14, NIV) Such a reading of this passage has seriously inhibited
Christians in trying to persuade non-Christians about the truth of their
faith: "There's no point," is the prevailing attitude; "non-Christians have
reprobate minds, minds which are darkened so that they cannot understand. So why reason with them? The activity is pointless."

We find a striking contrast to this attitude when we consider Paul's approach as seen in Acts. "Every Sabbath he *reasoned* in the synagogue, *trying to persuade Jews and Greeks;*" (18:4, NIV) "He . . . went into the synagogue and *reasoned* with the Jews;" (18:19) "he vigorously *refuted* the Jews . . . proving from the Scriptures;" (18:28) "[He] spoke boldly there [in the synagogue] for three months, *arguing persuasively* about the kingdom of God;" (19:8) "From morning till evening he explained and declared to them the kingdom of God and *tried to convince* them about Jesus . . ." (28:23) And so on . . . .

Now these examples of how Paul approached unbelievers — whether Jews or Gentiles didn't matter — indicates again the importance God places on the mind, even the mind of those who are, to use the Biblical expression, "dead in trespasses and sins." It is truth which is being communicated, truth which is "evident to all." (Romans 1:18 ff) Therefore, it must be addressed to the mind — and, of course, also to the heart and the conscience for, as we said, there is finally no separation possible between the thinking of those whom he comes in contact. He reasons with them, he explains, he argues persuasively.

In fact, he even describes his calling as being the capturing of all intellectual activity for God and God's truth. "We demolish arguments and every pretension that sets itself up against the knowledge of God, and we take captive every thought to make it obedient to Christ." (2 Corinthians 10:4, 5, NIV)

This attitude and approach parallels, of course, what we see both in Jesus' ministry and in the prophets of the Old Testament. Jesus condemns his opponents because of the evident folly of what they think and do and say: "You blind fools! Which is greater: the gold, or the temple that makes the gold sacred?" (Matthew 23:17, NIV) What he means is that they should be able to see for themselves that this doesn't make sense. So, "they are without excuse . . . thinking themselves to be wise," as Paul says in a parallel instance, "they have become fools." (Romans 1:22)

Isaiah says the same thing: "No one stops to think, no one has the knowledge or understanding to say . . . [he is speaking about the foolishness of idolatry, of making idols from logs of wood and burning one part while worshipping another!] 'Half of it I used for fuel . . . shall I make a detestable thing from what is left? Shall I bow down to a block of wood?'" (Isaiah 44:19, NIV) So, just as Paul does, he appeals to those who are opposing God's truth, "Come, let us reason together." (Isaiah 1:18)

To summarize then, the evidence of the whole Bible, both explicit and implicit, is directed against any repudiation of the mind, or even demeaning of the mind as has, regrettably, characterized much evangelicalism during the past century. This has been a completely unbiblical "tradition," and the sooner it is recognized as such, and more importantly, the sooner resolute steps are taken by individuals and groups alike to eradicate it from our midst, the better. Traditions, however, die hard. Hence, the opposition must be both resolute and informed.

The sole basis for such opposition, let it be repeated, is the evidence of the word of God.

The Development of a Christian Mind.

Having seen from Scripture that a Christian mind is a necessity, we turn now to consider how such a "mind" should be developed.

1. *Submission to God's Word*

A Christian mind is, above everything, a mind committed to the truth of God's word and its absolute authority. Its first concern is not, "What do *I* think?" or "What does society think?" but rather "What has God said?"

This is what Paul is getting at when he says in 1 Corinthians 1:21 that "God was pleased through the foolishness of what was preached to save those who believe." Throughout this passage he contrasts the "foolishness of the Gospel" and the "wisdom of man." " . . . in the wisdom of God the world through its wisdom did not know him." (1:21, NIV)

Paul has been taken by some to be suggesting that the message of the Bible is in fact foolish, that it does not and cannot make sense to the mind of man. But this is surely mistaken. If this were indeed his meaning we would have to conclude that he is contradicting himself. In Romans 1:18*ff*, he states categorically that the truth about God, that is, about "his eternal power and divine nature," is clearly to be seen within creation. Man, therefore, needs to "suppress the truth" in order to avoid its obvious implications — that he should worship God and be obedient to His word. Instead, he turns and worships the creature rather than the Creator. He is "without excuse" in this, for the truth is evident to him.

It is not that the mind of man cannot understand the truth. God's word is "true and reasonable" (Acts 26:25, NIV) — that is why Paul takes pains to explain it to non-Christians, and tries to persuade them about it, as we saw. It is that men *refuse to acknowledge* God's word. They are ignorant about the truth "due to the hardening of their hearts." (Ephesians 4:18, NIV)

We must insist, therefore, that when Paul describes the gospel in 1 Corinthians 1 and 2 as God's "foolishness," he is not meaning that it is, in fact, foolish, that it is unreasonable. He simply takes the Greeks' reaction to the gospel, that it doesn't make sense to them, and parodies it. One could imagine Paul saying, "What you take to be foolish in the Gospel,

(Christ's coming, death and resurrection, cf. Acts 17:32), is actually God's own wisdom made clear." The foolishness of the gospel is not a real foolishness, but only apparent — since man in his rebellion is inveterately foolish. (cf. Romans 1:22)

Furthermore, in contrasting (within the parody) the foolishness of the gospel and the wisdom of man, Paul is not implying that wisdom, in the sense of intellectual activity, is invalid. He is not expressing a distrust in the mind as such — else, as we have seen, he would be being inconsistent with his own state intentions and practices — but rather excluding the claims of the autonomous mind. He is contrasting, in other words, God's revealed truth and man's unaided reason. By the latter — without revelation — man is unable to arrive at the truth. Why? Because the truth man needs for salvation, depends absolutely upon God's revelation of himself to man, which reaches its apex in the birth, life, death and resurrection of the Son of God himself, the eternal second person of the Trinity.

This is why Paul interjects in 1 Corinthians 2:2, ". . . I resolved to know nothing while I was with you except Jesus Christ and him crucified." (NIV) He is emphasizing truth which is revealed. The gospel is not something which man's unaided reason can discover by itself, for it has been "created" by the free choice of God. It is not a "principle of nature" to be discovered as scientists discover truths about the world around us. It is sui generis, as all personal acts are. God has acted. He has provided us with salvation through the gracious work of the Savior. This is the gospel. It is God's work.

Paul is not suggesting, however, that the gospel is against reason. Otherwise he could not have replied to Festus in Acts 26:25, "What I am saying is true and reasonable." The gospel, including in that, as Paul evidently does, "the whole will of God" i.e. all of God's revelation stretching right back through the Old Testament to the beginning (Acts 20:27) — is the only thing which makes sense of human experience. So Paul can say, "Jesus Christ . . . has become for us wisdom from God . . ." (1 Corinthians 1:30, NIV)

The contrast Paul is concerned to maintain is between God's word and humanistic philosophy (i.e. philosophy arising from man). Note the parallel in Colossians 2:8, "See to it that no one takes you captive through hollow and deceptive philosophy, which depends on human tradition and the basic principles of this world rather than on Christ." (NIV) It is not philosophy as such, in other words intellectual activity, which Paul is warning the Colossian believers against. It is a particular kind of intellectual activity — thinking which ignores God's revelation (which centers in Christ) and finds its justification within "human tradition," within man's unaided reason.

But to return to 1 Corinthians 1 and 2: The vital point to keep in mind is that the Christian is committed above all else to *revealed* truth. He is committed to use his mind, to use it actively and broadly (as we shall see) — but, first of all, he is to use it *in submission to God's word*. If this is not present, a "mind" may be developed, but not a "Christian mind" — and history has examples enough and to spare, unhappily, of other "minds." They are all of them impressive in their own way, either because they include insights which are profound and true, or because they display remarkable ingenuity or erudition or complexity — but they are not for that reason a "Christian mind." A Christian mind is first of all submitted to God's word, eager and anxious to conform all its thinking to the truths contained therein.

Not *blindly* submissive, however; for there are good and sufficient reasons to elicit such a response. Just as there are good and sufficient reasons to cause us to accept, within the context of the earth's atmosphere at least, Newton's law of gravity. Such law is authoritative, it demands acquiescence — yet it can be seen to be true also, the evidence beign all about us. So it is with the authority of God's word: it need not be accepted blindly. It is evidently true.

Yet it is a *real* submission for all that. Believers have returned to a relationship of love with their Creator, in which they acknowledge him *ipso facto* as sovereign over the whole of reality (let alone sovereign over their own individuality — and very tiny — lives). So they "do not lean to their own understanding." (Proverbs 3:5) They submit their understanding, their mind, to God's revealed truth. Where it goes, they go, where it stops, they stop. Its information on all topics is received regardless of whether it is palatable to them at the time or confirmed by "the assured results of scholarship" — at the time. They scrutinize carefully, seeking by all means available to scholarship to understand its teaching better. They are thankful for those multitudes of confirmations and clarifications which have resulted from disciplines such as archaeology and etymology during the past century and a half. Yet they do not receive Scripture's teaching *because* it has been confirmed by the mind, by the science of man, but, first simply because it is contained in God's word written. So it is scrutinized — but not criticized and condemned, as has, unhappily, been the case in liberal scholarship since the 18th century.

So the Christian mind is esentially a *humble* mind, submitting itself absolutely to the authority of God's word written. No submission of this sort, no Christian mind.

2. A Christian mind involves *a passionate commitment to Truth.*

First, to *objective truth.* The statements within the Bible are true in the sense that they accurately describe, or, in some cases, define the way reality actually is. God is personal and not impersonal. God exists objectively and is not a figment of the imagination. Man is made in God's image. Man has fallen from his original perfection and innocence. Jesus is the Christ. His work on the cross is a "full and sufficient sacrifice, oblation and satisfaction for the sins of the whole world."

All this is not doctrine merely — but Truth. If it is expressed in creedal or liturgical formulae, it faces the danger of becoming formalized for us, of becoming "statements" rather than "reality." But that is a danger which all human expression is subject to: musical compositions, for example, can become lifeless within time if the reality of the original creation is not maintained. So with doctrinal statements. They are not wrong to be statements, for statements are necessary if truth is to be communicated. But they are not *truth* because they are religious. They are truth because they accurately describe what reality, in fact, is, or in the case of historical events, has been. Saul *was*, in fact, converted on the Damascus Road. God is, in fact, the Creator of the heavens and the earth and everything in them.

Again, this is so obvious we hestitate to say it. Yet it must be said, if only because truth has been undermined so seriously within our culture in the West. But Scripture, and the historic Christian faith, is committed fundamentally to the concept of *objective* truth. As Paul says (in dealing with the objective reality of the resurrection), "if Christ has not been raised, your faith is futile . . . [and] we are to be pitied more than all men. But Christ has indeed been raised from the dead . . ." (1 Corinthians 15:17-20, NIV)

Second, to *salvation truth:* The Christian mind is passionately committed to objective truth, but objective truth, happily, which centers upon the saving work of Christ. Because of Christ's work, it is possible for man, the sinner, to come to know God, or rather, as Paul so carefully points out, "to be known by God." (Galatians 4:9) God is holy. God is also the upright Judge whose judgments are "righteous altogether." How, then, can the unrighteous sinner be pardoned and received again into fellowship with God? Through Christ!

Hence, the Christian mind is centered upon Christ, upon salvation truth. And in this connection it is, of course, only right that the term "passionate" should be used of its commitment to truth — for does Christ's work of humbling himself and of laying aside his glory in order to become a servant to serve and give his life a ransom for many, does this work leave the believer's heart unmoved? No — "the love of Christ constrains me," says Paul. He is indeed "lost in wonder, love and praise."

So, the Christian mind is not a reasoning mind only, a dispassionate mind. Far from it. It is passionately committed to the Truth of God's word, both as objective truth and salvation truth. The objectivity of truth calls forth passionate praise: "Oh! the depth of the riches of the wisdom and knowledge of God! . . . For from him and through him, and to him are all things." (Romans 11:33, 36, NIV) And the center of truth, the reality of Christ's free and unmerited salvation, calls forth passionate love . . . "We love him because he first loved us." (1 John 4:19)

3. Finally, the Christian mind is *Universal in its Vision*

This principle reminds us that in Christianity there is no division between secular and spiritual. Politics, entertainment, nature, literature . . . all lie within the scope of the spiritual. Why? Becaue that is the way *God* has made man, to live within just such an environment, to be physical, social, creative, fun-loving, responsible, and so on.

The subsequent sinfulness of man, resulting from the Fall, brought division into human experience, but only in the sense that, now, right has to be distinguished from wrong, goodness from evil, love from hate. And that throughout the entire course of human experience — within the so-called "spiritual" experiences, yes, even the religious ones, as much as within the physical. Pride and envy are sinful; so are adultery and drunkenness. The former are no less sinful than the latter — if anything more so.

Hence, the Christian mind is conscious of distinctions which have to be made and maintained on the basis of sin — but not so as to divide religious experience from secular, or spiritual from physical. All human experience is good, because it arises from an original creation which combined both physical and spiritual without division and without sin. So the Christian mind is free to explore and gain knowledge about all the reaches of God's marvelous creation without let or hindrance, apart, that is, from sin.

Paul expresses this freedom in majestic words: "whatever is true, whatever is noble, whatever is right, whatever is pure, whatever is lovely, whatever is admirable — if anything is excellent or praiseworthy — think about such things." (Philippians 4:8, NIV)

We deduce an important principle from this which has far-reaching implications. *The truth of God's word written over-arches the whole of reality.* Just as in a large auditorium with an impressive dome for ceiling, the entire floorspace is overshadowed by the truths contained in Scripture. No experience, no fact, even (experienced or not experienced by man), is "free" from the surveillance of God's word.

However, two important riders need to accompany the principle. *First,
Scripture applies directly to only some aspects of our experience, Second,
even where Scripture does not apply directly, it applies indirectly.*

To continue the illustration of the ceiling: imagine a skylight in the dome
through which a shaft of light is shining into the auditorium below. The
light streams into only one section of the floor below — yet the whole
auditorium is "lightened" by it. So with Scripture and the world: not all
that man sees or knows is dealt with by God's revealed truth. Yet all is influenced by, and in a very real sense, controlled by, that truth. The Bible
gives information about what we call "theological matters," like the sinfulness of man or the person of Christ. It also give information about
"historical/scientific matters." In all such cases, God has spoken directly,
he has lit up those areas of reality directly. But Scripture is not a collection
of all possible information. Much about reality is left untouched by it;
much has already been discovered about the universe which is not dealt
with but which is nevertheless true, information from astronomy, for example or information from history. The fact that it does not appear in the
Bible does not mean it cannot be true.

However, the parallel rider is also true: all of reality is overarched, is
controlled — even though only indirectly — by God's word. Our understanding of psychology, for example, is "controlled" by God's word as is
our science, our history, our sociology, our legal and political systems,
everything. We may apply our minds to find out more about all these
areas of human experience and, in some cases, will arrive at knowledge
which is both original and beneficial. Yet, no areas of human investigation
and activity will be "autonomous" — literally, "a law unto themselves."
They will all be related in some form or another, even though indirectly, to
God's revealed truth. For example, in science many discoveries about the
world have been both true and helpful — many have not been, of course.
But even where discoveries are in themselves true, they can be misapplied.
Crick and Watson's discovery of the formation of the DNA molecule was
a true discovery and in many instances beneficial to the advance of
knowledge. Yet Crick used this discovery as a support for a thorough-
going materialistic philosophy, thereby contradicting God's clear teaching
about creation. Science is not autonomous. God's word judges it!

So with psychology. Undoubtedly, things have been discovered about
the human psyche which are not dealt with in Scripture but which are
helpful in understanding both ourselves and others. However, much
psychology has been an expression of a materialistic view of reality with
little or no place for individual responsibility, let alone guilt before a holy
God. To all this, Scripture addresses itself, sometimes directly, sometimes

indirectly. Man is fallen, so all human relationships are affected detrimentally, and man's relationship within himself is disjointed, even (and very
specially) within his own psyche. The causes and effects of these disruptions have been clarified by careful observation. This is not wrong. The
science of psychology is presupposed, one might say, in what Scripture
tells us of the abnormality of man. But then not all psychology is valid.
God has told us of the principal problem confronting mankind, namely
objective guilt because of sin. Whenever such a view is omitted or rejected
within psychology, it can be seen to be false. Psychology is not
autonomous.

Thus, the Christian mind must be panoramic in vision while controlled
by Scripture.

Three things flow from this:

a. *The Christian mind must receive what is good in culture wherever it is
found.*

It is not only Christians who can appreciate beauty and create it, have
keen insights, solve problems both physical and spiritual, care for the destitute, uphold justice, do deeds of heroism. The non-Christian can do
these, too, for he is made in the image of God.

Therefore, the Christian mind will expect to find the true, the whole, the
right, the pure, the lovely, the admirable within all human experience —
even though seriously diminished and hampered by sin maybe. this calls
for discernment for the sifting of good and bad. There are no easy solutions, neatly packaged. It is a matter of sifting and weighing, of "trying to
find what is pleasing to the Lord," of taking time and trouble, of discerning
and listening.

How, for example are movements in art measured? How are priorities in
political action decided upon? What responses have to be made to those
who criticize the church? What of education, of family life, of lifestyles, of
music? and so on.

b. *The Christian mind must learn to distinguish fundamental issues and
peripheral ones.*

All truth is important, but not all truth is equally important. God's word
is the criterion. Whatever is clearly and frequently taught must be maintained with greater strenuousness than whatever is mentioned vaguely and
occasionally. The classic illustration here is baptism. Baptism is taught explicitly in Scripture. It is commanded. Therefore, it must be practiced.
However, the subjects and mode of baptism are not spelled out clearly.
Therefore, these aspects must be considered peripheral.

By contrast, the Scripture's teaching about sin and salvation, of the person of Christ and the nature of atonement receive explicit and detailed

treatment — and upon them rests the entire superstructure of the Christian faith. They are fundamentals.

Not to distinguish in this way between fundamental and peripheral issues is to cause great mischief. Many of the conflicts and tensions within the church have arisen because this principle has been inadequately understood or applied. Is anything sadder than to find Christians unable to accept one another simply because they disagree on some peripheral issue? Especially in such a day when the fundamentals themselves, upon which they are almost completely agreed, are the real issue vis a vis the culture.

c. *The Christian mind is "to judge all things."* (1 Corinthians 2:15)

Paul explains in the second half of 1 Corinthians 2 that the Christian has something which no one else has, namely information from God himself. This is the wisdom from God to which we referred earlier. "No eye has seen, no ear has heard, no mind has conceived . . . God has revealed it to us by his Spirit." (1 Corinthians 2:9, 10) Therefore, the spiritual man (*i.e.* the one who is properly related to the Holy Spirit through faith in Christ) is able to "make judgments about all things . . . " (1 Corinthians 2:15) In other words, is able to really understand what is going on in the world, what things amount to, what is true, what is false, et cetera.

We have seen examples of this already in science and psychology. But the principle of "judging all things" must be universally applied.

Obviously, it is in this area that the Christian mind must be prepared to *confront the world*. When care has been taken to distinguish between things which are of central importance and things which are only peripheral, and when care has been taken, furthermore, to come with a positive attutude to all culture, seeking for what is good and not condemning indiscriminately whatever does not bear the label, "Christian," even then, there is bound to be confrontation. As Jesus said: "In the world you will have trouble." (John 16:33) Confrontation is inevitable, and the Christian mind must not flinch from it.

Man's false ideas, man's "hollow and deceptive philosophy" (Colossians 2:8), man's "pretensions that set themselves up against the knowledge of God" (2 Corinthians 10:5) — these are like a pollutant within the rivers of human experience. Everywhere they deceive and destroy — within our own culture especially, now that the Christian foundation upon which it rested for so many years has been supplanted by humanism. The media and academia, particularly in places like the United Kingdom and Europe, are steeped in one or another of the expressions of humanistic thought. Every discipline should now be clarified by the addition of a prefix, "humanist" — humanist-psychology, humanist-economics, et cetera, et cetera.

Are we then to sit meekly by, those of us involved within such societies and disciplines, and simply watch and pray and say nothing? The Christian mind will oppose falsehood with all possible vigor. This will be evidence enough that the idea of "developing a Christian mind" is not simply an intellectual concept. It is a passionate commitment to truth, as was said earlier. So passionate, in fact, that the inevitable result will be a confrontation with false ideas and evil practices no less severe than Jesus' own. But did he not call us to this? "Remember the words I spoke to you: 'No servant is greater than his master.' If they persecuted me, they will persecute you also . . ." (John 15:20, NIV)

This is the real cutting edge for evangelism in our own day and will be the deciding factor in the recovery — or loss — of our culture within the next two decades: that in each discipline and profession (doctors, scientists, lawyers, teachers — those of us who are, as it were, a promontary jutting out into the "sea" of our society) that there should arise those whose confession is not merely "we are Christians," important as that is. But who also make confession to the commitment arising from their Christian mind that all knowledge and all experience can ultimately be understood only in terms of the Christian world view. As Malik says: "We must recapture the universities for Christ."[5]

Of course, this is a radical departure from our traditional isolation and passivity, especially intellectually, but are we not called to be radicals? It is sobering to realize that it was just such radical commitment on the other side, amongst humanists, during the latter part of the 19th century which captured the culture for untruth. What, apart from our timidity, keeps us from doing the same, in reverse, today? The Christian mind seeks to bring every thought captive to obey Christ.

DISCUSSION QUESTIONS

1. Why does distinguished statesman, Charles Malik, cite anti-intellectualism as the greatest danger besetting evangelicalism?

2. What effect has the fall had in the importance and worth of the
   mind? Why did Jesus say love God with our minds?

3. What significance does God's choosing a written Word have for our
   appreciation of the mind?

4. How is Paul's phrase "the foolishness of the Gospel" so often mis-
   understood?

5. Though the Bible is rational, rationalism is to be avoided. Though
   the mind is valuable, the autonomous mind is a mistake. Can you explain how these terms distinguish the Christian mind from the
   secular mind?

6. Submission to God's Word is crucial, but blind submission is never
   required. Why?

7. What does it mean to be committed to truth? How do we do this?

8. If all truth is God's truth, how should we view all disciplines of
   study?

9. Which issues of Biblical truth are fundamental? Which are
   peripheral?

10. What kinds of humanistic views pervade the media and the univer-
    sities?

"The need to re-examine so basic an element of our life as our view of spirituality requires a level of honesty we would rather not attempt."

Being Human - The Nature of Spiritual Experience

Ranald Macaulay

Whenever I hear someone referred to as "a very *spiritual* person," at least a part of me wants to ask "What do you mean?" The reason is that I am deeply skeptical about some of the models of spirituality which we have adopted within the church today. Is it "spiritual," for example, for us to have nothing to do with "the world," to spend the greater part of our free time within the church or in church-related activities, to insist that every one should have a "quiet time" each morning, to read only Christian books, to try to "die to self" as if nothing about our "self" has value, certainly not to become involved in what are called "intellectual issues"?

The model we find in the Bible, I suggest, is very different. That is what I want to try to clarify. Its importance is obvious. If we are wrong at this point, about the model of spirituality, we are bound to be wrong, or at least seriously limited, throughout our experience — for spirituality covers the whole of human experience. It would be like having a wrong model for playing tennis: imagine someone holding a tennis racket upside down, or having only half the number of strings. The whole game would be affected, detrimentally of course. That is what has happened within our history as Bible-believing Christians: we have been using a false model for spirituality. Therefore, despite the highly motivated efforts, the various techniques for church growth and individual growth, the crusades, the seminars and all the rest, there has been an evident deficiency in our experience.

Some, unhappily, aware of this state of affairs within the Bible-believing constituency, have reacted childishly. It has angered them. So they have become abusive towards their "parent" like a young child throwing a tantrum, which is sad. Their diagnosis about the ill-health of the patient (to change the metaphor) is frequently accurate; it is their remedy which is at fault. For soon they start questioning the fundamentals of the faith and one realizes where their protest leads, to the shipwreck of their faith, or at least to the shipwreck of those who follow them.

Against both of these trends we must show courage. It is not easy to "confess our faults" — as we all know. The need to re-examine so basic an element of our life as our view of spirituality requires a level of honesty we would rather not attempt. It disrupts our life in order to reconstruct it. So, naturally, we draw back. Friends misunderstand our motives, others resist our conclusions about the Biblical material involved, which means further hard work to get at the truth. And, most difficult of all, if it is better spirituality we are seeking, we know we must be peacemakers. After all, it costs nothing to be critical. It costs everything to be constructive, as this following comment on Deism in the 18th Century makes clear. It stands as a warning to all who want to change (for the better of course, for change is never advocated for the worse!): "Its [*i.e.* Deism's] critical powers far outstripped its constructive capacity."[1]

It is change we are seeking, but change which is constructive. I believe the basis for this is simple and obvious and, best of all, comprises the warp and woof of the whole Bible.

We start with Genesis 1. God made a physical reality. He made it with countless degrees of diversity — all good, all relevant to the whole, all remarkable. But man was made different. Man was made in "the image of God." (V. 27) As male and female, mankind was made in "the likeness of God." And man, too, like the rest of the creation, was described by God as "very good." (V. 31)

Man's experience, though, was "spiritual." From the very beginning, as soon as man was made, man was made within a religious framework. Man was physical: he had a body with a bone structure, a blood system, nerves, muscle tissue and all the rest. But man was more than physical. Man was what we today call a person. Man was able to relate to everything, himself and God included, as a person. He could think, love, create, discern right from wrong, communicate in language, enjoy beauty and so on.

This was man's spiritual experience. He was being as spiritual in tending the garden of Eden as he was when communicating with the Creator, in naming the animals as he was when he was loving his wife. And let's not draw back from it (any more than Paul did in the New Testament, 1 Timothy 4:3) — this relation of love, husband and wife, included their union sexually. This was God's design. This was God's desire. He made man not merely to have dominion over the world, but to enjoy the world. And ruling it, and enjoying it, man was being spiritual. He was in fact having the *ideal* "spiritual experience." No churches, no hymns, no Sunday School, no Bible reading, no evangelism. Yet Adam and Eve were perfectly spiritual.

Their relationship with God, in other words, was being expressed in the whole of their human experience. To be spiritual was to be human — and vice versa. There was no diversion between the two. Adam did not have to remove himself from his ordinary human experience in order to "come closer to God." He was as spiritual as God himself wanted him to be!

However, Adam and Eve chose to turn away from God's moral framework. That was where their own lives started to fall apart, and, derivatively, where the experience of all human beings subsequently — and even the experience of nature too — started to fall apart.

The solution to this, many of us are familiar with. We have heard the Gospel enough times to be able to repeat it backwards. (I'm thinking here of the evangelical churches.) But, unhappily, the good news — which it most certainly is — of how God's own son became man in order to rescue us from the law of sin and death, has been expressed in such a way that it seriously vitiates its potential to heal and restore. For the human has been separated from the spiritual.

Some, for example, have seen the Fall in Genesis 3 as almost the end of man's humanity. As if, to use an illustration, Adam and Eve had jumped off the edge of a cliff and been smashed to smithereens at the bottom. Certainly Adam and Eve's rebellion back there in history was devastating enough in its effects to warrant that kind of description, but the Bible indicates that they continued to exist after the fall as human beings — that is, with all the normal experiences which attend human life. To use Jesus' words, there was "eating and drinking and marrying and giving in marriage" (Matthew 24:38 NIV) back at the time of Noah — as there ever has been and ever will be right from the time of the fall up to the second coming of Christ.

This point about the continuity of human experience after the fall may seem so obvious that some may wonder why it is being stressed. Yet it is vital; for even though we have to agree that the whole of man's experience was altered by the fall, that man became — to use the language of the Anglican service book — a "miserable sinner," yet man did not lose his mannishness. He did not lose those attributes which, from his creation, distinguished him from the rest of what was around him. In short, he did not lose his "image-ness." The image was horribly distorted, yet it was still an image.

He became, in effect, like a priceless painting from one of the great masters in European history which is damaged by a senseless act of vandalism. It is horribly defaced. Yet its former glory can still be recognized. And most especially, it continues to have value — so much so that a process of restoration is immediately begun.

This is why (in part at least) the restoration of man was undertaken. God did not have to save man, yet He purposely chose to. There was an inherent value in man which motivated the Creator to undertake man's rescue. "God so loved the world" means that the world was so precious to God that He designed its restoration: man was so precious to God that God even *became* man.

The fall, then, while it defaced man as the image bearer of God, did not remove his humanity. Hence, we can understand why it is that all men (as Paul says in Romans 2) have a conscience; why it is that even sinners (to use Jesus' expression, Matthew 7:11) can give good gifts to their children; why even our opponents who hate the truth of the Gospel can detect some truth about the universe around them. (Matthew 16:3, Romans 1:19) So all societies have stories of compassion and heroism and loyalty and love. All societies have some who long for justice, some who are creative, some who are honorable in their dealings. These qualities and achievements do not save them from the judgment. Yet they are valuable. They make a difference in the world and a difference for good. But they are what they are only because man, though fallen, continues to be "the image of God."

How, then, do we see salvation? How do we see the process of restoration, thinking of the illustration we used of the damaged painting? And, most of all, how does this relate to spiritual experience and being human?

Quite simply, like this: the process of salvation has this as its principal aim, to restore man to the kind of spiritual experience which he forfeited at the fall. This would be impossible, of course, apart from a Saviour. Man can now come back to a relationship with God, he can be accepted by God even as a sinner because atonement for sin is complete. He is justified by grace simply by trusting the work and promises of Christ, justified, in other words, by faith. But he is thus justified NOT to try to get away from his humanity, but to have his humanity re-integrated, to be as it was at the beginning when man was made.

That humanity, we saw, included all the ordinary things. Adam was not more spiritual when praying and less spiritual when gardening or having a nice time with Eve. All his experience was designed by God. All of it was also *God's* delight. All of it was spiritual. And that ideal of spirituality we must now recover. We glorify God when we are most "ordinary" — when we know how to conduct our relationships with others, when we have happy families, when we are radiant and creative, when we find ways around practical problems, when we delight in our physical being and revel in the delights of nature around us, when we enjoy beauty and create beauty. It is *not* the removal of our humanity. It is not even a grudging acceptance of our humanity — as if it is better to be a pastor or an evangelist than an artist or gardener, spending our lives in "spiritual" activities rather than in "secular" ones. Such an attitude must be seen to be anathema. It must be rooted out of our thinking, and also out of our churches.

The resurrection of the body is an outstanding finale to this renewed vision of the human-ness of spiritual experience. For what do we find involved here, if not that the whole of our experience, even the physical experience of the body, is of such value that God is going to restore our bodies at the last trumpet when, in the twinkling of an eye, we shall all be changed. Our humanity will then have been perfectly restored, physical and spiritual together.

In the meantime, we must work for the restoration of the whole of our experience — to the degree, that is, that this is possible within our fallen condition. We must value the human, the individual, the physical, the concrete reality in which God has placed us. To try to reject it is a futile exercise anyway — for it is always there, even at the point when we have died physically and are raised (once more) with bodies! But we must not just tolerate it. We must see that it is *this* which is important. To be spiritual is to be human.

If our model of spirituality leads us away from this, there is something wrong with it, very seriously wrong with it. Jesus was able to attend a marriage feast and even make wine for the pleasure of the guests. Was he being unspiritual doing this? Or does the miraculous side, the water into wine, remove the simple humanity of the event as if that side of things were unimportant — whether the wedding itself, the joy of the couple and their anticipated union, the pleasure of the guests in this important step within the community and especially within the two families concerned, the bustle of the servants, the responsibilities of the caterers, *et cetera, et cetera.*

Or, to take another example which we shall look at in greater detail elsewhere, the mind. Do we find the mind disparaged within the New Testament? Not at all. Paul evidently applied himself intellectually. As he says, he set out to "demolish arguments and every pretension that sets itself up against the knowledge of God, and we *take every thought captive to make it obedient to Christ."* (2 Corinthians 10:4, 5, NIV)

He also exhorted believers to be changed in their lives by "the renewing of their minds." (Romans 12:2, NIV) Elsewhere he went in the Mediterranean world, amongst non-believers as much as believers, he taught and discussed and argued. Why? Because the mind of man is important. It is part of his humanity, continuing into the present despite the fall.

Of course marriage and sexuality can be, and are, distorted. And so, too, the mind. This is the tragedy of man: that the good gifts given by God are turned to evil ends. But this does not mean that they are irrelevant and unnecessary for spiritual experience. The Christian is called to reject and to mortify the evil use of his self — whether mind, appetite, possessions or anything else. It is sin which is to be removed — *NOT* the self. Rather, the self is to be liberated from sin, the human released from its bondage — so that the image can be seen in something "approaching" its former glory — the self renewed in the likeness (image) of its creator. (See 2 Corinthians 3:18 and Colossians 3:10.)

DISCUSSION QUESTIONS

1. What are some distorted notions of spirituality currently held among Christians?

2. How have some Christians wrongly reacted to false spirituality?

3. What were the spiritual habits practiced by the first human?

4. What accounts for the persistence of love, loyalty and heroism in a fallen world?

5. How does salvation in Christ affect our humanity?

6. What kinds of vocational choices does God lead His truly spiritual followers to make?

7. How did Jesus show true humanity?

8. How did Paul's ministry show the scope of salvation, the fullness to which man is restored in Christ?

9. How has the *good news* been poorly expressed? Why has its potential to *heal* and *restore* been so hampered? Why does a dichotomy between "spiritual" and "physical" create such a situation.

10. How can we actually work for the restoration of the whole of our experience? Why is this crucial?

11. Why is the use of the mind and its regeneration a vital aspect of gaining true spirituality?

12. Explain the distinction between the Christian's call to *reject* and *mortify* the use of his self for evil and the call to *affirm* the self and *restore* it to its original glory.

13. Explain the distinction between the Christian's call to *reject* and *mortify* the use of his self for evil and the call to *affirm* the self and *restore* it to its original glory.

"The way to freedom is gladly to accept the law
of God and seek to do it . . . we have nothing
to fear from failure . . ."

Grace and Law:
The Pursuit of Freedom

Ranald Macaulay

It is not an exaggeration to say that the two words *grace* and *law* lie at the very heart of the Christian faith. One would expect, therefore, that Christians would be clear about them if they were clear about anything, for the Bible is replete with discussions of each and even with explanations about their interconnection. Unhappily, that is not so.

The problem is that grace and law have been opposed to one another in a quite unbiblical way. We have even arrived at the remarkable position that says that trusting and trying are mutually exclusive activities for a Christian, despite the fact that every page of the New Testament is full of exhortations both to trust and to try.

Take this extract from the well known book by Watchman Nee, *The Normal Christian Life* (first published in 1958), as illustrative of the confusion:

> What does it mean in everyday life to be delivered from the Law? It means that from henceforth I am going to do nothing whatever for God; *I am never again going to try to please Him* . . .[1]

Let us try to sort out the confusion, for the mistake is a serious one.

We start again, where we always should start in fact, at the beginning. Paul discusses the law like this: "The law is holy, and the commandment is holy, righteous and good." (Romans 7:12, NIV) Why is this? Because it expresses for the actions and attitudes of man what is consistent with the character of God. It is God's person which is at the center of all reality. God is, in fact, so personal that God is Trinity, Father, Son and Holy Spirit. God is not an abstract idea as in Greek philosophy. And God's character is the moral absolute by which all actions within Creation are judged. God's person is the foundation of all morality in the same way that He is the source of all existence. To quote the Greek poet referred to by Paul when he was at Athens, "in Him we live and move and have our being." (Acts 17:28) Existence is what it is because God exists. Similarly, morality is what it is, in terms of its essence, only because God's character is what it is. God is holy. God is completely moral.

The law, then, is the expression of that moral character of God; hence it is "holy, and the commandment is holy." (Romans 7:12) And it is to be found as much within the New Testament as within the Old. Take, for example, the moral injunctions in the Gospels or the letters: This is how you must behave, says Jesus, don't be like the Pharisees, concerned with externals, but be real, be genuine on the inside (Matthew 6:1-18); or Paul says, "Be imitators of God . . . and live a life of love" (Ephesians 5:1, NIV); or Peter says, "Submit yourselves for the Lord's sake to every authority instituted among men . . ." (1 Peter 2:13, NIV)

We must not be confused by the term *law* and think that it is only an Old Testament idea. It is New Testament as well, as the examples above indicate. In fact, the New Testament is chock-ablock full of moral commands and exhortation.

When we move, then, to consider the statements in the New Testament about the "bondage of the law" we must remember this larger context: (a) that law is itself good and spiritual because it reflects the character of God; (b) that law cannot be confined to the Old Testament because the commands of the New Testament, addressed to believers, are also law.

How then must we understand the insistence, particularly in Paul's writings, that we cannot be set free by the law because it is powerless (Romans 8:3)? In fact, he says, we have to be "released from the law" because we are held captive by it. (Romans 7:6) Does this mean that the law no longer applies to the believer?

The answer is yes and no.

The law is set aside as a means whereby sinners can be justified before God. Consider Galatians 3:10: there Paul expresses the dilemma. The law is good. It tells me how I should be living, covering not just external sins but internal ones too. For example, it says, "you must not covet." That is an internal reality which others around me may not even see — though God sees. That is a statement of the law; and as I understand it, it condemns me. (See Romans 7:7 on this.) This is the activity of the law — it condemns me, because it shows me that I have failed to live consistently with the law of God, and hence with what is really right. But more than that, it shows me that there is no way I can ever be accepted by God *through law*, because I fail continuously to keep its just requirements. No matter how fervently I may set myself to keep even one or two of the law's requirements — let us say not to be selfish or to be compassionate and forgiving — I cannot do that. Why? Becuase I am under the power of sin.

Hence, Paul draws the conclusion: if we are going to be accepted by God, it has to be apart from the principle of law. (*cf.* Romans 3:21) That is the way provided by God himself, the way of a Saviour who does everything I need so that salvation, reconciliation with God, is possible. All I need to do is to accept that work and say thank you. This the Bible calls *faith*. I trust in the work of Christ and the promises of God which are attached to it. That is the way I am accepted by God — not by trying to keep the law.

This is the first sense in which the New Testament speaks about the law. As a means of coming back to God it is like a "no through road" sign — there's no way here, turn back, realize that trying to be good is useless. That is why Paul describes the law as being "in charge to lead us to Christ that we might be justified by faith." (Galations 3:24, NIV)

Hence, we can summarize this section by saying that we must never look at the law as if we have to keep it in order to be saved. That is what we are constantly tempted to think, because we know wrongdoing is against the character of God. We forget that only Christ can save us. We start to look to the law, at our failure and successes, and we either become more and more insensitive and deceived about the real horror of sin — and think we're not too bad because we read the Bible every day, or pray frequently, or witness occasionally, or give money to the church, etcetera, — or we become despairing about ever satisfying God's perfect standards, and we slip further and further into uncertainty and then hopelessness about our salvation.

That is why Paul is so vehement about not trying to be saved by "works of the law." Galatians 3:1: "You foolish Galatians! Who has bewitched you?" Galatians 5:1: "It is for freedom that Christ has set us free. Stand firm, then, and do not let yourselves be burdened again by a yoke of slavery." (NIV)

It is in this sense that we have to be set free from the law. We have to be set free from the idea that it is law-keeping that reconciles us to God. It is not. It is Christ, and cnly Christ, that does this.

However, there is a second sense in which the law continues to apply to us, and from which we can never be set free. This is the law, as we pointed out earlier, as it faithfully represents the character of God. That we cannot escape — nor should we even try to — because it shows us what God is like, it shows us what real holiness is, what being like Him, therefore, must include. If you want to know how you should be living, look at the law of God — not at the law of the Old Testament primarily (though we can learn many things from it), because it was the law for the people of God within the nation of Israel — but to the law of the New Testament.

This brings us to another crucial step in the argument, one which is so important (because it is so exciting and practical) that I request you to ponder it even more carefully than other sections in this study. For the New Testament even goes so far as to say that by looking at the law and keeping it, we are set free. For example, James calls the law "the perfect law that gives freedom" (James 1:25), and he urges believers to look intently into it and to continue in it. Jesus says the same thing: "If you hold to my teaching . . . then you will know the truth, and the truth will set you free." (John 8:31, NIV)

How does the law set us free? It helps us to see how we are *made* to function. For obviously, if we are made to live in a certain way, and we live against that design, we make life difficult for ourselves. It is a little like treating plants, or animals or even machines according to their design. We have to find out the proper environment, temperature, food, attitudes, fuel, etcetera, which each requires — then, as we respect these design factors, things work, plants are healthy and produce flowers and fruit, animals are healthy and obedient, machines run smoothly.

The same is true for man. He is designed in a certain way, both physically and spiritually. Therefore, the closer he gets to living consistently with his design, the better he is, the freer he is. This is how the law has a positive function. This is why we must respect it, search for it, receive it gladly (even when it contradicts previously held opinions). The more we receive it, and the more we try to do it ("continue in it," "hold to it"), the more we are set free.

Here, however, we run into two problems:

First, there is the question of the connection between the two senses of the law which we have examined. This is a delicate business. How do we both reject the law and receive it at one and the same time? We must reject it as a means of justifying us before God, yet we must accept it as a means to set us free. How, practically, does this work?

The answer is really very simple. We must love God's law. We must receive it as being good in itself, as being "spiritual." Yet, as we receive it in this way we must remember — *and never forget* — *that we are already ex-*

cused whatever failures there are going to be in our keeping of the law. If, however, we forget this and slip back into the idea that our status before God depends on our degree of success in keeping the law, rather than simply on Christ, we are headed for difficulties. We shall find that "the very commandment that was intended to bring life actually [brings] death." (Romans 7:10, NIV) "Sin, seizing the opportunity afforded by the commandment, [will produce] in me every kind of [sinful-covetous] desire." (Romans 7:8, NIV)

The wrong approach to the law in such cases will actually increase the sense of sin, the power and tenacity of sin. We will be dragged further down. We will be "alienated from Christ," we will have "fallen from grace." (Galatians 5:4)

So, as we look to the law as holy and good, with a desire to keep it and so be set free, we must be clear in our understanding and resolute in our conviction that in the first sense of the law (as we saw earlier), we have already been set free from the law. We no longer have to fear it, for we have died with Christ, and that means we no longer have to fear judgment.

We welcome the law as our guide. We no longer fear it as our judge. Having been set free (through Christ), we labour to keep God's law to be set free in practice, *i.e.* living as we were designed to live, in righteousness and holiness. (See Ephesians 5: 8-10)

Second, we have to resist any suggestions that we don't try as Christians, as if the process of being changed has nothing to do with our willing and working. This is sheer stupidity, in view of the clear admonitions in the New Testament. The passage just cited (Ephesians 5: 9-20) contains at least eleven admonitions: do this, don't do that . . . Make the most of every opportunity . . . Do not be foolish . . . be filled with the Spirit . . . always give thanks . . . . Or, alternatively, 2 Peter 1: 5, 6: " . . . *make every effort* to add to your faith goodness; and to goodness . . . perseverance" . . . , which continues (verse 10): "Therefore . . . be all the more eager to make your calling and election sure. For if *you do these things*, you will never fall . . . ." (NIV) And so on, and so on — with literally thousands of examples in the New Testament as a whole.

The way to freedom, therefore, is gladly to accept the law of God and to seek to do it, but always only on the basis of the abiding reality (consciously appropriated) that we have nothing to fear from failure, for we have already "died to the law through the body of Christ." (Romans 7: 4)

DISCUSSION QUESTIONS

1. What is the "Law" and what is "Grace?"

2. How are trying and trusting integrated into the Christian life?

3. How does the law express the character of God?

4. How can we both accept and reject God's law?

5. What is our proper emotional response to the substance of God's law?

6. What are the consequences of failing to keep the Law?

7. How can we hope to experience true freedom?

8. The struggle of measuring up to God's perfect standard should not cause us to quit the contest. How do we approach this dilemma?

9. Can history rightly be divided into an age of law and an age of grace? Explain. Was there ever a period in which following the law could win God's favor?

"We must understand why losing ourselves
is not a negative idea. We must understand the value and
significance of every individual and every choice."

Self Affirmation &
Self Denial

Ranald Macaulay

Some of the most striking words in Paul's letters are those in 2 Corinthians
4:10, 11: "We always carry around in our body the death of Jesus, so that
the life of Jesus may also be revealed in our body. For we who are alive are
always being given over to death for Jesus' sake, so that his life may be revealed in our mortal body." (NIV)

So severe do they sound, in fact — "carrying about the death of Jesus"
— we are tempted to rationalize them away, to try to make them seem less
severe, for Paul himself, first of all, then, for ourselves. We try to escape
any application they may have to our own experience. Surely *we* are not
called to anything so extreme? Surely such morbid sentiments, such nega-
tiveness, is inappropriate in a Christian who is called to "Rejoice in the
Lord always"?

An examination of the context, however, makes it apparent that Paul
was not trying to be negative. Nor was he "showing off" as if to suggest
that he had had worse experiences than others and therefore was better!
Later in 2 Corinthians (11:21 ff), he says he realizes that is how it may seem
to his readers, this catalogue of all the experiences which were hard on him
— the imprisonments, the beatings, the danger in rivers, danger from
bandits, danger at sea, et cetera, et cetera. He actually says: "I am speaking
as a fool (in this boasting)!"

Paul's purpose, however, is deliberate. He is contrasting his own experience as a "true" apostle with the experience of those who claimed to be "super-apostles" but were, in fact, "false apostles, deceitful workmen." (2 Corinthians 11:5, 13 NIV) To summarize his argument he says, "Look at what I have done, because you can see from my experience that my apostleship is genuine, and particularly from the experiences which 'show my weakness.' These are the experiences I want you to pay special attention to because they indicate how weak I am in myself and therefore demonstrate more clearly than anything else could, that it has not been my *own* power at work in my ministry, but God's — for God himself said, when I complained those three times about my 'thorn in the flesh,' that His strength is made perfect *in my weakness*. So that is why . . . "I delight in weaknesses, in insults, in hardships, in persecutions, in difficulties. For when I am weak, then I am strong."' (2 Corinthians 12:10 NIV)

We are familiar with these last words, but do we really understand them? I believe their significance largely escapes us. Yet, I believe also that, as Bible-believing Christians within the affluent West, almost no other teaching in the New Testament is as relevant for us.

First, we have to understand that we are called to this same type of experience — which in itself is something of a shock! Paul's motivation must be ours. He says as much: ". . . I am not seeking my own good, but the good of many, so that they may be saved. *Follow my example, as I follow the example of Christ."* (1 Corinthians 10:33; 11:1, NIV) So we are called to imitate Paul's suffering.

Notice the association between Paul's example and Christ's. Paul is doing what he does, because he wants to follow the example of Christ. He sees Jesus as the great model to be imitated. That is why, when he describes the hardships he and his companions faced on their various journeys, he uses this particular language, "we carry around in our body the death of Jesus . . ." (2 Corinthians 4:10 NIV). He sees himself going through a similar kind of experience as Jesus' own — not that he was getting confused and thinking his experiences were of the same significance as his master's. NO! It was Jesus' dying, and that alone, which could make atonement for sin. Paul is thinking of another element in Christ's suffering, namely his motivation. It was this, after all, which brought him to earth to take upon himself the reality of a human experience within which "he humbled himself and became obedient to death — even death on a cross." (Philippians 2:8 NIV) As Paul says in that same passage, Jesus was in very nature God, but He did not consider equality with God something to be grasped, to be held onto, but He laid it aside, He came because He really loved man and sought to save the world.

In other words, it was the love which Jesus had for all of us which motivated Him, which drove Him on. *And this is the point to grasp*: Jesus was not doing this because He was being masochistic, as if He derived pleasure from pain and humiliation. He was not being negative towards life. He was not implying that life is not to be enjoyed or that we have to reject our physical and human desires as if those have no value.

He was simply doing what had to be done. There was no other way. Had Adam and Eve not rebelled against God, there would have been no "law of sin and death" to be overcome. But once it was there, this was the only remedy — that the Son of God should lay aside His glory and come to die. There was nothing wrong with His glory, there was nothing wrong with His life as a man, as if He had, being born, to hurry and get rid of it. Not at all. It was simply that, given the plight of man, if anyone was to be saved, He had to suffer and die.

Now the same thing is true of us; we, too, are called to try to rescue the world — not, obviously, in the same way Jesus did, for that is impossible. As the hymn writer says: "He *only* could unlock the gate of heaven and let us in." His work of rescue was unique. Nevertheless, we are to be His imitators, and we are to be similarly motivated, we are to go out, *and, at cost to ourselves*, seek to save that which is lost.

To this we are expressly called. In Ephesians 5:1 Paul says: "Be imitators of God, therefore, as dearly loved children and live a life of love, just as Christ loved us and gave himself up for us a fragrant offering and sacrifice to God." (NIV) The links in the argument are clear here: first, that Christ loved us and, hence, gave Himself up for us; second, that we are to be imitators of Him in this same attitude of love; third, that we should do this not merely because Christ is our example, but because God is our Father and we are His children.

This last point brings us to a further clarification. We are God's offspring. In Genesis 1:26, man's creation is described in this way: "Then God said, 'Let us make man in our image, in our likeness' . . . " As human beings, we are the image of God. We bear, if you like, a family resemblance. The whole of mankind is in this sense God's offspring, His special creations, because as "man" we are unique in the world. Hence, man is given dominion over the earth. But with the coming of sin, man is estranged from God, under judgment. He has, therefore, to be saved. Which means he has to have a Saviour, for he cannot save himself. When, however, he *is* saved, when he has been justified by grace through faith, he is called to the recovery of the image of God which he was designed to be. The heart of that is that he should love in the same way God loves. "Be kind and compassionate . . . just as in Christ God forgave you. Be imitators of God . . . and live a life of love . . ." (Eph. 4:32, 5:1, NIV)

We see, therefore, that the call to imitate Christ is not an arbitrary one. We are called to a life of love because that is what God's nature is. He loves perfectly. As John puts it, "God is love." (1 John 4:8) Since we are his image, it is, in a sense, *our* nature also. We were made to be like Him; yet the likeness has been disfigured through the fall. Having been brought back into a relationship with God, however, we are "being renewed in knowledge in the *image* of (our) Creator." (Colossians 3:10) So our inherent imageness is being gradually restored. Our calling to "live a life of love" in imitation of God is simply, then, the call to live the way we were designed to live.

This is an important thing for us to grasp, for when we first come across severe-sounding passages like the one we started with — others like Jesus' statement "whoever loses his life for my sake will find it" — we get the impression that this is a negation of our "self." We feel ourselves recoiling from the idea, because we consider it a threat to our very being. This is unfortunate, for the threat lies in the opposite direction. We are in fact *made* to live like this, and only as we do so are we satisfied as human beings. This is the force of what Jesus is saying when He says we must lose ourselves to find ourselves.

We are not imitating a model which is designed to cut across our nature, as if to take on difficult and painful things has a merit because they are difficult and painful. Far from it: they are accepted, because they are consistent with our nature as the image of God.

In addition, we see the example of Jesus' own life in this same light. He was prepared to lay aside things and take a hard road for our sake — but only because he, in turn, was living out the reality of *his* nature. It was because He was love itself, the perfect embodiment of it, that He was prepared and able to lose Himself. He did not, of course, need to "find himself" as we do, for He was unmarred by sin. Yet, He could speak of the necessity, like a seed, to "fall into the ground and die." (John 12:23) For if it does not, "it remains only a single seed"; there is no fruit.

Hence, we can summarize what we have said like this: in a fallen world, within which both man and nature are under a curse, there can be no solution apart from a Savior — a Savior who comes and gives Himself away because He loves the world. And since we are "his offspring" in the double sense that we are both His creatures and rescued by Him, we have to continue that same work. We have to be His "image" in this sense also. We have to lay down *our* lives, or, to use Paul's expression with which we began, we have to be prepared "to carry around in our body the death of Jesus." (2 Corinthians 4:10)

Two questions flow out of this. First, what motivates us to live like this?

What changes our attitude so that we no longer recoil from this exhortation (to lose ourselves, et cetera) and instead delight in it? Second, how does this work out in practice?

The first has a simple and obvious answer from Paul: he says, ". . . *Christ's love* compels us." (2 Corinthians 5:14) He looks to Christ's example, how Christ has loved us in our need, how Christ has "died for all," and, seeing this, he concludes that we should no longer live for ourselves but for Him who died for us and was raised again (2 Corinthians 5:15). So he focuses his attention upon Christ. This is the only way we can have the right attitude toward "losing ourselves." Looking to Christ, consciously and continually, is the only way our hearts can be changed so that we, too, become those who "lay down our lives for the brethen," but not only that, who are glad to do so.

We must understand why losing ourselves is not a negative idea. We must understand the value and significance of every individual and every choice. We must understand the greatness of God's truth, knowing it to be really true and, hence, the only thing that can set us free. All this we must understand. but only one thing will enable us to start to live as Christ did (and as Paul did), and that is to consider what Christ has done for us. This we must do consciously and continuously, and we must "remain" or "abide" in Him (John 15:5). Out of gratitude for Christ, and seeing the value He sets upon each individual, we will begin to lose ourselves for others. And doing that, we will start to find ourselves.

How this works out in practice — the carrying about in our body the death of Jesus — is not easy to express, for it includes attitudes and experiences covering the whole of life. Also, it is a delicate issue, easily misrepresented. Two things, however, it must include.

First, there is the basic choice to live no longer for myself, but for Him who died for me (2 Corinthians 5:15). This is included in the idea of *repentance*. When I first come to God through Christ and believe in Him, *i.e.*, trust in His saving work, what I also do is repent. I obey Christ's command: "Repent and believe the good news." (Mark 1:15) and that is not simply saying "sorry," though it includes it. It is a deeper thing. It is the turning of myself *to follow Christ.*

So it is nothing exceptional to follow Christ; I think I am doing what every Christian does when he first believes, when he first "repents." Also, I am doing what I am called to. I am saved from sin in order to live for God, which includes *preeminently* "following Christ." What was His example then? How did He conduct his life? What ambitions did He have?

"If anyone wants to be first, he must be the very last, and the servant of all." (Mark 9:35) "whoever wants to become great among you must be your servant, and whoever wants to be first must be slave of all. For even the Son of Man did not come to be served, but to serve, *and to give his life* as a ransom for many." (Mark 10:45, NIV)

You will notice that I have not emphasized the last five words — "as a ransom for many" — because Jesus' work was unique. He was the Son of God, and He came to die and be raised for our salvation — which He alone was and could do. That part of His "example" we cannot imitate. But we can, and I repeat are *called to*, imitate His attitude towards life — his willingness to lose everything, if need be, for the sake of those around Him.

This is the calling of *every* Christian!

The second thing is that we will look upon hard experiences differently. If we want to imitate Christ's love, there will be more than enough for us to do. Needs surround us on all sides. What about the people who live near us? What needs do they have, and can we help? The reality of living this way will surge up all around us. And that is where the problem comes, for, to continue the metaphor, we will begin to feel as if we are on high ground during a flood, with the water rising every minute, so that soon we shan't have place for our own feet, let alone anyone else's! Speak to anyone who is involved in helping people, doctors, nurses, teachers, social workers, et cetera — and very importantly, parents! — and this is their unanimous report: there is too much to do, always far too much!

Which means we have to be careful. First, because we can easily be swept off our feet. We can get into the habit of "giving ourselves away," so that we neglect entirely our own needs. But you will notice that not even Jesus did that during the time of His ministry: He went away to rest, He took the disciples to the other side of the lake to get away, He went off alone to be by Himself. He did not try to heal every sick person in Judea and Galilee, or raise every widow's son. He lived as a man must live, accepting the limitations of His humanness, though He was prepared always — and at the proper time in reality — to give Himself away completely, as He did on the cross.

Second, however, we must be careful the other way. We should know ahead of time that to imitate Christ is not going to be easy, that we will often feel tired because of the pressures involved, or confused about what's going to happen next. Then our response must be, as the Scripture so often urges, to take courage! Why? Because we need it. The same way football players need courage when they're in a hard match. If they need it — for an activity of very little significance really — how much more do we within the battle of reality (for reality after the fall, don't forget *is* a battle. *cf.* Ephesians 6:10ff).

This is where we, all of us, tend to get confused, especially as citizens of the affluent West where everything must be made easy. The technological revolution demands it! So we draw back from the first whiff or discomfort of the battle. We start to think, because life is "rough," that we must be in the wrong place, that we must have missed God's (perfect) leading, that we've married the wrong spouse, that we'd better go to Bible school and learn more about the Bible, or travel for a semester just to get away from things.

We absent ourselves from the roll call for battle. Hence, the enemy remains unchallenged, and we ourselves do not "find ourselves" but continue to "lose ourselves." The church wastes away, the believer wastes away. This, I believe, is one of the principal problems in our churches today — that we have failed to take seriously the clear teaching in the New Testament about our call to imitate Jesus.

The gospel saves us from feeling we have to "do more" in order to enjoy fellowship with God. The anxiety of wondering if we have obeyed God's commandments enough, or loved people enough and so on is forever set aside. Christ is the sole and sufficient Savior we each of us need.

However, it is this same gospel which calls us to imitate Christ's death — not because it commands it primarily, but because it illustrates it. It shows us, perfectly, what real humanness, real spirituality, involves. It is, if you like, what the cross of Christ has set us free (from condemnation) to do. It is preaching the gospel certainly — as Jesus did. But it is also *living* the gospel, imitating the life of the One who was the servant of all, who "gave himself up for us as a fragrant offering and sacrifice . . . " (Ephesians 5:1) That is why Paul says: "Be imitators of God . . . and live a life of love, just as Christ loved us."

It is also the reason why Paul, describing his own experience, can say — as we all should be able to say about our own experience, even if only in very small measure: "We are hard pressed on every side . . . perplexed . . . persecuted . . . struck down. We always carry around in our body the death of Jesus, so that the life of Jesus may also be revealed in our body." (2 Corinthians 4:8-10, NIV)

It may not seem like it, but this is the way (as it was for Paul, 2 Corinthians 12:9, 10) of life and power. Of life, in that we are increasingly brought into the experience of reality, the way it actually is and was intended to be, which Paul elsewhere describes as "being changed from one degree of glory to another." (2 Corinthians 3:18) Of power, because, although we may feel weaker within ourselves — hard pressed, perplexed and so on — we will be compelled to a more *real* trust in God, else we will not survive within the battles. And then we will start to see *God* at work!

DISCUSSION QUESTIONS

1. Why does Ranald believe this message is so important to today's culture?

2. What does it mean to sacrifice? Why should we?

3. How should Christians imitate the mission of Jesus? Why can our ministry never substitute for His?

4. What does repentance involve? Why is this important?

5. How long has life been a battle for people?

6. Why do modern American Christians find it difficult to identify with the task of "carrying around in our body the death of Jesus"? Is this task optional or mandatory?

7. How do we bring together the Biblical commands of rejoicing and dying to self? Define both.

8. How can fulfillment come through service?

9. How has "life and power" come into your experience as a Christian? What do you do when you get a "whiff of the battle"?

Susan Macaulay

Susan is Francis and Edith Schaeffer's second daughter. Although an American citizen, Susan has lived most of her life in Switzerland or England.

Her education could be described as eccentric — American schools, one room Swiss schools, family studies, correspondence courses, University of Lausanne, and Oxford University in England. While at Oxford, she met her husband-to-be, Ranald Macaulay. After their marriage, Ranald and Susan worked at the Swiss L'Abri for four and a half years, establishing a second student house. Then they returned to England and lived in London while Ranald was finishing a theology degree.

After a few years the Macaulay's moved into the English countryside to begin the English L'Abri in 1970, where they are living at present.

Susan recently has done some writing, publishing two books. One is entitled *Something Beautiful from God* and her most recent, *How to be Your Own Selfish Pig*. Susan and Ranald have four children.

*". . . the 20th century specializes in cutting
people off from each other and also alienating us
from the idea that relationships are
very important in our lives."*

Priorities in Family Life
Susan Macaulay

I've labeled this "priorities in family life," but we may think of family as
being something broader than the nuclear family. The nuclear family is
what we usually think of, that is, mother, father, son and daughter. The
typical family goes out driving in a nice car on Sunday and they have their
color TV at home and their carpet. When you say "family," that's what a
lot of people think of. But actually "family" includes broader relationships,
because all of us have families — all single persons, all people living in a
community. It depends on the exact definition that you give to this, but, in
fact, it's our human relationships — those which are closest to us — the attitudes that we have. This is one of the things that I want to bring out as
we think about what life is all about and its direction, what the priorities
are. It also very much includes ourselves. It certainly includes God, who is
there.

Now, we're up against a dilemma because, in the 20th century, we have
a Christian world-view, the one which has grown out of the base of the
idea that the Bible is actually truth, that the things which are told to us in it
not only make a difference and not only are good or right, but that this is
the way the world actually is. A lot of people think about Christianity just
like some sort of religion. They think of it perhaps as their own religious
experience or their own religious behavior. In actual fact, if this is truth, if
Christianity is really true, then, the world-views that we have around us

are false, and the conclusions and behavior that grow out of them are also very often wrong because they've come from the wrong base. Whatever sociological aspect we examine, we're going to find that this affects it, that the world-view that grows out of the base is going to make differences.

If Christianity is true, our understanding of the person is totally different from that of the culture around us. And right away we have a problem with language when we say, "the person." If we are a 20th century human being, affected by the humanist philosophy, we're immediately going to think of some sort of fancy machine, complicated programmed computer, animal — a rather advanced animal. If we're coming from the Biblical base, our understanding of the word "person" is going to be quite different; we believe that we have been created in the image of the God who is there. We have an eternal purpose, a relationship with Him; we can love; we're free; we're separate; we're not puppets. We're not just like a little match stick floating down a stream that has to be buffeted about as the stream goes along. We have direction within this world, with meaning, with framework, with relationship to a personal God who is there; we have significance and we can be creative, we can do things, we can make things. So right away we feel the difficulty that we're up against. You just use one word, "the person," the human being, and all the ideas are quite, quite different depending on where you're coming from.

Now, we've contrasted the "person" of the Biblical world-view against the "person" of the 20th century world-view. This person is unique from the Christian point-of-view — valid — and this is why the Christian world-view has produced, for instance, care for the down-and-outs, and for the handicapped, because, although we are all limited, and we have all been affected by the abnormal world, we're each of one of us valid in God's sight.

But as we know, in the 20th century, if you have no final meaning, no explanation for the person, well then, this individual — how valid is he? What about the problems of euthanasia with the old or the problem of abortion? The next problem which is cropping up now in the medical world is "should we let very handicapped children live? Wouldn't it be better just to let them die off right away within 24 hours, deny them a simple operation, deny them food?" This is the common practice now, because we no longer respect the individual as a separate person under God, and we're bringing in some sort of utilitarian criterion to explain its value. And, as we'll see later on, I think this gives us a sense that when people look for their purpose it's tied into this. The fact that we have eternal life, a perspective beyond death, makes our life, the whole thing — what life is all about — very, very different from that of people who are going to die.

I'm 40, and if I'm lucky, I have another 35 years. Thirty-five years isn't all that long if you really think that's all you've got. You've got to see the sun and another spring and to hold little children on your lap and to love and be loved and to do things. How miserable and how desperate we would be! Because of this, we have people in our society hiding themselves from reality, probably especially concerning eternity they hide themselves from reality.

It used to be that when you were bringing up children, you tried to protect them from sexual things, so babies came out of cabbage patches. Now days, what you protect children from is the fact of death, that we're going to die, and we shut people off to die. People don't like to think of people dying at home very much. I have friends who, if they see a funeral in the distance, will actually drive their children down another street so as to avoid questions about what's going on, and who will not take them near a graveyard to try not to discuss death. There is this fear as I discovered when my father was diagnosed as having cancer. You say, "My Dad has cancer, and I'm going out to see him." There's this kind of hush; it's a fear, and people are scared to talk about it.

Now if you're a Christian, and this is truth, you're in a different place. It's a different life — we're talking about a different thing as human beings. Our choices have meaning, have value. Now, right away, when you talk about the person, the non-Christian is not sure about whether there really is a morality at all, so good and bad become meaningless words. And if we're going to talk about society and behavior, this is terribly important. The Christian says what is right is right — not because I like it, not because it's convenient, not because most people do it, but because certain things are right and certain things are wrong. He or she has a moral framework, whereas the typical 20th century person is very insecure and isn't sure what's right and what's wrong. Maybe 15 years ago, when I was having children, it was wrong to have an abortion; now it may be right to have an abortion. Three years ago, it may have been wrong to deny food to small children because they were handicapped, and I would have ended up in jail; this year it may be right. To our generation, morality is an evolutionary thing, it's changing. So it gives people my age with teenage children great insecurity who aren't Christians. They say, "Well, we didn't sleep around when we were teenagers, but we guess our daughters and our sons are going to do so." At a conference I attended recently, a doctor who is working on environmental research in this country was saying how very bad it is that a 16-year-old girl in this country is given the pill. Now, automatically, she's given the pill because it is assumed that she'll become sexually active. That is an assumption. And even 20 years ago, even 10 years ago, I dare say even 6 years ago, this was not the case. This doctor was saying what havoc it was making in these girls' bodies: by the time they're 22, 23, their hormonal systems are upside down. But the thing is the assumption that what was wrong can turn into right, that our social patterns can still be in the air.

As soon as we're going to talk about anything sociologically oriented such as the family, we see that we're miles away from our culture's views in all sorts of ways. We realize that our experiences, our relationships, have meaning, because 5,000 years from now, you're going to be there, and I will be there, too, and just think about that. We may talk about the laundry. We make jokes about old L'Abri people getting together in heaven and finding old cabbage leaves and making soup! We will actually be there. Our relationships are ongoing; they have meaning, value.

It may seem that I will never see this person again, or I'm with him for a very short time. This is a feature of 20th century life, that people feel the transition of relationships, and families move away from each other very quickly. Married couples do: if it doesn't work out, you may not be to-gether even in five years time. As an antithesis to this feeling of transition of change (that nothing really matters and that, if I make a mess, I can go try something else, and if that doesn't work out, I'll go try somewhere else), the Christian view is that each relationship, in a sense, is a permanent one and we have a responsibility that is ongoing. The love that I have, the care that I show, the joy that we together share in a relationship, whether it's for a lifetime, as close as a marriage, or whether it's just a friendship which may last for a summer, this has meaning, it's worth it.

Another aspect which is very different in our two world-views, which has an effect on a practical subject, is our view of truth, which ties in, of course, with the moral aspect. We have an absolute framework. People are very shocked with the idea that you say, "I have a definite objective framework which I believe is right, which I believe is truth." It sounds very arrogant to the 20th century mind to say that my way is right. They say, "Well, why do you think your way is right? Maybe it's right for you." And they get this smile on their faces and say, "That's nice for you," and, "I wish I had a faith."

Well, that's supposed to be a great compliment. You turn around and say, "Perhaps this is really truth; I believe it is as true as that beam is there, and if I tried to walk straight through it, I'd get bruised. If I ran at it, I might get a concussion because that is the way this beam is constructed." And then you say, "If Christianity is true, this is the way things are, and this is who I am as a human being. And if I try to behave as a machine, I'm going to have a concussion of the soul because what I'm trying to do is live in a world that doesn't exist." So, for instance, you have the picture of the fish, which says, "I'm going to be free." It's swimming around, and it has the whole ocean — the Atlantic, the Pacific, the Indian, the whole thing — and it comes along and says, "But I'm going to be free. I'm going to get out and go on the land. I'm going to go up on the beach." It flips up on the beach and the poor thing just very shortly dies. It doesn't have freedom at all because it wasn't created to live on the beach. If the Bible is true, this is what modern man is doing. That is, we are trying to behave in a way which isn't the way we were actually made.

Take, for instance, sexual fulfillment. Is it a limitation? Is it puritanical? Is it old fashioned to say that there is meant to be a relationship between one man and one woman? Does that close off all the fun and fulfillment that you could have in your life? Well, that might be so. There are two possibilities. If Christianity is true and if we, as human beings, are sensitive persons, then being created in this particular way, we will be like the fish in the sea when we work within the framework for which we were created. In the sexual thing, we will find real freedom, real fulfillment, real depth, when we are living the way we were meant to live. That is, when we confine our relationship within the love and trust and security of marriage.

We look around as Christians and we say, "Well, in this so-called promiscuous society, are they having that much more fun, fulfillment, inner peace, security, joy in their relationships? Is it so much fun, even?" And you have two opposing possibilities. They both can't be true. Either the framework, the way of living, which the Bible teaches is just a silly old prison which should die off with our grandparents and good riddance or, if this God is actually there, that is the only way that we are really going to be fulfilled as human beings and be free to be who we actually are. Otherwise, we'll be like fish flopping up from the sea.

If Christianity is true, what are the priorities of our human life and our family relationships? What is actually meant, and what is actually enjoyed *if* the Christian framework is truth? It's very difficult to communicate this. I have found this true as a woman trying to talk about the Biblical view of men and women. People who are very angry about feminism find it terribly difficult to receive the communication because their sense of status and worth is dependent on such different things from those which grow out of the Biblical view. It's difficult to build bridges to them.

If Christianity is truth for human beings, the picture is a family picture to start with. So God himself, in this amazing relationship in the Trinity, gives us the words of a family relationship. You have the Father and the Son, and God has said that we are His children, that we can call him "Father." Of course, in the New Testament, Jesus also gives the picture of himself as the bridegroom and us as the bride — the Church as the bride.

There are all sorts of pictures, not any one of them complete because we are finite, and we only see a part. We can only comprehend a tiny bit of this infinite God and of His relationship, but, if the Bible is true, then what we enjoy is valid because this God has said, "I will create you as persons." And so we share in this mysterious way, this very deep way, something of the essence of God himself in his personality, of his own experience. The essence of this is a relationship, because God doesn't have a body; all of the physical things that we quite rightly enjoy, the food, the beautiful day, the beach, the symphony — whatever it happens to be — are tied in with the created world which God has created, and we are part of it — my hands, my feet — we are part of this created world and, indeed, our bodies will be raised from the dead, so there is no separation of our experience. There isn't this "spiritual" floating six inches above the other part of me — I'm a unity.

There is this aspect of myself, however, in my personality which I share with God, and when I come before him as his child, it won't be so foreign and alien. We can understand something of the depth of this experience. And what is it? It's a relationship. We know this very well as human beings because, apart from the death sentence, one of the worst things that anybody can do to anybody else is put him in solitary confinement. In desperate, horrible governments that's what they do to somebody — they stick him in a hole all by himself. They also disorient him and remove him from the physical world so he doesn't know if it's night or day. There is something particularly sad and difficult about the existence of a human being who is cut off and who doesn't have other relationships. It is the very essence of our lives.

Yet, the 20th century specializes in cutting people off from each other and also alienating us from the idea that relationships are very important in our lives. So we're led to believe through out education, through the media, through social pressures, that what matters in our lives — what really matters — is how much money we're going to earn. To some people, that's a criterion so they will work extra hours and not go home for supper and not be around to be with the people that they do love and do care about, because they're so busy earning all this extra money and climbing up the ladder.

Another thing which is very important to people is status, and that usually is tied in with money. So, for instance, if you're an airplane pilot and you're earning a lot of money — a pilot for TWA or British Airways — that has some status. If you say, "I'm a cleaner in a geriatric ward," people immediately sort of slot you down in their scale. (People have these ladders in their heads.) It is so utterly different from the Biblical view of what life is all about. There's no resemblance to it, unless you just wanted to turn it upside down, because most of the things which our generation says are important — if you read the New Testament, you'll find Christ saying quite clearly that, not only are they unimportant, it's even wrong to be thinking about them. So he more or less scolded the disciples when they asked who was going to be the most important, who was going to sit up at the head of the table. And yet, people will work their whole lives to move up those notches at the table; that's what matters to them, and it matters to them for their children. They will push their children right against their natural grain and sacrifice all sorts of things because "You not only have to fit into society, my son, my daughter, you must be high up, you must be presentable. We're winners — you have to be a winner. And if not, I'll kill you to make you try or prop you up to get you there."

As a Christian, if you actually look at the priorities of our society, there's something terribly ugly, and I think it's a stench in the nostrils of God. He said in the Old Testament that when the Canaanites would burn their babies, he loathed it. It was a stench. Then you have our society with all the possibilities and benefits and what do we do — what are we actually doing? It's not good just using words, sort of using our lips on Sunday and singing or talking about things that are important. The proof of the pudding, whether you really care, is from Monday until Saturday night. It isn't just the words. So I care for all black people, or I care for children, or I care for old people. Well, who have you cared for today and yesterday? And did you take the time to write your mother a letter, which you should have done because she's waiting for a letter? It will mean something to her.

I'm afraid the Christian community can do the same thing — it can talk about the "non-Christian" at great length, and it's all a great theory, and how are we going to evangelize, and what are we going to do about the non-Christians? And then we sit down and say, "Who are your non-Christian friends? Who are the people you are having relationships with, that you've discussed things with, that you've shown that you care, and are acting in their lives?"

Or you have people who spend their lives doing things for children. They may be educators, they may write curricula, but they don't know a child. They have never known a child. They haven't had a child, they don't particularly enjoy children, they don't go out with them, and they spend their lives producing things for children. This is ridiculous. We have people specializing, even dedicating themselves to great ideas, and yet they won't get down to the nitty-gritty.

We see this in priorities. We can talk about how important other people are, and we never get around to getting somebody else a cup of coffee or saying, "Look, I see you've come home and you're tired — I'll do all the dishes." Actually, putting into practice the realities of the ideas.

They sound great, these priorities. What does this mean? It means that it's very, very easy in the 20th century to zip through the New Testament and spiritualize things, to make them feel holy as you read them, feel uplifted, and then afterwards to go out into the rat race and behave as though there's no difference at all in your life, as if the careers, the amount of money, what you're going to do really is what life is all about.

What we have to do as Christians is to turn this around if it's going to make any difference at all in life and try to be honest and make choices which may seem ludicrous to other people. For example, take a man and a woman who are married with two or three children. The career situation is hard enough. Now, are one or two of them going to have a career? That's a good first question, and if both people have a career, can they actually serve the family? Is it even possible physically, mentally, emotionally? It may be. I'm not saying it isn't. Think about it carefully. Is it possible to make the family a priority, relationships a priority? I mean, after all, we're going to die and be put in a grave, and whether one has $3,000 or $30,000 or a million dollars isn't going to make any difference at all. Nor, when we stand before God, is it going to make any difference at all if we were a corporate executive for General Motors, Ford Motor Company or whether we collected the garbage cans on the back of the garbage truck down the road. It really won't make any difference. It's very difficult for us to believe that.

What will make a difference is other things. What are the other things? The Bible says, first of all, that we have a duty to have a relationship with God because that is what we were created for, and that is not just some sort of religious phrase, but it should make a difference in my life. it should be so important that maybe sometimes I don't do something in a career, perhaps I'm not so fulfilled in a hobby or a particular talent that I have because I actually think it's important to have a relationship with God.

If we're going to have a relationship with anybody, it's going to take time. That's the rub — 20th century persons don't like time. They will say to me, "Oh, don't you have a lovely relationship with your children. I wish I did." Again, it's like what they said about faith. It's as if they said, "You've caught it. You've caught the good relationship and I didn't." When, in actual fact, it takes time. People's clubs and their hobbies and their own church work can be so important to them that they're never sitting there in a relaxed way so that children can come up to them and sit on their laps, and be together and talk about things. They must do things together, take a walk, look at ants crawling in and out. Relationships take time. The relationship between ourselves and God takes time. It doesn't happen just because we know God's there. We've read a few of Schaeffer's books a few years ago, and we thought, "Oh yeah, that's true. There is a God and He's there, He is there and He is not silent. So I've got the Bible. I do go to church on Sunday morning and I do this, that and the other thing." We can say that we read the Bible quickly every day and get down on our knees and pray for a few people. But is that a relationship with God? Do I trust Him, do I enjoy Him? The feelings can be scary, too, because as we actually look at ourselves and say, "Oh dear, I guess I really don't have a relationship that I enjoy very much," it can turn into the wrong kind of a thing. But as you go along through life, if you take the time, and if you pay attention and obey what God has said to us, thanking him, talking to him about things, you will have a relationship with him.

Now, who else do we have to have a relationship with? A relationship with ourselves, and the Bible talks quite a lot about this. For instance, we're supposed to have peace and self-control and joy. These are all things inside me. I'm to love my neighbor as myself. I count, too, and I'm somebody — somebody so unique, so precious that Christ would have come and died just for me, and that's not being proud. That is what God has said to us.

I think very often Christians have a false modesty. They get kind of nervous about themselves, and they say, "Not me, but Christ. And everything I do is kind of dirty rags." Well, there are moments in life when you do look back and you do have this kind of sinking feeling, that everything has been a bit of a mess, and you haven't succeeded very well. We all feel that because we're caught up in the abnormal world. We are not as good or as intelligent or as beautiful or as perfect as we'd like to be. But, if the Bible is true, I matter. Now it doesn't matter how much I earn, or what my status is in life, or what anybody even thinks about me, or what I look like — that doesn't matter. It's just that I am. If we grow in our understanding of God's truth, we are going to be able to appreciate ourselves, accept ourselves and not forever be angry or upset because we're not another way. We can give ourselves things, and that's a funny sort of an idea. We can be pulled into thinking that we always have to be doing things for other people or working; that I can never just sit down and do something for myself or that I can never say, "Well, I will arrange my day because this is what I need."

If we're going to forgive other people for their sins the way we're meant to, it starts out with forgiving ourselves and accepting ourselves. The only way we can forgive ourselves is by accepting our own limitations and real-izing that God has forgiven us for the sins that we feel miserable about. So we do change, and we aren't stuck with what we did 20 or 30 years ago, so that our lives are ongoing if we have this combination of a relationship with the God who is there and a proper self-appreciation and self-respect, accepting ourselves, enjoying ourselves, enjoying the things we like, hav-ing a certain amount of cheerfulness and also being able to live within the limitations of what we've actually got and not always looking at the grass on the other side of the fence and thinking it's greener over there.

We sometimes fall into the "if only" syndrome — if only I was married, I'd be happier, if only I didn't have this, that, or the other thing. If only I had money or education or lived somewhere I could have a job that was halfway decent, or a house. The sort of feeling that everything then would be all right. We never give ourselves any breaks for where we actually are, who we actually are, because our minds are always somewhere else and imagining something which doesn't exist. So if you've got this combination of a personal relationship with God and a growing relationship with your-self, then you're ready (now this doesn't happen one, two, three and you spend five years on each; they're all happening simultaneously). You don't have to look very far for your relationships with other people. Some of us are married, and so we're already stuck, as it were, for better or worse; that's it. If we are accepting this particular framework, we don't hop around every three or four years trying out somebody else. Those of you who aren't married, are in a very good position, because if ever this choice comes before you, you can think about it very seriously within this frame-work. It's quite a big step to say "This is the person I will live with for the next 'x' number of years."

Who are these persons that we are going to have relationships with? We may or may not have a husband or wife; those who do may or may not have children. Most of us have parents alive, some of us have parents who have died, but most people do have parents. Some have sisters and brothers, nieces and nephews, uncles and aunts. We have neighbors. We also have people that we bump into every day. So, if you live in an apart-ment house and you're forever seeing this young woman struggling in with shopping, baby crying in her stroller, and a toddler being dragged along, and she's slapping at them and screaming at them, she's obviously desper-ate. It's not just one day, it's more or less a pattern. Do you ever take re-sponsibility for that person? Do you ever go up and befriend her and say, "We live in the same apartment house. I wonder if you'd like to come up for a cup of coffee one day, or we could take the children for a walk and have a picnic?"

Where does the line between family and neighbor end? It's a very wavy, loose line. We have different responsibilities, if we are married, to our husband or wife. We should have very different responsibilities, to our mothers and our father, and, I believe, our sisters, our brothers, our cousins and our aunts, as Gilbert and Sullivan said. There they all are, like it or not, breathing down our necks. But we also have responsibilities to the next person. How about in the church? How much are we going to serve, how much are we going to take responsibilities for other people?

I think that, to get this into perspective, if we read the New Testament, what we see is that when we stand before God and look back at this rather pathetic bit of life that we've lived on this planet, there's one question that is going to be very important and that is: How well did you serve other people, and how seriously did you take your responsibilities? If you notice in Timothy, for instance, when they're talking about the church social work in which older women were workers, he said if they still have dependents, they shouldn't come and do this. They should take care of their own families. It isn't just women — there is this primary responsibility to take care of family before we start gallivanting all over the place to do other things. We have to fulfill these responsibilities. Now, if even 70 percent of human beings were serving each other in some poor way, the way the New Testament tells us, what a different world it would be! A lot of the problems that we encounter today in our society would be non-existent. The figures are climbing up very rapidly in terms of breakdown, need of support of all sorts, children in need, old people abandoned, unhappy people, marriage breakdown, all sorts of frustration. If everyone started taking care of his or her own particular circle of people and then his or her neighbors, still we couldn't take care of everybody. We have to draw the line somewhere, and that's painful. So, for instance, you are busy and have a job and family and a few other responsibilities — say your mother lives in the next town and she's widowed and you go and visit her and take her to dinner, and say you have a brother who has had a divorce recently, and he's going through a bit of a rough time, so you say to him, "Well, you can come stay with us for a bit while you look for a new job." And so you're dealing with all this, and *then* you bump into the young lady who is slapping her children and screaming at them and you think, "Where am I in this?" Well, you can't just rush in; it's a very painful question because, at some point, you have to stop helping other people or else, in the end, it's like water in sand, it's gone, and you're not going to do any good to people.

There's no magic in Christian relationships. It's a very sad and painful thing to hear a person saying, "Well, I'm sure everything will be all right because I've married a Christian," or "Our children will be all right; we've prayed for them, and I'm sure the Lord will take care of them." If you're going to have a marriage that works, it will take time, time together. You're not going to have time to do other things, even if they're good works, and you're going to have to put that other person first. You're going to have to be flexible to a certain degree — of course, we experiment and we make mistakes, we have to change the way we do things, but that is what we're working towards. It's going to take energy and discipline to have a relationship that works; it means that because I'm tending to this other person or writing a letter to my mother, I'm not going to be doing something else, and that has to be a priority. If the Bible is true, these relationships have to matter more than these other things in our lives. They have to count. There has to be perseverance in a relationship — carrying on.

Now, sometimes people have relationships with parents that are very painful and difficult because perhaps the parents weren't good parents in the years past, perhaps they're bitter, perhaps they hurt your feelings still. I have friends who are 40 years old, and their parents can still hurt their feelings. They're still full of anger and difficulty at this stage of life, but even so, we're meant to persevere.

Now, you have to find out what that means. It may mean one thing for one person and another for another. There's nothing that tells you exactly what these relationships are going to mean to you — whether in marriage or with children or with parents or with friends or neighbors. But you must think about it, and you must take responsibility. It is important and it is going to take time and energy. It's also going to take creativity. No relationships in the fallen world "just happen" as something beautiful. People have this unreal idea — they look in and they say, "Oh, that looks like a happy couple or parent/child or friends or people working together." There's going to be friction, and, because we're sinful, we're going to do things which are wrong, so there's going to have to be forgiveness and forbearance. And also, there's nothing perfect, and people, from a non-Christian background who come into a Christian one, or people who are just sliding along — from three or four generations of Christians — assume that things are going to be all right because they are Christians, and, in fact, it's not so. The Christian also has a temper, the Christian also hates himself and so is judgmental towards other people, the Christian is also selfish; we're all suffering with these common human problems. The things which are going to help human beings in general are going to help all of us. We aren't in some different category because we are Christians.

Because of this, we have to think of creative ways within our own situation. Now, one of the things about reading Christian books on marriage or children or being Christian friends or being single or your working relationships or whatever it is — one of the things to watch out for is some sort of catalogue or list of things which tells you what to do. Some of them actually have little checklists, and you're supposed to check them off and that's the way to do it. But we're all so different from each other, and our situations are so different. We can share ideas of what it means to us to make a relationship in marriage a priority in our lives, but other people may do it a totally different way.

Because of our own life, Ranald and I don't spend our evenings together. For most of our friends in the church, that is the time that the couples have their relationships — in the evening. The husband gets home from work at 5:00, and from that time until "x" time, that is their marriage. They break off the next morning again. So, we're living a totally different life.

Or, you say, this is what it means to build a relationship with a child: to do this, that and the other thing. But other persons may have different details in their lives and may not even like doing the thing that you're talking about. It may be so unnatural to them, that it would be forced for them to try to copy it. So, for instance, we could say that we read a story out-loud every evening with the children and the whole family comes together — there are exceptions, but that's what usually happens. Another family may think, "That's the blueprint!" Well, I can think of worse blueprints. I think that would do everybody good to read books together in the evening, but, even so, you might have people who enjoy doing quite different things — they're making music, or they have horses that they're out there taking care of. So we shouldn't be telling each other what's right and what's wrong. We need to use individual creativity to decide what all of these things are going to mean in our own lives, in our relationship with God. For each of us, it's going to be a different thing. We may talk to Him at night when we can't go to sleep and somebody else may set the alarm clock and get up at 6:00 in the morning, and yet another person may do it in quite a different way. We each must find our own way of having those relationships.

We have to find ourselves in different ways. What it means to have a relationship in marriage and to have the priority of serving the other person is going to be different for each one of us, because we're doing different things, our personalities are different, where we are is different, it's a different relationship. But one thing will be constant, and that is the willingness to serve each other, to give, and that, again, is in total antithesis to the whole climate of what we have today in the 20th century.

The climate today is: be independent and be fulfilled. Yourself — that's who counts. If other people are getting in your way, you knock them over. You plough through like a snow-plough. What counts is getting there yourself. The New Testament's view or perspective of priorities is different. Jesus said, "If you are willing to lose your life, you will gain it." And these people snow-ploughing down the road, chasing after their own fulfillment rather like somebody chasing a pot of gold at the end of a rainbow — they go on and on and on and on, and it's never there, they never get that fulfillment. It all seems to elude them in the end. The more they look for it, the more they don't find it. And, in fact, Jesus said that if you just turn around and you think about that other person and what he needs, and you start taking responsibility for fulfilling some of that, then *you* will be fulfilled yourself. But it's not going to happen by looking at yourself — it's as you give, as you serve. It's terribly practical; it really is in the nitty gritty of Monday morning until Saturday night.

And so, as a woman and in marriage, this means that I'm told today through the media and society in general, "You just look out for your own interests and don't you dare serve too hard. That is menial and then you'll just turn into a slave, and people will take you for granted." There is this attitude today which says, "Don't ever pick up your children's things for them or sort out their toys," because everybody from the age of three years old should have to do his own thing and not be served. Jesus puts it the other way around, and that is, you give yourself to another person, you look out for him. So, you're aware if they're coming home tired and you try to do something which is really nice for them. You're trying to give, and this isn't just the woman who does it, it is all of us as human beings. This is supposed to be a priority in life. We're looking out for the other person. We don't just say, "I'll do 50% if you'll do 50%." That is not the attitude of the New Testament. I'll do everything, and not make a big song and dance and not talk about it five years later either, and not be martyrish about it. Usually, it's quite a good thing to be able to do things like that, and we should be thankful if we've got health and we can do it, because a lot of the reality, the bitterness, is just right here in our head. Not because we've cleared the table, washed the dishes, or made a meal for the 60th time. People get tied up, they're slaves, because they think of how much they're doing instead of putting their attention on these other people, on the relationship.

At one point, we were thinking of living and working in Africa and having our young family there. I was quite clear on one thing, and I said, "If I have to have babies and young children here in southern Africa, I won't have servants — not until they're grown up." I wanted to do things around my little children. I didn't want to just go out and play with them, as that's very artificial. But if you're making beds, vacuuming, hanging out the wash, and you've got a baby on your back or crawling around on the ground and a toddler who is running in and out, it's a lovely, natural relationship. You're free to talk to them, you're free to stop, but it's not artificial and contrived. You're not sitting there hovering over them, so they can run in and out and not be spoiled in that way and yet have the peace and the quiet to communicate. It's lovely, it's very beautiful.

The relationship between a man and a woman is so precious, is so worthwhile, that it's worth the perseverance through our limitations; through our imperfections, through our disappointments — there are disappointments: I'm disappointed in myself and I'm disappointed in the other person; through our failures and the things which happen to us from the outside which are difficult to live through. It's worth it. Very often, people blame the particular relationship and they're so quick to jump out of it. And what do they find? They're still the same old persons. At least they've still got 50% of the problem. The other person, if they find one, is also going to be sinful and they've just inherited another set of problems. And then if they've taken along with them the poor little children — the nightmare of it for the children!

I was reading a book which isn't from the Christian viewpoint at all which studied the psychological dilemma of children today by the hundreds and thousands — the terrible nightmare of a home here, a home there. When you study it in detail psychologically, it's quite haunting. Different sets of grandparents and children are brought together, and invariably the stepparent and the child have a very sticky relationship. It's bad enough when somebody dies and you try to work within this creatively, but to have a whole society that keeps doing this! About three months ago, a paper came out saying that they interviewed parents who had a divorce, and I think 70% of them had not considered the children at all and their dilemma. That, to them, was not a factor. So you have these extraordinary families, almost Victorian-size, where children have been put together.

I was flipping through my mother's new book called *Lifelines* on the Ten Commandments, and I saw one bit on the family. She tells about this little boy of seven who sighed, "Oh, I can't wait to be grown up, because then I can have a home of my own." This little boy's parents had been divorced, remarried, and divorced again. He had been in and out of so many combinations of houses, grandparents, all sorts of different relationships, shuttled back and forth. This is not an uncommon experience. Shortly, those of us who are interested in children in any way at all will find that this will be the normal child's experience. A very fragmented, lonely existence, because, whatever our society says, the child psychologists tell us, "Well, of course, what is really best is for the child to have a mother and a father who show mutual love and respect and who perhaps fight and make up afterwards and put up with each other." In other words, the good old-fashioned Christian picture of marriage. This, in fact, turns out to be the good thing. Not only that, the other thing that turns out to be good for children is to be taken care of by one of these parents consistently, be loved, be talked to, have time spent with them. Not to be herded into wonderful plastic nurseries with every little gadget — but to be puttering around their own house with their own parent. There's no substitute for it.

The more that we have studied child psychology, the more — and this is where the schizophrenia of our generation is quite extraordinary — we have said that those first five years are so important. In our courts, for instance, we can excuse the most extraordinary acts because we say, "Well, this person had such an upset and such an unhappy early childhood experience." And then we turn around and say that we know how important children's adolescence is and how insecure they are and what a difficult transition that is and how they need to be communicating with someone, to have someone who accepts them, who loves them through all their ups and downs, and failures.

What do we give them as a society? We know one thing, and when we stand before God as a society, as a generation, we are not going to be able to say we didn't know this. You just have to turn to all the libraries full of books on developmental psychology; we have never known it so clearly. It has been written *ad nauseum*, and yet, how are we behaving as a group? Nobody wants to live in a way that actually works. It's very telling that while we know all of this, we know how important the individual is to society as a group, we're still bouncing around telling young women who are starting out on their experience as parents, "Well now, your education will be wasted if you just stay there taking care of two or three young children. You should be out doing something really important — capital 'I.'" At least that's the feeling that's communicated. You're not paid, and, if you listen to people, that is very crucial to them. I'm going to be teaching Ranald John, and I won't be paid anything. Is that any different from the tutor who gets paid by the hour for doing exactly the same thing? What is the difference? People are so mixed up, because they *think* that things are only valuable if they get money for them.

If we're looking in life at the whole perspective — and we started out by saying how different our view of the person is and where we're going and how the extent of our life is totally different — things like the bank account or my status don't matter. Some of you may be very successful in the world's eyes and some of you terribly unsuccessful. Let's all get together in heaven 150 years from now, and sit around and exchange notes. These things as we look back will not matter very much — what kind of a house we lived in, how much tax we had to pay, what kind of a car we drove, will all be terribly insignificant. What is going to matter is how we accepted the human responsibilities that we had. What kind of a wife, what kind of a husband, what kind of a parent, what kind of a child was I, what kind of a neighbor, what kind of a friend?

And, of course, there are other things that matter, so people can say, "Well, how many people became Christians through my witness?" Well, that is, of course, very important, too, but if I am holding onto the truth on the one hand and I understand it, and if I am functioning as a neighbor, as a friend, as a family member, this is going to come across and all fall into place fairly naturally. Because you take that young woman who is desperate, and she's slapping her children and she's screaming, and she's very alone and you bring her in and have a cup of coffee, and what are you going to find out? Well, you're going to find out that she might be worried that her husband is going out with another woman, and also she doesn't have as much money as she used to have, because she used to have a job, and there was a second salary. Actually, she's not budgeting very well, and so she goes out and she gets things which actually aren't very important, like extra clothes, and she hasn't got good toys for the children to play with, so they're always fussing, they're always irritable, and she doesn't know much about them. She's terribly lonely, she's afraid, she doesn't have anybody to talk to. What are you going to do as a Christian in this sort of situation? Well, if you are going to be her friend, of course, the words of Christianity are going to come in; this is going to be very important at some point in the relationship, because the knowledge of who she is and her relationship is going to be terribly important. But it's also going to be important to say, "Well, listen, you can leave the children while you go down to the post office." I found as a young mother, if you have your own children, that with such people, as they come in and you are a friend to them, perhaps their children start playing with yours, they notice things. You don't have to give them lectures. They notice that you can get some cardboard boxes from the grocery store and line them up and you have a train and it didn't cost you anything. And they watch, and if you're not being judgmental and you're sharing it, you say, "Well, yeah, that sort of thing makes me feel very angry, too. If you try this, if you try that, maybe the children won't be so fussy." You can start helping them as people, start talking and start caring. This is what we desperately need in the 20th Century. If there's anything that we need, this is it because we're rapidly becoming a society of people who are lonely, people who lose contact — the old, the urban people, disturbed children. Who do they go to very often? Well, the only person they can think of going to is somebody who is paid — maybe psychiatric guidance or a counsellor, or maybe the doctor, and maybe they'll ask for tranquilizers. What they're doing is saying, "Help, help, help! I'm alone. I want somebody. I want to talk."

There are two things. There's the dilemma that I talked about that you cannot serve everybody that you're going to see, and you have to be able to go to bed at night and be quiet. We have to accept our limitations and live within them; you have to be able to go out and throw a stick with your own dog and watch your own child run across the grass and not be hounded by all these other needs. In so doing, in being solid and healthy and having your own relationships straightened out and well taken care of, you are going to be an example, first of all, for other people. So this woman coming in is going to be helped, because you are doing the things you ought to be doing. For instance, I as a mother could be spending much more time sitting around and talking to people who come into L'Abri and answering their questions. I would love that, I enjoy it, it's something which is very good. But I feel through the years, looking back, that having a family which is happy and settled, not without its ups and downs, not without its failures, not without its difficult moments, but which is persevering, has done more for people coming through perhaps than any amount of sitting around and talking. I once had a young man who came to me and said, "If only I had been somebody else — a student coming to my parents' Christian work — my father would have had time to talk to me, but because I was one of his children, I could never talk over these things. There never was time as a child." A wife could feel that way — if only I was someone else. If I was my husband's patient, then maybe he would sit down and listen to me. Or a minister's wife can feel that way. Or a man can feel that way today because women, too, get caught up in the rat race just as much if not more than men — have to do this, have to do that, and there's no place for you, there's no time for you. You're a big grownup person, so why aren't you taking care of yourself? If you read American magazines now — I think they're very horrific — the attitude is to the child: "You take care of yourself. It's probably good for you to come home after school and have to paddle your own canoe until 6:00 when I'm home. At least you're not dependent on me then." What you have is a horrible ugliness, and this is what I think is a stench in the nostrils of God because it's so unnatural. Everybody is trying to take care of himself, trying to be fulfilled, and if you've got a talent, you're being done in if you can't express it fully, and if you don't have as much as you can have, you shouldn't be anybody's servant or else they might use you.

And in the end, what do you get? What kind of an old person do you want to be? You're going to sit there one day and you're going to look back over your life — this is before we get on to this nicer perspective a little bit ahead of us where we'll be able to chat about it — we'll sit there and we'll look back and say, "Okay, what was that life all about?" And it's not very nice to sit at that end of life, as I have seen old people doing, and really weeping; there's not much you can say to them because they are regretting their lost opportunities. The child grows up, and he's angry and alienated, and maybe even hates you. The husband goes — okay, you didn't serve him, you couldn't give in, you couldn't be flexible to the other person. The parent dies, and you can't write the letter anymore. Your neighbor goes away. You've watched the woman coming out the door and the children have been taken away from her. The marriage broke up. She's going to disappear into the city, and you're never going to see her again. The people in the church had a baby which died. Okay, it's finished now — the wound is closed over. You weren't there. You couldn't take the time. You couldn't go and sit and listen to them. The girl got pregnant and, she didn't know what to do about it — whether to have an abortion or not, but you didn't have time. You didn't have time to go and listen to her, talk to her, be her friend. And how about the person with a handicapped child? What have we done for people with handicapped children? We said we cared, maybe we gave donations, but did we have any of them back home again? Did we help anybody with one? Did we babysit so that the family could go on a vacation once in a while or the mother could go out shopping? And the old people? We're going to have a lot to look back over just in our own lives. Suddenly as people look back over their lives, things come into a different perspective. The money and the jobs shrink.

The Biblical perspective is totally different from the advertisements you see every day, from the media, from your education, what your family wants for you and their ambitions. A lot of people's parents are very, very angry if they choose to do something which doesn't fit into this projection, because that is, after all, what they sacrificed for so that we could go to school, and that's what they did so that their children would have this immortality of being winners. So you have this totally different upside down view of what life is supposed to be about and what its priority is.

DISCUSSION QUESTIONS

1. When we hear the word "family," what relationships should come to mind?

2. How does a twentieth century humanist think of the notion of "person"? What difference does having a Christian world view make in our notion of "person"? What are some dangerous modern practices arising from a humanist view of "person"?

3. How is morality viewed as an evolutionary trend? How does this conflict with the Christian view?

4. Why is it important to constantly view life from an eternal perspective? What are practical aspects of this practice? How does such a view affect our actions concerning the "worthless" in society?

5. To what extent is western man's perceptions of value and status in human beings utilitarian? How does this manifest itself in our society, especially concerning abortion, euthanasia, etc.?

6. Why does living outside of the Scriptural mandates and principles resemble a fish beaching itself and attempting to walk?

7. To what extent are interpersonal relationships a vital and necessary aspect of truly being human? For the Christian, how do such relationships affect our views of status and worth? What has modern secular culture substituted for relationships as a basis for worth and esteem?

8. Why is taking time in a relationship with God stressed as a *first priority* in every person's life?

9. Why is it difficult to befriend a stranger? Who is responsible for the stranger?

10. How pervasive is the "if-only" syndrome — "if only I were married, single, rich, educated, etc., then I would be happy"?

11. Why are "checklists of Christian living" dangerous?

12. Comment on Susan's statement: ". . . there's going to be one question that is going to be very important and that is, 'How well did you serve other people, and how well did you take your responsibilities?'"

> "... we are not puppets, and our very make-up is that our choice has meaning and it matters to live our life that way."

Creativity: My Thinking, Choosing and Acting Counts!

Susan Macaulay

As we think of any part of our lives as Christians — loving our neighbor, or taking care of our families, or witnessing to the non-Christian — all of these ideas or relationships — we have to start off with ourselves, always. Even when I'm thinking about marraige, about two people, in the end I stand before God *alone*. And *I* live my life, however long it's going to be; I'm responsible for my own life.

Remember that Jesus said to the people, when they kept criticizing the person next to them, "Don't look for the straw in your neighbor's eye; look for the beam in your own eye." As we read the Bible, thinking about the truth which God gives us, thinking about his law and about those things which are right, it's easy (perhaps the easiest thing of all) to worry about the next person and to take responsibility for somebody else. This is very often the trouble in marriage, and between parents and children, and between friends, and among people we work with; that is, that people we work with are always looking at us in a critical way and through this sort of veil, and we feel this, and we think, "Oh, I'm not as good, not as strong, not as nice, not as generous as this other person would like me to be, or as *I* would like to be." And of course we criticize ourselves, too, we let ourselves down, we're very disappointed in ourselves. Now Jesus quite firmly kept saying to us, "First of all your responsibility is yourself." We're not supposed to be judging the next person. And the next thing we're not supposed to be is the Holy Spirit for the next person. That's not our job, to wonder whether the next person is becoming kinder, more patient; that is not our concern. My concern in life is "me," Susan; each one of us is alone in our relationship and responsibility before God.

The Biblical view of who I am as a person is totally different from the view around us in the 20th Century. When we go and have coffee with our friends — just the ordinary relationships — we have to understand that the way we're looking at ourselves is totally different from the way our friends and other people are looking at us. They do not know who the human being *is*; they do not know that we are persons created in the image of God. Now this means we're not going to have to achieve a status in order to have worth. You notice today that people determine your importance by your salary, how much education you've had and how high up the ladder you get; these sorts of things are terribly important. And people say to their children, "You *must*, you *must* work hard because I want you to succeed, I want you to win, I want you to be a *top* person." But as we look at the Bible, our whole sense of values gets turned totally upside down. I think about my life . . . "I have worth and value before God; He has accepted me because of who He's made me to be." The beauty, the excitement of being a human being in God's eyes isn't altered by whether I earn 2000 dollars a year in some third world country or whether I'm earning 35 or 40 thousand dollars a year and I'm very well-off. It doesn't make one little bit of difference to God about my status.

Another thing that doesn't make any difference before God is a person's sex. There is no top person and no bottom person before God because of whether we're male or female, or whether we're Jew or Greek, black or white, whatever; these secondary things don't come in before God. Neither does our intelligence. Recently, in the last two or three years, there has been an increasing sense in medical ethics that if a baby's born and perhaps it's going to have Down's Syndrome, or is not going to be as clever as you or I, that maybe this person doesn't even have a right to live, that this person has no value, that somehow we check in as valuable people at a certain IQ level. This means nothing to God; He said, "let the children come unto me, because of such is the kingdom of God." This is a human being who is, in a sense, an example to us, not the other way around.

So we can come before God with a sense of tremendous relaxation. We don't have to pretend to be better — first of all, He knows we're sinful and we've failed, and He's accepted us the way we are — and we don't have to invent things for ourselves — play little games and pretend. We can be relaxed just the way we see little children running around the yard . . . they rush in and they've got chocolate ice cream on their faces and they've got mud 'cause they fell in the pond . . . and they know that they're loved and forgiven. This is our strong position before God. Therefore, we're not living to sort of tick things off on some sort of scale and be accepted.

Now one thing some Christians have gotten sort of mixed up on is thinking that God, being a spirit, is more pleased if we live our lives in a "spiritual" way. That is, "If I go to two or three prayer meetings a week and two Bible studies and rush around — perhaps on my two free afternoons I'm down on some street corner witnessing — I will really please God a lot." "If going to church once on Sunday is quite a good idea, then perhaps going three times on Sunday will make God extremely happy." And we get like little children who are trying to earn gold stars. We keep falling back into this mentality; we keep thinking God wants something "other worldly" from us.

Now in fact, if we'll just sit back and look at it for a minute, we can think, "Now God planned us to be creatures of this planet, that was His intention." If I try to run away from who I want to be, say, if I love rushing around the lawn with bare feet, or going to the seaside, or throwing myself into music, and I think, "Oh *dear*, I mustn't do this, this isn't very spiritual," then I'm negating who God made me to be, and it's a slap in His face, because He wanted me to enjoy the seaside and music; He made me to enjoy a sexual relationship in marriage; He made us to joy in having small children, or a dish of ice cream with a piece of chocolate in it; whatever scale of things we think of as human beings, these are good gifts from God, and they're part of the unity of "who I am." I'm woven together like a piece of cloth, and God said it was very good, the wholeness of myself.

Now part of this is to have a relationship with God and to grow in the knowledge of his truth, but He tied me down to this planet, and not only did He tie me down, but the Bible says that when I die, I'm going to be left for just a little while, and then I'll be raised again, so for eternity I'll have this link. And this is not "just a lump of clay," the way some people have said "death is a release" — not at all; this is a gift of God, this is planned, this is creation. And so, as I think about my life as a person, what I'm working towards is a unity within myself, who am I.

Now "who am I" is slightly different for each one of us, because we've been made differently, and there isn't any rubber stamp Christian, there isn't such a thing as a "spiritual person" that I should copy. What I should look for is who am I, now, because who I am now is very different from who I was 20 years ago when I was 20 years old and first married. Who am I now is different from who I was even five years ago — I know that for a fact; I've changed quite a bit in my ideas, in a lot of things that I understand. So I'm not even static, and I must have this self-understanding to know peace in life. We in the 20th Century pant after peace. And we live in a most frantic generation where there is often no peace, no self-understanding, no sense of unity or sense of rest. We as Christians should know this better than other people. Although the sad fact is that often we don't. We're going to work at this for a long time, and we're limited, and we're never going to have the perfect situation, so we won't reach a real unity like this 'til we're raised again from the dead and in the next step of our lives. But we work towards it, and the Holy Spirit who is in us will help us work towards this self-understanding, this unity. It's all linked up with the ordinary things.

Now you can have someone say, 'I feel depressed." There can be various reasons; perhaps after ten minutes of conversation, you find out that someone loved very dearly by the person has just contracted a very serious illness; or they will be no longer able to rent their house, and they don't have money for anything that's on the market in the area; and you find that there's a very good explanation for this depression. Now you could have a "Christian" answer . . . "If you'll just pray about this and trust in the Lord, then your fears, your low times, will disappear; you're not being spiritual." And I say, "Rubbish!" If someone you love very very dearly has contracted a serious illness, or you suddenly realize that you're going to be homeless and you don't have any money to go anywhere else, you have every reason to feel sad and depressed. And in fact, if you don't allow yourself to feel this, you're creating a tension . . . you're denying the reality inside of yourself. Now we know this, for instance, from the last war; the people who had the most serious, permanent psychological damage when they went through a difficult experience were the ones who couldn't cry, couldn't grieve, couldn't say "how terrible it was," could not face the reality of what was inside.

Often Christians have been brainwashed into thinking that they must act, must seem, both to themselves and to others, as if everything was always okay, and joy-joy-joy, happy-happy-happy; or that they are going to be on their knees all day long, that they're not going to get hungry or want to go for a long walk, or do this or that; they're trying to pretend they're somebody they're not, and that's a kind of dishonesty. When I'm dishonest with myself, that's going to have very serious consequences. I'm going to put a tremendous tension inside myself; I won't understand myself; I'll be creating all sorts of disunity, or "unpeace." We have no need of this. First of all, we do live in an abnormal world, and each one of us has problems both outside and inside; we all share in this. Second, we don't walk through this alone. This is what "walk the gospel" means, and that is, "I have come to you in your real life, when you're very discouraged, you're very upset and you feel as if you want endless amounts of sleeping tablets because you've turned and tossed for the last twenty nights, where you're not sure how you're going to go on." This is where God comes to us. It's the crunch. It's reality. You can say, "Yes, I am depressed, yes I am very sad, yes, I am tempted, I'm afraid," and be able to admit how you really are. Or, "No, I'm *not* going to church fifteen times; I'm going to decide on my priorities, but I'm not going to deny other things about the way God has made me. These are also good, these are also necessary, this is who I *am*".

Now, I'm not saying that every little thing we find inside ourselves, every little grain, has to be fulfilled, because obviously it can't be; our life is something like the frame of a picture, defining our limitations. For instance, we're all born with all sorts of possibilities and we could grow this way and that way, and be fulfilled in all sorts of different areas, and we *aren't*. Each of us could live out maybe six lives which would be very interesting and very fulfilling out of the seeds of possibilities which are in us. We may have different combinations of gifts. But the years are short. The responsibilities are great, and so we are limited in what we can actually do. This is sometimes a little disappointing if we think, "Oh, I *could* do this, this, and this." But I can't. God has only made me *one*. And this is what I'm talking about . . . I'm talking about the "me." I have to accept this limitation; I have to accept that the years I'm young and strong are short. This is almost a paranoia today; people can't admit that they're going to get old, that they're going to get tired; we have a sort of "myth of youth," and we hang on to this, turning away from reality again, the reality of the fallen world, which is a limitation. If I choose to get married, I'm going to be very limited in some areas; there are some things I could've done as a single person, for myself and for others, that are now closed off to me. On the other hand, if I'm single, there are other things that are cut off to me that I could've had if I'd been married. Each one of these things become part of our picture. We're limited by our physical energies. We think, "I *would* do this, I *would* do that, but I'm unable. There are only 24 hours in a day, and, unfortunately, I need so many hours of sleep, and I *can't* do it."

Some people live their lives like little birds, always fluttering on the edge of that limitation and are always discontented. "If only the sun had shown today, then it would've been a great day," or, "if only I had gone to college," or "if only I didn't have this bad foot," or "if only I had lived in another country," or "if only I could write," or maybe "I *could* write but I never had time to sit down and do anything about it." And they're always pushing against the edge of that. Now it causes trouble as soon as they get married or have a job or child or any sort of responsibility, because this is also dissatisfying. "If only the person I married was a little bit different"; "if only my job gave me slightly more scope, or the people were more sympathetic, or perhaps I had more money . . ."

This being content and being creative *inside* of our limitations is, I think, the secret in life. First we have the base of who we are and the knowledge of who we are, so we understand what the whole framework is, and we know where we're going.

Second, we have the idea of this limitation not being some sort of a prison, but a boundary inside of which I'm going to be creative, and I often tell this story, but I think it's very appropriate. Say, you've planned a Youth Hosteling vacation, and you save up for it, and you say, "After I've been at L'Abri, I'm going to go off for a month, and it's very important to you. You may never get back to England again, and you've planned all these things, and you go off, and as soon as you get out there, the sun stops shining, and the birds stop singing, and we've got a month of rain — I'm sorry, but it's all too possible.

It's rainy, and it's windy, and it's cold. Now you can have two reactions: You can be the person that lets that ruin his whole time . . . or her whole time. You may say, "Oh, I had a lousy time Youth Hosteling, it was awful, rainy and wet . . . The whole time was ruined." And you've allowed this, the framework of what actually was, not like the travel brochure where the Lake District sun always shines — though, in fact, it hardly ever does — but you've had this idea, and you've been unable to accept the reality. And then you have another person who may go out and find it's rainy and say, "Well, we'll go to the town, we'll go and look at Bath, and they go and look at the architecture, and they enjoy something slightly different. And they make capital of it. It's as if they have something, and they spend it wisely; they're creative with what they have, and they're able to enjoy it. They're able to change and be flexible. And that, to me, is the secret of life.

You say, right now I'd rather be married; how are you going to be creative in being single? Or say a person is married and says, "Oh, what a terrible mistake I made in marrying this wretched person. I'd rather be single — look at those lucky people who are single. And then you say, "But here I am. This is my framework, and I will be creative in this." Now we have God's help, and it's a very ordinary thing; and yet, if you look for it in the Bible, you'll see that that is often given as the reality. And it makes for contentment, it makes for happiness, but it also makes for a tremendous creativity. The most creative cooking in the world came from people who couldn't go down to the local supermarket and get every last ingredient that was in a cook book. And so, for instance, you get your pizzas from Italy — where some people had very limited resources, and they made the best of what they had. The same with Chinese cooking, so you have a little bit of this and a little bit of that. Now your most creative lives are made that same way. Take the ingredients of what I've got today, not tomorrow, or next month — from *now* and make the best of those — work with those. And that's very exciting and interesting, and you make the most of it. It's like taking the bull by the horns. Instead of sort of cowering under life — it's embracing, it's getting on top of it and thinking about it — and we won't always feel that way — we very often feel squashed, we feel crushed, and we feel as if a big rock has landed on us, and we are flattened underneath circumstances which are limiting us. I can't move, I can't do anything about it. Now there are certain things we can do so that we don't get into this rather miserable situation — or the equally miserable one of getting into a rut so deep that I cannot again, be creative at all — like some muddy road that wagons have gone down for months, and then your wagon gets in those ruts, and you just can't move, and you're not being creative in any way.

Because God made us — the theology of this and the philosophy of this is that we live in a structured universe. God is infinite, and there's not any *chance*, but, on the other hand, we are not puppets, and our very makeup is that our choice has meaning, and it matters to live our life that way. It matters not to just feel as if I'm squashed by events, but that I look at it, and I accept limitations, my own limitations. "Oh, I'm not so clever as I would like to be. No, I'm not, perhaps, as resilient emotionally as I would like to be." "No, I'm not so good at personal relationships as I would have imagined, but I will accept who I am and I will work with that." I work with what I have here. Jesus said, "Don't just be hearers of the word, but doers." Now it's easy to keep all that we read in a nice little Spiritual compartment and not to ever start putting it into practice in my own nitty gritty daily life.

Now what is the nitty gritty? — well, first of all, I've got a big secret — it is this relationship with God; there isn't a blue print for it. Nobody can tell you how or when or how long you should read the Bible. But we're told to grow in the knowledge of the truth, and what that means for you will be very different from what it means for me, perhaps. What it means at one point in your life may be very different from what it means at another, but this is our bread, this is our meat. Just as much as we're tied down to planet Earth physically, so, if we want to have a sense of unity and well-being, we're also tied down to this "good nutrition." Ranald preached a sermon once that I liked very much where he said "What are we filling ourselves up with for our spiritual nutrition? Is it junk food?"

And, of course, one thinks about one's diet. It's not good to say, "I feel so awful. I feel so terrible. God hasn't been good enough to me or maybe Satan's tempting me," and, in actual fact, you're living on Coca-Cola and potato chips — that's not going to do you any good, and there's nothing spiritual or unspiritual about it.

In the same way, we are meant to be responsible for what we put into our heads — and our use of our time. I think, having grown up in a Christian family, one of the things which is bad is the tendency to think of having a relationship with God only as a duty — to think, "Oh, I should be reading the Bible, or I should be praying" and we feel a little bit guilty. A magazine just came in, and you're reading it — about the Falklands, or something — and then it's awfully late and you think, "Oh, dear" — (it becomes guilt) — "well, then I'd better do it (read the Bible). *There*, there, now, I've read two pages, that's pretty good." That sort of thing. Now, I think we have to think about our relationship with God the way we would think about our relationship with a friend, and that is, you have to plan to have time together. The hallmark of 20th Century life is we're run off our feet. We're run off our feet the whole time we're growing up — homework is thrown at us, exams; we're rushing around here and there, earning money if you're American and you can't get grants; trying to make ends meet together, and we're dash, dash. The electric lights are on, so we get very few hours sleep; blinking television keeps us awake and is always stirring up little bits and pieces of things, and so then, I haven't got time to talk to my husband, I haven't got time to listen to my children — "What? You read a story every night? Where would you find time?" That's ridiculous! My appeal is, just sit down! You're only going to be around here for a few years — what on earth is worthwhile? What is really worthwhile? Because if you just let it happen to you, you're going to end up having wasted what is most precious in life — we're really in danger of selling our birthright for a mess of potage. Who wants that? Your birthright is *life*. Now it's damaged, of course, — we all are fallen, but there you've got your birthright.

Now it really matters that you have a relationship with another person. Say you have somebody that you like very much. And you never make time to be together, and you never have time to spend with each other in any way at all. What kind of a relationship is that? You say . . . Oops! Ten past ten. I've got ten minutes . . . there, I've done it. Now I can get back to another television program or my magazine or whatever. That's ridiculous!! Now if you're going to have a good relationship with a person, as well as with God, what you must do is think ahead. Think, "Well, now, I'll finish my work, and I'll take a picnic out into the garden. Or, "It's horrible weather — we'll build a fire in the fireplace, and we'll make a pot of tea or a cup of coffee — we'll go out for a walk, and we'll spend time together." What makes me saddest is when parents say to me, "Oh, you have such a beautiful relationship with your children. I wish I did." And they act as if it's something that falls out like radioactive fallout from heaven — it fell on you, and it didn't fall on me. You have a good relationship, I don't. They don't realize that anybody can have a good relationship with anybody, practically. If you think about it, if you spend time, if you accept that other person, if you enjoy her, if you look into her eyes and find out how she is.

Now we can do this with God. And I think it's very important. Say you're working, you're rushing around at your job, you're very tired, and then your church is putting a lot of pressure on you, or maybe it's something else — or maybe you have a lot of hobbies — think ahead during the week — when you are going to sit down and relax and be with the Lord? It's very important to treat Him as if He was a friend — make a pot of tea or a cup of coffee, build a fire, sit out in the garden. Say, "I'm sorry, no, I can't do this, no, I can't do that" because you have an appointment and it's very important. Make it nice, it's a friendship, it's pleasant. Now that's not the way it'll always be. There's a moment in every relationship for an "Oh, help!" or "Quick, look!" But you're rushing along, and it's amazing what little pithy bits of goodness you can have both in God-person relationships and in interpersonal relationships when you have the groundedness. We can't judge each other, but we can plan. Now this means a certain kind of discipline, doesn't it? Because if you're going to plan to spend time with somebody, plan to spend time with God. That means you are disciplined, and it means saying no to certain things; and it means also deciding what's top priority and saying, "I can't do everything, and this one is on the top.

Now I think, too, of another priority (and remember, now I'm thinking about myself, so I'm not thinking of all the things that God will be telling me to do as I read His word). I'm thinking about my relationship to myself and my responsibilities right here. I also have to have a priority of my *mind*. God has given us a mind, and it's very interesting that where people have had the word of God and started growing, they have become much more interested in thinking. After all, you only need to read this, really read it and you have an education. We are meant to use our minds, and very often if you take a person who is just rushing around and vegetating and feeling vaguely dissatisfied and miserable, he's not letting this part of himself grow. And the evangelical church hasn't had all that good a track record about this. And so, for instance, am I reading any books which are pushing me a bit or are interesting and making me grow? I'm sure I've

quoted this before, but I was reading that the average American college
graduate reads one book a year. Now that really knocks you over flat
when you think that this is the main means of serious communication.
What do we know about contemporary literature or drama? What do I
know about art? What do I know, perhaps, about the Renaissance? I have
so much to know — and I should be a growing person. That's part of being
alive. Incidently, it's a very good way of not getting senile — to be feeding
your mind. We should go on being creative as well. Now it may be in the
kitchen, it may be with drawing, it may be with bringing up children, but
we should think about our creativity; that's important. Conversations are
important, too, to be able to express what I'm thinking, to be able to communicate. To receive is important for me, too, because I'm not living in
isolation. I stand in relationship to my neighbor, always, whoever that
neighbor is. I have a responsibility to examine the principles of what I'm
thinking and talking about and doing — to not be parroting. And I have a
responsibility to not just turn myself into some kind of tape recorder. Now
if I'm schooled, or if I'm studying at L'Abri, and I go in and listen to a tape
recorder, or I go to church, or turn on the television to look at news, or I
read my newspaper, I must not just accept what I'm given ever. I have a
responsibility to think, to judge — is this true? is this right? Or, what's
wrong about it? Where's it leading? Where has it come from? That's what I
should be thinking about.

   Now we have a tension today because, in a way, I live in a generation
where I am told repeatedly who matters is only *you*, so we have a kind of
worship cult going for the *me*. It's great to go jogging if that's what you
like to do to keep fit. But there are people who live for only that. So this
has to be kept in balance. It's important. Some people live only for the *unity* aspect. After all, who is looking for unity in the 20th Century? Very
often it's not the Christian; very often it's people sitting in the lotus position on the floor or with their hands out trying to make their minds blank.
And it's come from an eastern philosophy and not with this wonderful
sense of "I know who I am and know I'm important, and I can find a unity
and a peace in that way, in that reality." So here we have to be very careful, because the things we're looking for can suddenly become the center
of our lives. Understanding who I am and serving myself are only spring
boards for living life. As I become involved with other people and start
taking responsibilities, in fact, my eyes will be taken off myself. You find
some people who are tempted to put themselves miles and miles behind
and to give, give, give, serve, serve, serve, serve. And then you have other
people who are always sort of making a little circle, like a dog who's been
hit in the head. Sometimes we can go round and round and round. That's

not living life. It certainly isn't. So we have to find our balance or we'll make a mistake and say, "Oops, I've done too much for myself, thinking about myself. Oh, dear! Now here I am, I've left myself miles behind, I'm as dry as anything, I'm empty, I'm not really even alive." And we have to look for this, this is part of the maturing. This is balance.

DISCUSSION QUESTIONS

1. Why must the primary starting position of all relationships be "my-self"? Why is this healthy and necessary, and how can it be warped into hedonism, selfishness, and complacency?

2. Why must the status and worth we accord ourselves and others come solely from God's acceptance of us all as we are? How do we subtly deviate from this basis of value?

3. Why is it necessary to have man in the image of God as a proper starting point for any proper evaluation of creativity? How does this both exalt and humble our self view and view of man in general?

4. In what ways do people attempt to be the Holy Spirit for their friends and relatives?

5. Contentment and creativity inside our limitations is vital in life. Who should define our limitations?

6. In what sense is there no such thing as total fulfillment?

7. Facing decisions is a difficult fact of life for most people. Would you prefer that others make decisions for you? What difficulties do we face in the truth that each person is responsible for his own life?

8. What parts of our twentieth century life must we resist in order to live contently and creatively?

9. Why is choice so needed in our lives? How can having an ability to choose wisely affect our lives?

Udo Middelmann

Udo was born in Frankfort, Germany in 1940. He attended high school in Bonn which included a year as an exchange student in Washington state. His university studies at Bonn, Lausanne, Berlin and Freiberg resulted in a law degree in 1963. After graduation, Udo pursued a second field of studies at Covenant Theological Seminary where he received a B.D. and a Master of Arts in 1967.

Since that time he has been a full time staff worker and member of L'Abri Fellowship in Switzerland. In 1973 he was ordained a pastor in the English speaking church (International Church, Presbyterian - Reformee) in Huemoz, Switzerland. Besides working at L'Abri, he travels frequently to lecture in Europe, the USA and Australia.

He contributed to the research of the film series "How Should We Then Live?" and "Whatever Happened to the Human Race?". His book, *Pro-Existence*, was published by Inter-Varsity Press in 1974. Udo and his wife, Debbie, have four daughters.

"The Christian is the one who, from his own understanding of the structures of the real world, has insight into the needs and possible solutions for societal struggles."

The Christian and Government
Udo Middelmann

The question of the place of the Christian in relationship to the government is one that has been raised through the ages by people who are conscious of the moral obligation of man to historic realities. It is not new, as church fathers, Christians and the Church have dealt with it in various ways depending on historical realities of different governing bodies and different theological emphases. These influence our perspective at any time, and any suggestion must be seen to relate primarily to a matter of principle rather than practice. Our concern is not a master plan for action, but a wider consideration of the place of the Christian outlook on all of life, society and politics.

Such a question would never arise in a perspective that minimizes the place of man in history. Any withdrawal into a spirituality that does not relate to the here and now of human existence, but emphasizes a spiritual existence in which the body and historical life are seen as appendices or necessary evils, would not concern itself with the question of the political responsibility of the Christian. But would such a view even be Christian?

Starting either with the given of our historic life as human beings confronted with the need to make choices that affect all of life into the next generations, or starting with the Biblical record in the Old Testament, we are faced with the affirmation of the correctness of living in a material and definite universe that is the creation of a God who has a character. By that, the Bible means to show that to God, not all things are the same, that He distinguishes, even as He created matter and shaped it into ever greater differentiations. At the end of it, He looked at it and saw that it was very good.

We find here the basis and starting point for the Biblical affirmation of the rightful place of man in a created order. Into this order, Christ was born, and it is this order that Christ will change, when at His coming all death and tears will be removed and righteousness will reign forever.

The Biblical perspective does not start with the moral demands on man in obedience to Christ, but with the affirmation of a God who has created a definite universe, in which law and order are aspects of His character and the character of the universe. There is no other place to be for man, but in his body and soul occupying space to form it, fill it and bring glory to God through it. This is the scope of human existence. It is the attention of God to that detail that is the expression of the grace of God, his law and love.

In this world of basic differentiations, man was to live as a choosing creature, expressing imagination and variety, creativity and responsibility. This is the context of human existence, the unity of body and soul and spirit, of man and nature, male and female, God and Man.

When the fall of Adam affected all this and tore apart the created relationships, man did not cease to be the image bearer of God. And thus, in real human history, valid human relationships are forged and need protection. The commands in the Bible, the need to fit into the form of the universe with its characteristic limitations on one hand, and the protection of the person against superior physical might on the other, require a basic distinction between good and evil.

The Bible, word of the creator and living God, speaks for the need of the rule of law in order to protect and further human existence.

This view must be guarded against at least two misconceptions.

1. For many people today, the foundation of modern democracies is found in the Bible. All democratic decisions, unless they directly violate God's commands, are seen as right and wise. Democracy is seen as the protector of Christian freedoms and human liberties.

2. For others, out of a mistaken view of spirituality, all involvement in the politics of the day is seen to play into the hands of humanism and an undermining of the larger Christian concern to lead people to a knowledge of the Lord through the teaching of Biblical Christianity. Heaven is our goal and a spirituality that denies the involvement of daily life is seen as the way to heaven, where neither politics nor human situations corrupt.

The first misconception fails to recognize the basic change in the concept of democracy in our own century. In Greece, the vote by the people was protected against a wrong use of voting power by having only the free and accepted share in the common responsibilities of the public interest. Others were excluded. In the 18th and 19th centuries such an exclusion was not necessary to the same extent, for a common view of the world and man was held due to the prevalent rule of the Biblical understanding of man and history. This was not held universally, as votes were curtailed by color and social associations. But the choice to have all people participate in the formulation of the public will was based on the assumption of a common value system and goal for all of life. That goal and concern was largely maintained by the underlying Biblical foundations.

As long as that common concern was held, a limit existed for the exercise of free political choices. Government for and by the people worked, as long as the definition of ultimate values, especially the value of the human being, was given from outside of man. Then, in opposition to the authoritarian rule of absolutistic powers of the court or the church, the wisdom and insight was sought from the minds and hands of those who bore the brunt of social responsibilities.

When, at the same time, the basis of the Biblical world view was undermined by the philosophical changes in Kant's objection to revelation, the naturalistic interpretation of the Bible, and the evolutionary thinking in sociology, the former limits were removed and the boundaries pushed outward. What had been the selfish rights of the potentates now became the rights of the public will. Having no control over the political choices, the majority became a potentate in its dictatorial imposition of law as might. Mathematical considerations triumphed. The result is that democracy from the end of the last century found a kinship in the notion of peace in the polis of the Greek world, rather than in the common responsibility of Biblical man to serve God and man in the boundaries of Scripture.

Democracy in this modern sense leads to a softening of the rule of law, an abolition of man, and an abandonment of irrationality. Law henceforth describes the rule of power for time, man is readily redefined according to the needs of the greater whole and collective, and the distinction between rationality and irrationality is abandoned, as all things become equally possible. What was right, was right as long as might was there to support it. Opposites become acceptable, love without commitment, humanism without man, law without legitimacy, the state when there is no solidarity between mother and child or husband and wife or employer and employee.

The Biblical concept of law and society is based on a different foundation. It is not left up to human imagination or mere concensus. The focal point of Biblical law and society is based on the existence of a knowable

God, whose character is the law of the universe. By this it is understood that God has created a universe that corresponds to His own character. His commands are then not the imposition of arbitrary power demanding blind obedience of the weaker to the stronger, but are the description of the kind of world we live in. Law aids in the discovery of the boundaries of the world created, rather than attempting to create a world by force. Morality is based on the choice of God, not on the shifting values in a society determined by mathematical constellations. Law is control over our imagination and fancy and leads to a discovery of what is best for the human being and society. The one who has created the universe describes it to us much the way an architect would describe the house he created for us to live in.

In this view, absolutes are grounded in the character of the God of the Bible, who is eternal as a person, and whose work reflects his character. Neither God nor his creation is up for reelection. There is no question of whether they might strike our fancy or convince our imagination with newer models of media dreams and consumer varieties. Rather, God is true to what He has made. Law must then reflect that shape of things in all areas of reality to man and against mere imagination. Truth, not consensus; life, not popularity, are central concerns. This fixed point is not of human imagination or of faith, but results from the understanding of the creator and creation.

This view is very different from the Roman and Greek view of the modern state. The latter is concerned with peace in the polis. It is an approach of consensus among men's imaginations and desires, but fails to respect the universe in its boundary conditions. It affirms nature, but denies morality. It favors history, but denies judgment. It confirms significance, but is amoral and indifferent to consequences. It denies the reality of true evil, making of evil and good relative moral outrage. It speaks for humanity, but has no place for man. It is for law, but knows no anchor for legitimization. It finds no objection to the rule of inhumanity, because it has replaced the power of the king by the power of the mob.

It is based on the assumption that man is basically good. That assumption is based on the liberal ideal that man is evolving, that there is no real basis for a distinction between good and evil, and that nature is the primal mover of human reality in its amorality.

Against this we must speak and work for the reasonable foundation of moral existence and law and compassion, based on the starting point of God's existence, in whom human life, law, morality, praise and blame have their foundation. Only here is there room to demand and justify the outrage against all that is less than good, just, human.

The opposite view so often taken by Christians is at the base a misunderstanding of the Biblical framework. To abandon public and civil responsibility is explained on the basis of a mistaken view of the work of Christ. It is much closer to the gnostic view of spirituality of the second century or the eastern mysticism of our own day. It is the view that Christ has redeemed us out of daily existence. This emphasis on the second article of the confessions of faith in the Church fails to take note of and respect the context in which that relationship to Christ is established and maintained.

The Bible does not start with man's need for salvation. That subject is not touched until the setting is made plain first. The context speaks of the affirmation of creation by a God who desired to create a universe of definite materiality and have man share in this as a unit of body and spirit.

The fall of man is portrayed as resulting in moral separation from the creator with results also touching the material world. The history in the Old Testament shows the rightful place of man is materiality, with love and hate, space and time, glory and cruelty, whole and broken existences, obedience and revolt as part of the humanness of man's created existence. Death, with all its ugly faces, as a falling apart of what God has made to be whole, pierces through all of life and society. To show that this is not normal, that what is of now-nature is in fact unnatural, the promise of redemption draws all existence towards the coming Messiah as the only sufficient substitute. But this redemption is seen as a redemption of all of history, beginning with the moral need of man and going on to the hope of everlasting righteousness. It is this going together of the Old and New Testament, of life on a created earth in real history, into which Christ was born and into which his return will take place, that is the stage of human existence. Here society exists as the collective of individuals.

It is in this framework that the state and the collective of society function. The responsibility of the Christian is not to accept all of society's reality as the normal, to withdraw from real human and passionate existence into some other spirituality. In this real history, the battle against all forms of evil must take place. The brokenness of the universe, the reality of the fall and the manifestation of all sorts of evil challenge us to do battle against death in all its appearances. History and all evil are to be placed in the seat of the accused. Government on a larger scale and personal action in the limits of our lives are to be used to stand against all indifference to nature, including human nature.

Biblical man is called to stand with the proper arrogance and passion against everything that is mere nature, indifferent, lacking compassion. Science and Art are based on this arrogance, judging things as they are to

be amoral and lacking in human worth until they are handled and tem-
pered by moral choices and creative gifts. But this must also be so in public life and societal responsibilities.

First we have the responsiblity to demand a solid intellectural foundation for the affirmation of man in distinction to non-man. This has become increasingly more important as the Biblical view of the person
created in the image of the personal God of the Bible is abandoned or re-
legated to the realm of faith. When only the data of repeatable natural
phenomena is admitted, all reality is reduced to the mathematical. Man
is reduced to the machine in a determined system. Whatever is natural is
seen as proper. Thus the foundation for law and justice is in nature, not
in morality. When the public (teacher, legislator, doctor) speak of man,
they ought to be challenged to define their point of orientation for the use
of the word *human* or *man*.

Second, the educational system must be challenged on the level of discussing the point and goals of education. Is it to prepare the human being
for industry and the needs of the market, or is it preparatory to the introduction into human existence in history, literature, the sciences, because
the tools for grappling with the world as it is in order to work in it and
improve it are valuable in their own right? Utilitarian concepts must be
kept in the second place where they belong. The first concern should be a
concern for a better fight against indifference in the goal of a better education.

Third, the responsibilities of the individual for the state's task to be a
force for order and law against a violation of the same must be clearly
presented in a culture that worships the self and selfish goals, and also
denies the existence of real evil. Much of the pacifism in today's political
associations and church groups comes out of a misunderstanding of the
basic battle of man for life against evil and death. Romans 13 gives a
clear mandate for the maintenance of law, and the Christian is called to
take his stand with the state against all attacks of man against man.
Where in personal relations, the individual may choose to forgive, such
benevolence is not admissible in the larger context of the public life.

In our post-Christian age, where much of the state is based on
humanistic ideas coming from Greek and Roman thought, many of the
programs and issues established may not be in line with genuine Christian concerns. Here the distinction between those battling for the same
goal but out of different motives is important. For the Christian has the
only basis for real evil and the grounds to stand against it. The fall and its
resultant basic injustice and the affirmation of choices bringing results in
the Christian world view lay the foundation for passionate involvment.

The Christian is the one who, from his own understanding of the structures of the real world, has insight into the needs and possible solutions for societal struggles. It is here where, from a basis of understanding, he can be a challenge and an encouragement to work toward the integration of law and freedom, morality and compassion, reason and religion. For Christianity starts with the affirmation — for good and sufficient reasons — of the existence of God, whose word is the revelation of God's character into the human existence in a real world. Here is the boundary condition of all human life and private and public morality, of justice and mercy in human relationships, of creating a breathing space for the perfect and the injured, the young and the old.

When this sounds like more than we feel comfortable with, is this not due to the horrendous failure of much of the Christian church in the recent past, when we have not dealt with the thought forms of naturalistic philosophies intellectually, or with sane human existence in the areas of art and science, or have not exhibited in our own lives and concerns much more than justifications for our own personal greed and immorality toward God and toward our fellow man? The condemnation of Romans 1 might touch the non-Christian in our own day and age. But we are addressed in the second chapter as those who had a basis, but have not availed ourselves of that which God has given in the past. Instead, we have too often withdrawn into some false separate existence and shown very little concern for the day's life that is before us. And we have been too quick to speak of sin as an explanation of all evil without having compassion on the situation after the fall, in which all our lives are mortgaged by the sin of previous generations and in which there is no normality until Christ returns in glory.

DISCUSSION QUESTIONS

1. Why does Udo stress that what he is sharing are *principles* and not a *plan of action*?

2. Udo maintains that the basis of truth is neither human imagination nor faith. Why?

3. What is the basic change in the concept of democracy that has occurred today? In light of that change, why is it a misconception to continue to advocate democracy in its original sense?

4. To be naive is to give an ultimate loyalty to the state or to a political party. To be an escapist or isolationist is to retreat from political life. The Christian way is to work for the redemption of political institutions. How is this responsibility transformed into action?

5. Why is there no basis for law in society other than the existance of God?

6. What difference does the doctrine of creation make to a Christian's approach to work and to social life?

7. How can we know whether man's written law corresponds to God's universal law?

8. How has the modern liberal view of man blurred the distinction between good and evil?

9. How should a Christian respond to the evil which surrounds and infects him or her?

"It is Biblical Christianity that established the
basis for true human life in the common things of the day,
dealing with real issues and offering realistic solutions
in anticipation of the return of the king."

The Christian Mind
Udo Middelmann

The concern about the place of the mind in the life of a Christian is often
voiced in discussions. This concern has been increasing in our present cultural situation, where the critics of Christianity have been gaining ground
and are increasingly carrying the day in public discussions and political
realities.

This should not surprise us in the least. The Christian consensus of
former days has been replaced by a consensus of supposedly scientific rationalism and evolutionary humanism. Our philosophers since Kant have
closed the possibility of metaphysical speech and created a situation of
silence when it comes to speech about values and morals. This has filtered
down into the general public in such forms as: truth is opinion; we all have
our own faiths; the message of a work of art is contained in its form and
statement with integrity. Sincerity is seen as judge of quality.

This metaphysical silence — about which most people would still complain in language that would only be meaningful if there were the possibility of metaphysical knowledge — has led to the embrace of the criteria of
natural science as the only possibility to arrive at an understanding of
truth. This is influenced by Descartes' statement about "true" being only
that which is distinct, definite and measurable. Nature and our scientific
studies of it are then the only references for life and morals. It is assumed
that whatever is true to nature has a right to be. And one can make only

quantitative statements about all of life.

This perspective of the European Enlightenment has not been darkened by the emphasis or, at least, silent support of some who would place themselves in the Christian camp, but whose outlook is far from being Biblical. Pascal is often quoted in his suggestion that the heart has its reason which the mind does not know. Kierkegaard introduced into Christian thought the acceptability of the irrational through his re-interpretation of Abraham's sacrifice of Isaac. From then on, a basic irrationality was seen to be the nature of the Christian faith.

With this change, not only were irrationality and the distrust of the mind made acceptable, but it became almost a matter of obedience and faith to be able to believe that which made no sense. Nothing could be further from the Biblical emphasis.

In the Bible, obedience and faith are always placed into the context of a questioning man who is dependent on revelation, *i.e.* information given to the human situation from outside of his intelligence-gathering capabilities. The informant is not *totaliter aliter* (wholly other) in Kant's concepts, but the creator of a rational universe that expressed his own choices as a personality. Man as the image bearer of God is understood to be God in so far as he is capable of understanding God's word and using it for judgment (John 10:31 ff; Psalm 82:6). The incarnation of Christ in all its mystery is the incarnation into a form that had already been made in God's image. There is a continuity of categories from the God of the universe to the creatures made in His image, so that rational speech and communication are possible as the framework for the relationship between the creator and the creature. Both are personal; neither is an infinite everything of Kant's limited view of infinity.

Obedience in the Biblical sense, then, is the recognition of what is true objectively in the word of God and creation and one's willingness to be duty-bound to one's finding by acts of the will. Faith is believing God to tell the truth about all of life and salvation, rather than calling Him a liar. It is to trust Him on the basis of good and sufficient evidence.

Obedience and faith, then, require the use of the mind, that rational faculty that allows us to distinguish between what fits and what does not fit in rational continuity and proper grammatical language. It is that portion of our personhood that is appealed to when we ask, or when we listen, in order to discern between reasons given for or against a proposition. This applies not only to the area of linguistic propositions, but to any information that comes to us from whatever source.

The word of God, just like any other proposition, appeals to the mind first. As I attempt to understand what is being said and differentiate that

from what is not being said, I may feel the message to be appealing, artisti-
cally enticing, pictorially rich, but it is only true if it can be placed into
some rational relationship to all that I know and have to live with in the
external space/time world.

The fall, with its effects on the whole spectrum of human and created realities, has undoubtedly also affected the use of the mind. Yet, what I find
in Scripture is not a rational statement ("there has been a fall with effects")
about the basic impossibility of understanding rational statements. I cannot "understand" the Bible to make statements about the non-understand-
ability of the Bible!! God reasons his case, pleads with our whole person
including the mind, appeals to our senses, condemns our irrationality and
failure to differentiate between what is consistent and what is inconsistent.
We have no excuse, if we hold the truth in unrighteousness.

The Bible's basic confrontation is not against something that is rational
but against something that exits only in our minds. There are no other
Gods. The gods we are not to bow down in front of are imaginary gods.
They have no rational existence. If we reason ourselves to them, we do so
only by avoiding the created reality of the daily life in a definite universe
to get there. Professing themselves to be wise, people have become fools.

And yet, the onslaught of rationalistic thinking in a universe that has
been declared silent by the philosophers has led to the acceptance of mean-
inglessness by the secular thinker. His orientaiton is a basically meaningless nature, history, or the state. None of these phenomena gives a justification for intrinsic value judgements.

On the other hand, to place the foundation for values outside of rational
comprehensibility is to invite nonsense and foolishness into the discussion.
This has been done not only by those whose embrace of Eastern mysticism
leads to the denial of some aspect of reality (either material or personal),
but increasingly also by those whose basis is the evangelical affirmation of
salvation in Christ. There is no justification in this, for it requires a fundamental denial of truth.

Paul's statements in 1 Corinthians 1 about the word of the cross being
foolishness must be understood in its normal grammatical meaning. How
many there are who find encouragement in their own foolish misunderstanding of what Paul is saying! Not in the word of the cross, but in the
mind of the Greek is the foolishness. For Paul proclaims truth and wisdom
in Christ (1 Corinthians 2:6ff). Our minds must no longer be darkened.
The word of God is not sound by its basic irrationality, but because it is
fitting and true. The resurrection does not take place when I become a
Christian and the resurrected one dwells in me, but took place at a certain
time in a certain place. If it were not so, our faith would be without foun-

dation and vain, empty. There would be no hope and no salvation.

Many reasons for the hesitation among so many who called themselves Christians about the place of the mind could be cited. Here are some suggestions: the battle for the mind was fought in the last centuries, when scientific insight was used by some to suggest the irrationality of the Christian faith. Rather than dealing with the charges on their own credibility and merit, a *totaliter aliter* faith was suggested by those who advocated a reaction against rationalism by a refusal to think rationally. Their obedience to the Lord had nothing to do with a basic trust in the truthfulness of God's work and action in history. Their confidence was shaken by the suggestions of a merely materialistic world view. Rather than doing their thoughtful homework, they doubted God's intentions to communicate truth into our daily lives and the human condition. The result was an escape into an irrational faith, the proud submission of their reason, not to evidence, but to their new theological views which paralleled the rationalistic views in their common acceptance of non-reason to validate their faith.

This led to the result that could have been predicted to flow from the other element of Cartesian thinking. For, as for the human person, the only certainty exists concerning the thinking consciousness in the "cogito ergo sum." This is a pursuit of the selfish, subjective, emotive and merely psychologically helpful at the expense of the thoughtful and true, evident and rational. The result is a blind faith in faith. This expresses itself not only in the basic impossibility of talking to many such Christians about matters of the common life, but also in their unwillingness to listen to the non-Christian's insight and sometimes wisdom across all human life, on one hand, and to their proposing theological messages that have very little to do with the questions that human life always raises. Their position is one of theological security which cannot be challenged by real life. Their view of death, work and compassion, sexuality and civic responsibility is colored by their theologies; their theos is not the creator of this world and not the author of that complete message that the Bible suggests to be. Their safeguard is a series of quotations out of the context of the Bible or the reality to which the Bible speaks. They belie the Lord of creation and father of the Lord Jesus Christ in their misquotations. Where the rationalistic liberal decides to be God by prescribing what God can and cannot do, the Christian here described is one who does exactly the same. He also does not stand under the sane and healthy word of God, but has made the word subservient to himself.

The suspicion cannot easily be supressed that much of this kind of mindless Christianity serves those who find people gullible and willing to accept a mindless spiritual mush. And with the democratic climate having produced a soft culture, in which there are no further possibilities to distinguish between truth and falsehood, good and evil, the people, in fact, choose what they get, whether among the politicians or those that speak for some church.

The emphasis in the Epistles to stay away from mindless chatter and philosophy is also often used to justify an anti-philosophical stance. However, a more careful reading of these passages in Colossians 2 and 1 Timothy would show very quickly that Paul is not arguing against the need to think and analyze. He is doing the very thing himself in the thoughtful and logical presentation of the Gospel and the evidences for God's present work in people's lives. Rather he is speaking against a philosophy that is precisely separate from the needs that real existence poses, such as a gnostic removal, from the body or the mentality of theologization so common also in today's people. When confessionalism is a person's concern, rather than truth, when patterns and structures are of greater import than understanding, wisdom and humility, are we, then, still using our minds to discern what is of God?

Furthermore, the suggestion needs to be made that possibly the fear of a humble use of the critical faculties of the mind is due to the reaction in our culture against an over-mechanization of our lives. In reaction to the rule of the machine and the computer, to the pattern of legislation and governmental interference into ever larger areas of the private life, there is a tendency to turn to the inner world where alone privacy is allowed and remains uncontrolled. In a culture that has produced an overwhelming amount of publications that tell you all the standards for what is normal in every area of your life, people in confusion tend to turn inward into subjective mysticism. When we add to this the thrust that only society's view of a person and what can be counted on the balance sheet of one's life is of value for society, where is the unique personhood of the self, but in the "other" self of mindless feeling, experience, and escape?

This has a Christian counterpart in the emphasis on a dichotomy between the spirit and the body, the spirit and reason. Where the Spirit is the spirit of truth and discernment, such a dis-pair is not called for; but when, under the designation of the spirit, one's subjective feeling alone is addressed, much confusion and irresponsibility must be feared and can be felt. For then the control of the mind, of the outside world in its form, and of the word of God in its grammatical precision and meaningful content, are abandoned. It is here where so much damage is done to individual human beings, first, by presenting them with a hope that has no substance, a heightened experience that gets easily deflated when confronted with reality. And then the damage is there where a God is reflected who is not the God of creation nor of salvation, but the stirrings of human vanity in a lost generation. Paul's admonition to those who emphasizesd spirituality was that they should no longer run hither and yon in confusion but become more discerning in their outlook. For there is a Spirit who is the Spirit of God. But that Spirit leads to truth, is a real comforter and reminder of the things that same Spirit has spoken through the words of the prophets and apostles as they bore witness to the living Christ.

That same mindless faith is expressed when there is so little concern for the common things of life among many Christians. A general lack of compassion for the human condition in a fallen world, little joy in human existence here and now (which are the only days we have to so live) and minimal concern for quality life in the arts, human relationships and social concerns have become characteristic of many Christians. It stems from a mistaken view of faith and spirit. For Biblical faith and the Lord's Spirit call for an engagement in life, a battle against folly and ignorance and always for the human being against death in all its ugly faces. It is Biblical Christianity that establishes the basis for true human life in the common things of the day, dealing with real issues and offering realistic solutions in anticipation of the return of the King. Here is the foundation for true thinking, a challenge to cope with life's injustices and a command to state against the majority, the state, impersonal history or mere social condition that God is Lord, that His word is true, that Christ is really our Lord in this life and that the Spirit gives us power and imagination to demonstrate the validity and sanity of our hope of the resurrection. When Christ comes, He will bring in everlasting righteousness. We are to live and build in such a way that we anticipate His coming.

DISCUSSION QUESTIONS

1. Why isn't sincerity a proper ground for judging quality?

2. Define "scientific". What are the inherent biases in this term? What does it fundamentally assume about nature and the supernatural?

3. What dangers do scientific rationalism and evolutionary humanism pose to modern man?

4. Why is Biblical obedience never "blind"? Is there a distinction between blind obedience and obedience when the reasons for it are not known?

5. Why is the mind so important to determining truth? How does one go about determining what is true? Why can we say a person has *no excuse* if he doesn't hold to *the* truth?

6. Why is *truth* such a vital concern for us as Christians?

7. Why is any dichotomy between the Holy Spirit and reason basically false? Why does this provide a harmful foundation on which to build the Christian life?

8. Most people are unaware of the philosophical bases of their lives. Why should Christians accept the responsibility of examining and criticizing their own and opposing ideas and thoughts? How can we do this?

9. In making value judgments, we too often respond with a reflex rather than with thoughtful reflection from a truly Christian perspective. In what areas (purchasing, politics, church work, etc.) are you most vulnerable to slipping from a thoughtful Christian life?

"The Biblical perspective is not one of exploitation and submission to undercut the significance of the individual. To serve God or man is seen as an expression of personality."

Self and Serving

Udo Middelmann

There is something very puzzling about the concept of service in an age that has long ago freed itself from serfdom and has come to the enlightened view of the liberated person. To be subservient is to put oneself under service to someone else who has rights and privileges over the servant. That form of a relationship has the ring of something not only archaic, but also subhuman and exploitive in its center. We shrink away from it when it would touch us, either as a servant or as one holding servants, *i.e.*, having a say over people who serve us. We think in terms of the enlightened liberated person of our day. We feel a closer kinship to the free expression of personhood. We like the sound of the Bill of Rights. Our culture advocates the expansion of personal rights.

Our present reaction is not new. In Greece, any kind of restraint to a person as a *doulos* or to a thing or to work as a *diakonos* was seen as a restraint on the person, preventing an unfolding of the self in the deep folds of the personality. One shared in the complex workings of a harmonious universe, each in his or her own place and role. But to serve, *i.e.* to be constrained into someone else's desires, was seen as the place of the slave, the unfree.

Likewise, in Rome, the servant was the *servus*, an exploited person, even less than a person. It was the next better thing after death. The servus was tied into the ropes of someone else's commands and wishes; he took

orders, never gave them; he stood in the fetters of someone's freedom, doing his bidding. He paid with his back for the freedom of others.

The total dependence on the grace of the church during the Middle Ages
in terms of knowledge, salvation, work and protection, even government
and law, was a more recent form of the service given by man to another
authoritarian class. Man served the church, and from the church came all
direction, hope, and protection.

In our own day, service is seen by many as a further form of exploitation, making use of the ignorance, economic dependence, market conditions and need for sustenance of some by others. It is capital against labor,
mind agains body, privilege against necessity. Service is seen as a violation
of the equal rights of everyone, who, by his existence, has an equal right to
share in the larger pie that history, the state, the law, the economy provide.

The rediscovery of the Bible as the truth for all of life and knowledge at
the time of the Reformation renewed the emphasis on the centrality of each
person. Not the church, the group, the professional guild, the tribe or the
city, but each person was reinstated as an image bearer of God and with
personal responsibility. The artist became free and independent from the
churches' commissions, the bourgeois saw his incentive rewarded in becoming an entrepreneur, risks and rewards were seen in a definite relationship. Banking and lending became a possibility also for the common man.
This led to the commodity capitalism of northern Europe, founded on the
worth of the individual and his credit rating based on his ideas as a person
and also on the rationality of God's created universe.

This Reformation-Biblical basis came under fire during the Enlightenment and led to the abolition of the Biblical view of man, history, work
and the common battle against death in any form as a result of the basic
fallenness of God's creation. There is no basis for a view of man and life
outside of the realization of a moral universe before a personal God.

With the 17th century and the 19th, something which might be called
cultural mannerism occurred. The person was seen as central without the
Biblical foundation or controls. Under the pervasive influence of the
philosophy of Descartes, the benefits of a Biblical view of man gradually
became hollow and unable to support the pressure of selfish man in enjoy-
ment of the pleasures that Biblical man produces. With Descartes'
philosophy, the foundation of a unified rational human existence becomes
virtually impossible. Descartes' purely subjective projected consciousness
of the thinking *I* stands in no relationship to the mathematically precise
and impersonal universe. One one side, no relationship to basic rationality
and practical existence can be affirmed; on the other side there is no room
for the discovery of man as a person. Much of our thinking today stems

from Cartesian influence inside and outside of the Christian church. The only certainty is that area which can be expresssed in mathematics, growth charts, statistics, entitlements, projections; meaning and morality are sought only in the areas of subjective faith, feeling, experience and personal relationships. When truth is only what can be measured, weighed and counted or only what can be felt and experienced without rationality, we have moved into a Cartesian world view.

The other influence that affects us is the general assumption that we live in a universe in which all discussion about values and meaning must be met with silence, since nature — the natural phenomena — is neutral and amoral. There can be no talk about compassion, mercy, and submission; there can be no more trust in the moral obedience of man to the word of God, since finite nature, in Kant's view, is incapable of being the carrier of God's word. The Bible, then, is not the word of God, but only meaningful to those who have a disposition to seeing in it God's word. This has nothing to do with Christianity, of course. Rather it shares in the conviction of a basic silence of the universe when it comes to moral obligations, personal commitment and values. A fundamental irrationality between the mathematically precise universe and any discussion about values is introduced, supported by secular and Christian writers: e.g. Kirkegaard's study of Abraham's sacrifice.

Where all this enters into the discussion about service and our responsibility to man and history, as well as to God, is at the point where we must realize that outside the thorough Biblical view there is no foundation for even the concept of service. It is seen as a subjective and emotional need, an idealism on the level of an aberration or a disease.

For a long time already the values and the perspective of the Biblical world view have been abandoned. The new perspective is quantitative, numerical, and objective, scientific. The new values are an attempt to mathematically redefine boundaries, entitlements and shares in the cake of society and economic possibilities. The model is the machine, not God; not responsibility, but integration of the parts as necessary for the whole unit is central; thrift, hard work, reward and sensibility are replaced by an industrialization of waste, participation and remuneration, as well as a new sensuality of possessing things. Man training himself to become industrious has been replaced by the man trained for industry. Utilitarianism, production cycles, raises in consumption, efficiency and cost benefit ratios are devoid of the life of the human spirit. The calling of a person becomes his job; obedience to God and man in nature is replaced by obedience to market conditions. Quality is increasingly repalaced by quantity; quality of life describes the quantity of things and privileges. The *oikonomos*, the householder who is responsible for human existence, lends his designation to "economics"; the human society of chosen and created relationships out of the common battle for humane existence to deal with all forms of human needs is turned into the goals of socialism, an artificial and fictional composite of atomistic and individualistic people whose relationships to each other are not on the basis of human compassion and responsibilities, but legal and mathematical in the forms of obligations and taxes. Laws no longer stand to protect and describe human relationships across all of life, but are made to create relationships between man and the collective.

It is easy to recognize the difficulties any emphasis on service would have to be accepted in such a cultural, philosophical and psychological climate. Our present moment of history presents us more or less openly and without subtlety a perspective that proposes the opposite to each of us. A still expanding economy, the overwhelming abundance of things, the facilities to travel physically and mentally, the books that offer us forever new experiences that we "naturally" have a right to have, that we deserve, make it difficult to consider service as anything more involved than the appeasement of a slight feeling of guilt quickly turned into self-praise. We see ourselves even entitled to that!

The center of the crisis and the reason our humanistic culture has produced it does not lie in the absence of resources, manpower or jobs that remain to be done; the dilemma is not with the inadequacy of service institutions or with ignorance of the problem. Rather, there has been produced a deeply felt absence of meaning to sustain human existence, and to serve man in his battle against nature, mere impassionate history and the horror of death. It is a crisis that cuts across the political will, the motivations of people. It instills a sense of cynicism and lets you grab for your life ring first and undercuts the civic will. *Carpe diem*, let the state provide!

The Biblical perspective is not one of exploitation and submission to undercut the significance of the individual. To serve God or man is seen as an expression of personality. It is expressive of will and imagination in an *unfinished* situation. Adam was to dress the garden and enjoy Eve, leave father and mother to cleave to her in commitment to their unique relationship, in which the two would become one and exhibit the image of God in their unity and diversity. Even after the fall, work was to continue in spite of the sweat of the brow required in a now-fallen world. But even between people, the servant was not to be exploited, underpaid or ill-treated, whether Jew or Gentile. The common produce would be shared.

In this respect the various illustrations from the New Testament throw light on the Biblical attitude. Luke 12:35-46 shows two wrong attitudes of the servant, while the lord tarries. He is not to live without responsibility out of his might and power, beating and using others in harshness and arbitrariness. Nor is he to enrich himself at the expense of others. They are like shepherds that do not care for the sheep, but only for themselves, as in Ezekiel 34. In Luke 17:7-10 the emphasis is on the need to see service not as a matter of special work, proud submission, but of life and truth in the most normal of human existences. In Luke 22:24-26 the chief in the kingdom of God is the one who fits into a hierarchy of humility. Paul adds in Galatians 5:12 that through love we ought to serve one another.

When we understand the reduction of modern life to either the heightened quest for selfish fulfillment with talks about rights, natural needs and entitlements on one hand and, on the other, the anchoring of values only in the mathematical redistribution of a certain mathematical unit into equal parts among the claimants, we must take a stand for the sake of those things that are forgotten in today's outlook. For with their disappearance, our culture, with its foundation in the Biblical view of man and life and social relationships and a judgment by history and God, will also disappear in an enormous outbursts of hedonistic lifestyles or massive imposition of legalized theft and rape by the state.

When we consider service, then, not as a job, but as a lifestyle in affirmation of the human being's personality and thus response-ability and of the Biblical framework of a fallen world that groans until the coming of Christ, service represents our understanding of the human condition and a willingness to war against it. When we are called to serve the Lord, it is not due to His having a need, but it expresses our willingness to battle side by side with Him for a removal of the practical and intellectual consequences of the fall. To be a servant is to express solidarity with the human condition; it is a matter of respect and courtesy. It expresses a desired relationship, as Mary was the handmaid of the Lord. It expresses a deep appreciation of man and a willingness to take a place in the battle to overcome that need.

A need can be in different areas. There is the need for life and its sustenance, but also the need for space, time and human communication. There is the need to be encouraged to keep on, to be taught to overcome ignorance or poor coordination. To serve is to choose to do a job well, to protect the weaker person, the one in need; it is to charge a fair price, to not stretch the truth. It is to be a critical challenge in a context of respect for the artist. It is to care for the body and soul as a medical person; it is the willingness to be made insecure by someone's questions and doubt. To serve is to create that protective umbrella that allows someone else to stand dry from the attacks of a hostile world after the fall.

To serve is to be a human being as God has made us, in the relationships

He intended us to have. It is to be a parent for a child, a lover to a man or woman, an artist to work against the bleakness of mere indifference, an employer for the needs of the employed, a caring person for the neighbor in need, a family for the single person, a person in politics for the maintenance of order and compassion.

Service is also an expression of outrage at the injustice and unfairness of a fallen world, in which often without fault of the people concerned, inequalities exist and pain, depression and real problems are placed on each of us by the choices of others. Service here is the statement that we care and consider ourselves first of all in solidarity with man against the unfairness of an impersonal and uncaring universe, history, state. It is here where humanness and willingness to give stand in opposition to resignation, indifference and irresponsibility. As we all have more and less than we deserve on the basis of our choice, we are to serve each other against all that is arbitrary, accidental, historically conditioned. To serve is to make a judgment for man against a common enemy, which is nature. It is here where we find the challenge extended from the God of the Bible who was willing to serve us in His Son for us a hope of life through His own willingness to do the will of the father by making propitiation for our sins and going on to that time when he shall return to remove all the abnormality of a broken world, all injustice, sickness, all groaning of the whole creation. (Romans 8) Service is, then, the recognition of the need that we all face to stand up to the impersonal nature, history and statistics and to speak in our lives for morality, justice and beauty in correspondence to the God of creation and redemption.

DISCUSSION QUESTIONS

1. How were the Greek words "doulos" (servant) and "diakonos" (deacon) changed when these words became part of the New Testament revelation of a new lifestyle?

2. Was man created to serve? Why do you think people respond with repugnance at the notion of service?

3. How did church officials during the Middle Ages resemble authoritarian rulers? How did the reformation recover the meaning of the person?

4. What view of man was adopted by those who developed "cultural mannerism"?

5. Under modern forms of thought, nature is said to be silent. In what sense does the Christian form of thought "hear" the voice of nature?

6. How does the idea of service as a lifestyle contribute to our performance at our job or activities?

7. Most people passively accept the culture they are born into. Only a few ever attempt to change it. How does "service as lifestyle" help formulate an effective strategy for significant social change?

8. How important are motives to sacrifice? How important are sacrifice and service to the gospel? Can there be any true service without regeneration through the gospel?

9. Why is service to be a normal aspect of the Christian life and not a matter of special work? Why is humility necessary to serve and live a life pleasing to God?

10. Discuss some practical aspects of service and things you can begin doing in your efforts to serve.

Wim Rietkerk

Wim Rietkerk was born in Holland the 11th of 12 children in a Presbyterian family. He grew up in a seaside village in German-occupied Holland at the beginning of World War II. During early adolescence he became a believer although his realization of the depth and height of Christian discipleship came later through his contact with Dr. Schaeffer and the Swiss L'Abri.

Wim studied at a Theological Seminary at Kampen and earned a doctorate from Leydon University, specializing in Philosophy of Religion. He worked closely with Free University (Amsterdam) art professor Dr. Hans Rookmaaker, and then helped found the Dutch L'Abri. He lectures at L'Abri conferences throughout Europe, the States, Canada, and Australia. Wim currently pastors a church nearby the Dutch L'Abri. He and his wife, Greta, have three children.

The Reality of God, Introduction

Wim Rietkerk

In the 20th century the battle is not so much on the level of the attributes of
God and of who God is. We live in an age in which His reality is ques-
tioned. In the first half of this century this has been done by two influential
thinkers: Freud and Lenin. Freud said: ". . . God is a projection" and Lenin:
". . . Christianity is an ideology."

There are two scriptures in the Gospel of John that I would like to start
with. You could say they are two contradictory scriptures. One is John
8:31,32, where Jesus is saying: "If you continue in my word, you are truly
my disciples, and you will know the truth, and the truth will make you
free. (RSV) In contrast to that is a verse from Chapter 18 where Jesus is
standing before Pilate and saying: "I have come to bear witness to the
truth," and then Pilate, in verse 38, shrugs his shoulders and says: "What is
truth?" Jesus, on one side, is saying, "If you continue in my word . . . you
will know the truth, and the truth will make you free." On the other side is
Pontius Pilate saying: "What is truth?"

I think these two verses are a good introduction to make clear what I
want to talk about because Pontius Pilate stands as a symbol, you could
say, for all those men who, when they hear someone talking about the
truth say: "But what is truth?" By contrast, we read again and again in the
words of Jesus Christ, that it is only the truth that can make you free.

When I think about the people I talk to in Europe, I think you could say that the mentality of Pontius Pilate is very powerful there. If you look beyond the beautiful surface of the mask, you find beneath it the deep skepticism of the European mind. It is the old skepticism of Pontius Pilate. I think if we understand the gospel, we should take the same stand today as Jesus took against this mentality of Pontius Pilate. He always emphasized that it is only the truth that can make you free.

These questions are, as far as I can see, the ones that mainly occupy the minds of modern men when you ask them why they rejected Christianity.

Recently, there was a poll in Holland to establish how many people believed in a personal God, not just in God as a higher power. They asked a very sharp question: "Do you believe in the existence of a personal God?" Only thirty-four percent of the Dutch people answered "Yes." In 1966, there was a poll on this same question and forty-eight percent of the Dutch population answered "Yes." In a period of fourteen years, you could say that Biblical Christianity, which always centers around the question of whether or not there is a personal God, lost fourteen percent of the Dutch population. Why have fourteen percent of the Dutch population in a period of fourteen years lost their faith in a personal God?

If I were to ask them the question: "Why do you not believe in Christianity?" then three subjects would come back again and again. Therefore, I want to talk about these three questions. Those under the influence of Marxism would answer: "Christianity is an ideology," and those under the influence of psychology — such as Freud — would answer: "But God is a projection." Those who imbibe the religious mood of today would say: "But aren't all religions the same?" As I meet these questions again and again, I have thought about them, and I hope I can help you to answer them.

"Without God we are left with a world
that is a closed system of cause and effect — just
protons and neutrons circling around one another
without any meaning . . ."

The Reality of God,
Part I: Is God
A Projection?
Wim Rietkerk

In *The Sunburnt Soul* I read:

> In the 25 years from 1956 to 1981 there has been a slow but constant decline in the num-
> ber of people in Australia who say they believe in God. In the early 1950's nearly all
> Australians said they believed in God, 95 percent. It was an assumed part of life in Aus-
> tralia. But the latest estimate of how many people believed in God was in 1980, 15 years
> later and that was 78 percent. We lost almost one of five Australians in not yet one gen-
> eration.[1]

This quotation provides the information I need, because exactly the same
thing happened in Holland.

What was the main reason? If you were to ask a non-Christian here in
this country for his main argument against the Christian faith in God, I
think he would say the same thing that I hear over and over again in Holland. When you question him, he will answer with the doubtful question
"Isn't it all self-imagination?" — and that is the idea of projection. As a
result of this, I have studied that question and I have made it my title: "Is
God a Projection?"

Years ago I gave a lecture on this question. Now I would like to repeat
the first half of it, using some different arguments, and then move on to the
deeper problem, which is the question: "How do we know we know?" Dr.
Schaeffer wrote in the book *He is There and He is not Silent*: "Our real

problem is not psychological. It is an epistemological problem."[2]

Now you may feel puzzled by this terminology, but it is not as difficult as it first looks. The word simply means that the statement "God is a projection" leads us back, not to the analysis of psychological feelings, but to the questions, "How do we know that something is true?" and "How do we know the truth?"

Applying this to God, how do we know that we know Him? They call that epistemology. *Episteme = knowledge* in Greek; *logic* means the thoughtful reflection on our knowledge. That is what I want to do here. I want to reflect thoughtfully on my own knowledge, and I hope that it will help you in your understanding.

But let me start first by explaining the problem — maybe you have not understood fully what I want to talk about. To make the problem clearer I will use a well known parable of John Wisdom, the parable of two explorers:

Once upon a time there were two explorers making their way through a dense jungle when, to their surprise, they came to a clearing where there was a beautiful garden with grass and all types of flowers. One explorer said: "Of course, this must be the work of a gardener." But the other explorer exclaimed: "That's impossible, there must be some other reason, a gardener could never have been here!" (Because it was in the midst of the jungle) The first explorer kept to his explanation: "There's no other explanation, this must be the work of a gardener."

So they made a tent and waited for the gardener to come, so that they could see this gardener. They waited, but the gardener did not come. "All right," said the first explorer, "Maybe he will come in the night or in a hidden way. Let's put up a fence and bloodhounds around it, then the gardener will be caught."

They waited and waited, night after night, and nothing happened. The skeptical explorer concluded: "There is no gardener." The other explorer maintained his belief in a gardener: "He is invisible, insensitive to dogs and fences, doesn't make any noise, and comes secretly to take care of the garden he loves." Then the skeptic at the point of despair says: "What's left of your original claim? What's the difference between what you call an invisible gardener and an imaginery gardener?"[3]

There you have the problem verbalized. That's what I want to talk about. That is the doubting question that suddenly hurts and touches the heart of many people today. Suddenly the thought arises; even though we are raised in a protected Christian family, doubts are kindled in our hearts. Is our Christian faith a product of our self-imagination?

In order to understand this question, we should take a moment to consider historically its origin.

It is always helpful when you are faced with a problem to try to find the root of it. Where did it come from? Where did it start? When did people first start to think like this? Now the first man who expressed this doubt was a German thinker in the last century, Feuerbach. As I said earlier, his name means "fire creek." Marx said that you can never really be a 20th century man if you do not go through this "fire creek." This man Feuerbach came after Kant and Hegel — both thinkers who led modern man beneath the line of despair. Feuerbach was their disciple and drew some conclusions from their thoughts in relationship to Christianity. He did this in a book called *The Essence of Christianity*. In this book he said:

> You start from man and his autonomous reason. If you want to understand why he believes in God, you should first investigate his unconscious motivation for his belief in God.[4]

What do you discover? One overwhelming fact! Christians believe in God because they are poor in themselves. They are alienated from their real selves, and therefore they project the ideal image that they have of themselves into an existing God:

> Every person has an ideal of himself, but because he is unable to come into union with that ideal image, he projects it outside himself into an eternal being, which he calls God![5]

And again:

> Man strives after happiness and harmony. He finds in himself only weakness, so he projects an all powerful God. He looks to himself and finds mortality, and, because he finds a desire for immortality, he projects an immortal life in heaven. He feels alone and small, so there arises the desire for a godly father. He feels unloving and searches in heaven for a perfect love. Man gives a character of reality to his own deepest wishes. What a man fails to be himself: perfect love, immortal, almighty, righteous and holy he expects from his God.[6]

Another quotation:

> The absolute personality is God as a projection of man's own being.[7]

The most cynical remark that I found in his book is "The poor man has a rich God." That is, I think, the most profound and cynical statement about faith in God that I have ever read. The poor man has a rich God — here we find the sharpest expression of the idea of projection. We understand the word *projection* better than Feuerbach did because we have a machine like it — a projector — and now everyone knows what projecting means. You put a slide in the projector, and the picture is projected onto the wall. Even a child knows that the real thing is not on the wall, the real thing is in the machine. This is exactly what Feuerbach wanted to say. Theology is, in effect, anthropology. It teaches us nothing about a God who is not there and everything about realities in the mind of man. He ends this whole life with anthropology and hedonism. "Man is what he eats, that is the definition of man," he said. "My first thought was God, my second thought was reason, my third and final thought was man." He even went so far as to say: "There is one God for man and that is man himself." Feuerbach had written on his grave, "Man is a God for man."[8]

A second man I want to mention in this regard is Freud. Sigmund Freud tried to give scientific proof for the criticism that Feuerbach verbalized philosophically. Freud introduced the whole idea of the subconsciousness of man. He observed that people project images, thoughts and fears that they themselves suppress deep in their subconscious.[9] When you suppress something in your subconscious, it suddenly pops out, and you project it on your relationships. For instance, you could meet someone who has a suppressed self-hatred; he's hardly aware of the fact, but when you get to know him better, you realize that he has a suppressed hatred against himself. Because he suppresses this threatening negative feeling toward himself, he starts to think that all people hate him. Do they really hate him? No, but he projects his own self-hatred on the people around him, and he thinks that they hate him too.

We have a proverb in Holland that runs as follows: In the same way his host is, he trusts his guests. We use it when someone is oversuspicious about the honesty of his fellowman. In this case we say: "Maybe you are dishonest yourself, and you won't face it, you suppress it, and now you are projecting your own dishonesty on your fellowman." Like the host is himself, in the same way he trusts his guests. An example of projection.

Up to this point, we can agree with Freud. However, he extended this thought and applied it to all religions. He said: "Everywhere, when man is religious, he is so because he suppresses his deep need for protection, his desire for absolute authority, even his feeling of guilt towards this absolute authority." All these suppressed feelings lead to that activity in the human mind which Freud called projection. Man is born with an earthly father, but as he grows up, he discovers that his earthly father, whom he first thought to be eternal, almighty and infinite, in fact is mortal, weak and finite. Once he has made that discovery, he starts to project his suppressed needs for an infinite father on the screen of heaven in the existence of a personal god.

I believe that this way of thinking has become powerful today. Even when we keep our doors closed, it penetrates our homes — like an old-fashioned London fog. Therefore we should be forewarned and armed to face this question. Even though it may hurt you to hear me talking about it, I would say go through it because you need to be warned, and you need to be ready.

This leads me to the next question: How do we answer this doubting question on whether or not God is real? First, let's look it straight in the eyes. If we do not do that, it keeps nagging at our insides. I remain threatened by the thought that this is so. Like a black cat that jumps on my back, I do not have it in front of me but I can always be threatened from behind. This is a general attitude in which we at L'Abri train ourselves. If people come with doubting questions, we have learned to put ourselves in their shoes. That is the first step. You would say it is rather dangerous. Yes, but isn't that exactly what Paul has taught us in 1 Corinthians 9:19? Paul is saying:

> To the Jews I became as a Jew . . . to those under the law I became as one under the law — though not being myself under the law — that I might win those under the law. To those outside the law . . . (RSV)

Do you see what he is saying to those outside the law? "I became as one outside the law that I might win those outside the law. I became as one outside the law."

In the same way, for one moment we will be an atheist with the atheist in order that we may win him — that is what Paul is saying. Where do we end? Suppose for a moment that the question has a projection and should be answered with a "yes." When we think through the question and look it straight in the eye we should then come at least to the first conclusion — that we are left behind in a world of matter and chance, without any revelation! But how do you know what a world without revelation looks like? Go to the Museum and look at the paintings of Francis Bacon. Dr. Hans Rookmaaker used one on the cover of his book on modern art — man caught in a closed system of cause and effect. He always paints people in a glass box — this man was in a glass box with his hair standing on end, shouting with no one to hear him.[10]

What the modern painters like Bacon have made visible, C. S. Lewis, the well-known novelist, has verbalized in one of his children's books *The Silver Chair*. Scrubb and Jill, the main characters in his book, have received a very difficult command from Aslan, the Lion. They must go into a cave in the middle of the woods, and as they descend into this cave they will discover that there is another world beneath this real one. But it is an enchanted world. There is no life. Everyone and everything is petrified under the spell of the witch. The children's task and duty is to search for the silver chair. As soon as the prince takes a seat in that silver chair the enchanted world will awake and become alive. But — and this is my point — as they move on in this world and meet the witch, they begin to become enchanted themselves. Then the nagging doubt starts to arise — isn't this the real world and wasn't Narnia a dream? When the witch talks with them she says: "Please describe to me the sun and Aslan and the trees and the flowers." As they try, they fail and feel silly. They start to doubt themselves and finally say: "It cannot be true; it was all a dream." In the end they start to believe that everything — the sun, Aslan, the trees — were self-imagination. Then the character Puddleglum stamps his feet in the fire and hurts them. At once he awakens. Listen to what he says:

> "One word, Madam," he said, coming back from the fire; limping, because of the pain. "One word. All you've been saying is quite right, I shouldn't wonder. I'm a chap who always likes to know the worst and then put the best face I can on it. So I won't deny anything of what you said. But there's one thing more to be said, even so. Suppose we have only dreamed, or made up, all those things — trees and grass and sun and moon and stars and Aslan himself. Suppose we have. Then all I can say is that, in that case, the made-up things seem a good deal more important than the real ones. Suppose this black pit of a kingdom of yours is the only world. Well, it strikes me as a pretty poor one. And that's a funny thing, when you come to think of it. We're just babies making up a game, if you're right. But four babies playing a game can make a play-world which licks your real world hollow. That's why I'm going to stand by the play-world. I'm on Aslan's side even if there isn't any Aslan to lead it. I'm going to live as like a Narnian as I can even if there isn't any Narnia. Thanking you kindly for our supper, if these two gentlemen and the lady are ready, we are leaving your court at once and setting out in the dark to spend our lives looking for Overland. Not that our lives will be very long, I should think; but that's a small loss if the world's as dull a place as you say.¹¹

I do not think that Lewis ever meant this as an argument against projection. He meant it to help people, to give them a kind of a shock. He used it only to shock all those people who say: "We do not believe in God. It is all a projection," and who continue to live as if nothing has happened. To them, this story has the same function as most of the paintings in a modern art museum. It shows us that there is no alternative without God. Without God we are left with a world that is a closed system of cause and effect — just protons and neutrons circling around one another without any meaning — "This black pit of yours," as Puddleglum says.

Now we are moving to the real argument — What do we say about the theory that God is a projection of the human mind? We will judge its truthfulness in three steps. First, I will give a psychological argument against it; second, a philosophical argument against it; and third, a Biblical argument against it. It is not because the last one is less important, but I think we should first argue with someone who is saying this with intrinsic arguments, with arguments he can understand, because he is a man, and I am a man.

Psychological Argument

Now let me say that there is an element of truth in this Freudian theory. His example of the projection of self-hatred on my fellowman is an example that speaks to me and provides a convincing argument. It is important to study this mechanism of projection. If God is really a person, why shouldn't we pollute our relationship with our fellowman through what he calls projection? I do not call it projection. I think it is better to call it wrong observation, exaggerated observation, associative observation — but that doesn't really matter. We should all understand that there is some truth in what he says about our relationship with God. We can pollute that relationship by what Freud calls "projection." The real question is: Is faith in God itself a projection? What is my argument against this? I would say that the argument has two sides, not just one. His whole argument depends completely on the presupposition that man has a hidden suppressed need to affirm the existence of God. That was Freud's observation. However, my observation is different. I meet more and more people who have a hidden or suppressed need to deny the existence of God.

I would dare to defend the statement that in our society today there are more people with a need to deny God than there are with a need to affirm God. This makes Freud's whole argument like a boomerang — you throw it at someone else's head, but it comes back at your own head.

Why didn't Freud come to the same conclusion as anyone else would? You do meet people who have a suppressed need to affirm God, but you meet just as many people who have a suppressed need to deny God. Why didn't he make that last observaton? Could it be that he suppressed his own need to deny God, and, therefore, he created this whole theory of projection?

Now I have only put this as a question. I don't really want to argue on the level of having, or not having, a need for God. I do not want to argue on the level of what I consciously or unconsciously suppress or do not suppress or feel inside of me. This is what Schaeffer calls the psychological level. We do not want to talk on the psychological level of truth. Therefore, I will merely put it as a question, because I do not want to use it as an argument against Freud. I only dare to question his whole mentality. Why do I not use it as an argument? I think we are taking the wrong approach with our fellowman when we do not listen to *what* he is saying, but only observe *how* or *why* he is saying something. I think it is important to listen more sharply. You can never use the *why* or the *how* as an argument to deny the worth of what someone is saying. It is even impossible to argue from a suppressed need or an unconscious need and come to the conclusion that if you suppress a need for something, the object you need cannot exist because it is a projection. I will explain why this is a wrong form of reasoning with the following example:

Just imagine that I get homesick next week. It looks silly to be depressed after having been away from my wife and children for only one week, so I suppress my homesickness. The symptoms of my illness increase and I decide to go to a psychiatrist. Now this psychiatrist happens to be a Freudian. Immediately, of course, he helps me to discover my suppressed longing for my wife and children. Wouldn't it be amazing if he told me at the same time to stop projecting, because there is no one there in Holland? This is literally what Feuerbach said: "Man gives a character of reality to his deepest wishes. It is an illusion to think that the object of his speculation is not his own self but another, a godly self."[12] Do you see what he did? I hope that I have made it sufficiently clear with the example of my homesickness. This sort of reasoning leads to absurdity.

You cannot conclude from any need — in whatever form the need exists — that it denies the existence of God. The *how* and *why* of what we believe cannot be used as an argument against *what* we believe. That is an argument on the psychological level, and I observe the same kind of problem with Freud.

Philosophical Argument

Now the second argument is the philosophical argument — that is, there is always a hidden philosophy behind this psychological criticism of religion. That hidden philosophy consists of unproven prejudices, and the unproven prejudice is the reality that God doesn't exist. It, therefore, consists of two layers of realities and is divided into two aspects. There is an objective outer world where everything works after the law of cause and effect — the closed system of cause and effect, and then there is the subjective inner world — man in his subjectivity. Man in his subjectivity, must give meaning to the meaningless objective outer world. this way of thinking has deeply penetrated the mind of Western man since Descartes. Since Descartes and after the Enlightenment, Western man in our society lives in that dichotomy — this is how Schaeffer expresses it: the dichotomy of upper story and lower story, the one story being the physical world, the mechanical world which functions according to the law of cause and effect, but the other higher story the one where we have to give subjective meaning to the outer world. Into this philosophical world view fits the whole theory of projection, but it is based on unproven prejudices. I don't want to go into this now because you could find it expressed in more detail in the book *The God Who Is There*, by Dr. Schaeffer.[13]

Biblical Argument

Now I move onto the third counter argument — the Biblical one. What do we discover in the Bible when we study the Word of God? Regarding this whole idea of projection, we find two amazing things:

a. The Christian faith is never based on emotional feelings or suppressed desires. To the contrary, the Christian faith is based on historic facts, in which God reveals himself to us. I can prove that to you from the whole Bible.

b. And the second fact that we can discover in the Bible is that the Bible itself hates nothing so much as when man creates, projects himself an image of God on the screen of heaven.

I want to explain both statements in more detail. I will explain the second one first. In the Bible you will discover that the second commandment is directed against any form of projection. I believe that the second commandment is the best word from the Old Testament against the whole theory of projection: "Thou shalt not make unto thee any graven image." In Deuteronomy 4:15 Moses said:

> Take heed to yourselves . . . you saw no form on the day that the Lord spoke to you at Horeb out of the midst of the fire . . . beware lest you act corruptly by making a graven image for yourselves. (RSV)

Do you see what the Lord is saying? Faith should not be based on what they themselves felt to be true about God but on the fact of God's self-revelation in Horeb. They were forbidden to do what is presupposed in the theory of projection, and that is to take anything out of the creation and make it into their God.

In Psalm 50 this is applied to mental images. In Psalm 50 God rebukes Israel for making a mental image of God which springs forth from their own needs instead of truly relying on God's revelation. In this Psalm the nation of Israel has an image of God. To them He is some kind of merchant. We give Him something, and then He gives us something back. So we can make a deal. There is nothing that the Lord hates as much as this. The Lord said: "You imagined." (In this context it is self imagination.) "You imagined that I was one like yourselves. But now I rebuke you and lay the charge before you!" This ends the first Biblical argument.

Now I want to turn to the New Testament. I could quote many passages from the New Testament to illustrate clearly that the Christian faith is not based on emotion, but on that which we have seen and which we have heard — this is what we proclaim to you. I now quote from the first letter of John. Right in the beginning of his first letter, John says several times:

> that which was from the beginning, which we have heard, which we have seen with our eyes, which we have looked upon and touched with our hands, concerning the word of life (RSV)

He then repeats it:

> that which we have seen and heard we proclaim to you, so that you may have fellowship with us

We also find the same thing in the letter of Peter, especially 2 Peter 1:

> For we did not follow clearly devised myths (We could say that we did not follow projections of the human mind) when we made known to you the power and the coming of our Lord Jesus Christ, but we are eye-witnesses of his majesty. (RSV)

Again, he emphasizes the fact that they were eye witnesses.

Now when I consider Luke and the way he wrote his Gospel, particularly Chapter 24, I think that he must have wrestled with some of the doubts that I have been speaking about. Maybe he did, because he wrote to a Greek man, Theophilus. It is the only Gospel that is clearly written to a non-Christian — for the Greek world. Now when you read Luke 24, it is amazing that Luke emphasizes that when Jesus was risen from the dead, none of the disciples, or the two men heading for Emmaus, or Peter, said, when they heard this good news for the first time, "Oh, that was exactly what I wanted to hear, so let me believe it." The opposite happened. When the women came from the grave and spread the good news that the Lord had risen, they said that they did not believe — it seemed to them an idle tale. I think they must have thought that these women were projecting. Early in the morning they went to the grave. Of course, they had a suppressed desire to see Jesus, and when they saw the open grave, they thought they were hallucinating. They were so convinced, that they really believed it. The only thing to finally convince them was that they really saw Him. Even when they saw Him, they still thought it was a ghost. Then He said: "You have something to eat." They gave Him something to eat — fish and bread — and He ate before their eyes. Then their eyes were opened.

It is very clear in Luke 24, both for the disciples individually and as a group, that they were convinced by the presence of Jesus among them. The historic fact of the resurrection was so important for the disciples. To quote another man, Paul, who based his whole gospel on the message of the eye witnesses, in 1 Corinthians 15, says that the whole message of the resurrection is based on that which the disciples heard and saw — at one time more than 500 at the same time — and then he adds, "many of whom are still alive." A strange addition says: If you want to verify it, go to them. The whole New Testament is making clear that the Christian faith is based on what was proclaimed to be true and what the eye witnesses have seen and heard and what they have communicated to us — not a suppressed need.

These are my three basic arguments against the theory of projection. You will remember the psychological one, and the one on the hidden presuppositions — the philosophical one, and then the third one — the two Biblical arguments.

I want to come now at the end to the more positive exposition on what is now a sound epistemology. How do I know the Bible is really true and God is really there? Now I do not want to talk about this academically, but personally. How would you answer the question: "How do I know that the Bible is true and that God is really there?" Now if someone asked me this question, I would answer with another question: "Did you ever read the Bible?"

It may sound strange, but a lot of people want absolute proof that the Bible is true before they are willing to read it. Now that is an impossible attitude because:

a. The Bible carries its evidence of truth in itself. It is only in reading the Word of God for ourselves or by listening to it that we can hear the voice of God.

It is not that we as men with our autonomous reason set up a standard of who God is and what He should be, and then start to measure Him according to our standard. I could use marriage to explain it. When you think about getting married, you don't first set up a standard and verbalize ten conditions — ten characteristics of the woman you want to marry. You meet one another and you think — one, two, three, four, et cetera. Finally, you have found the one who fits all the criteria and you accept her. That's not really how it works. But how does it work? It's very simple. As we communicate with somebody, we fall in love. That is the whole secret. The same thing is true of our relationship with God.

To sum up this point: As we read the Scriptures, we fall in love. As we read the scriptures, God speaks to us, and so the Bible carries its evidence in itself. Is that a matter of pure feeling which my words "falling in love" might suggest? Is it a matter of pure feeling and experience? No, it is also a matter of reason. A good marriage should be, too!

When Paul went to Berea, Acts 17:20, we read that he preached the gospel by actually reading the Scriptures with them, but then a remarkable thing is added: "They received the word with all eagerness, examining the Scriptures daily to see if these things were so."

This is the first cornerstone in coming to a knowledge of God: the consistency of the Biblical teaching: solid enough to be examined — not irrational — a system of teaching that has a remarkable unity and coherence, which is the more remarkable because it is a book written over a period of at least 1400 years. And as we read the scriptures — reasonably, emotionally, honestly — the Lord will speak to us. We will get to know Him.

b. Not only do we listen to the Bible and examine its integrity, we also apply the truth of it to the reality which is there. Is it true to what is really there — the universe, our own human existence, the history of man? In Romans 1-3, Paul teaches us how to do that. But this is a main point: we may look for the evidence of the truth of the Scriptures in the world outside us as to whether it is true to what is there.

c. Finally, I come to the question: Having done both of these, how do I know that I know God? Someone asked me that, and I have thought about it for a long time. How do I come to the assurance that it is really God who is speaking to me? The consistency of the Bible is very important. Acts 17:12 is very important. The evidence in reality in Romans 1-3 should be very clear to me. What is my final assurance that I really know God?

I would like to know what you would answer if someone were to ask you. My answer would be:

> I know that I know God *not* because I have built up with my human reason a certain standard of what God should be (when I read the Bible and see that it fits). This is not the way I know God. I would say that it is just the opposite way around. Once I read the Scriptures or listen to the word of God, I hear someone speaking to me, who knows me by name and knows who I am. To put it in Paul's words: "It is the fact that I am known that gives the assurance that it is God speaking to me."

1 Corinthians 8:1-3 is concerned with the problem of knowledge. Paul speaks against all the people that say "we have knowledge." It is in a situation where there were conflicts about food — whether or not you should eat food which had been offered to idols.

> We know that "all of us possess knowledge." "Knowledge" puffs us up, but love builds up. If anyone imagines that he knows something, he does not yet know as he ought to know. (RSV)

This knowledge we build up with our own human reason. If one loves God, one is known by Him. This last statement is a very short summary, but we would need to say more. I will explain it in my own words. At the time Paul was speaking to the Corinthian Christians. Many of them were saying "We know God."

So Paul says that, when we say we know God, we have not yet known Him as we should know, because true knowledge of God is a love reaction to the fact that we are known by Him. "Now that you know God," Paul is saying in another place (Galatians 4:9), then he corrects himself, "or rather that you are known by God, how can you turn back to the idols?" Here, again, we see that Paul corrects himself and says: "True knowledge of God is not proud knowledge that we have built up whatever basis we have. It is rather the opposite — it is God knowing us." This is when God's revelation is self-evident. He who has come to know God in Christ — and Him crucified — he truly knows God, because he feels fully understood, and he feels fully unmasked. He knows himself to be judged and forgiven and sanctified and even glorified through Christ by the God of the Universe.

Here, alone, is the final answer to all epistemology — the assurance of God's loving knowledge in the person and the work of Jesus Christ. In conclusion, we can say: only a sound Bible epistemology can help us today to face the threatening questions of Freud and Feuerbach. To reiterate, its three layers are:

a. Acts 17:12. The consistency of the Scriptures is a miracle, it is a wonder. How is that possible throughout fourteen centuries — one message of a personal God acting through Israel and the covenant through Jesus Christ to save the world?

b. Romans 1:3. The evidence that indeed brings us to a real conviction of the truth. We test the Scriptures with the universe that is there.

c. First Corinthians 8:3. The most personal one! The assurance that I am known by God through Jesus Christ. That leads me to the final certainty — being called by my name. We read in the Scriptures, for instance, at the meeting between Mary and Jesus, the risen Lord, that He said, "Mary," and she answered, "Rabbi." Now that's where I want to end. We started with a garden, a garden in the jungle, and with people wondering whether or not there was a God. Indeed, if there was a garden in the midst of the jungle, we could imagine how these questions arose.

But his is not where we stand. We stand in another garden, also in the midst of the jungle of human history. This is the garden of Joseph of Arimathaea, a garden in which there is an open grave and where we are met by the risen Lord!

The grass and the flowers cannot bring us to the final assurance that

God is there, but only the open grave and the risen Lord. That open grave can never be taken away out of our human history, and, as we wonder while reading the Scriptures what they may mean, the risen Lord himself stands right behind us, and it is He who calls our name! Like Mary! Only He can break through the enchantment — as C. S. Lewis called it — the spell, the enchantment, which is, I think, the deepest secret behind this whole idea of projection.

DISCUSSION QUESTIONS

1. To what extent has such "projection thinking" permeated Western society? Why is it necessary for Christians to think through this concept thoroughly?

2. How is the idea of God merely meeting a suppressed need communicated in today's world?

3. Freud tried to give scientific basis to Feuerbach's projection hypothesis in the idea of the subconsciousness of man. Why was this supposedly "scientific" theory and explanation biased from the start concerning its appraisal of religion and God?

4. Why must Christians be willing to step into the doubter's "shoes" and consider what he is thinking and feeling? Is Paul a valid example of this in his letter to the Corinthians? (1 Cor. 9:14)

5. As related in Lewis' writing, how do Christians in western society become "enchanted" and doubt what reality is concerning the kingdom of God, judgment, society around them, etc.? Why is pain and sacrifice necessary to keep us always trusting in the "real"?

6. Explain what Wim means by "Why and How questions"? Why are they not valid questions to determine whether something is true?

7. Why is the Christian faith so radically different from emotional feelings and suppressed desires?

8. What is the difference between a psychological and an epistemological problem?

9. What is crucial about the antithesis between Rietkerk's statement that people have a suppressed need to *deny* God versus Freud's conjecture that people have a suppressed need to *affirm* His existence?

10. Why is the stress on Christianity having an historical basis so important in these discussions?

"So behind the idea that Christianity is
an ideology lies the deeper idea that faith and
Christianity are the result of
wishful thinking."

The Reality of God, Part II: Is Christianity an Ideology?

Wim Rietkerk

"Christianity is an ideology" is the main statement that you hear from the Marxists. Their argument is based on an even deeper feeling that not only is Christianity an ideology, but it is an invention of the human mind. Man made up this whole system of truth, because he wants to fulfil a human need. So behind the idea that Christianity is an ideology lies the deeper idea that faith and Christianity are the result of wishful thinking. In fact, the Marxist is saying not that man is created after the image of God, but just the opposite, that God is created after the image of man.

To illustrate this way of thinking, I want to start with a little story written by Bertolt Brecht, the well-known German novelist. He once wrote a little story on the question of whether or not there is a God.

Someone asked Mr. K. if there was a God. Mr. K. answered:

> "My advice to you is, think about this: would your behaviour change if you were to discover the answer? If your behaviour remains unchanged, drop the question. Why should we talk about a question that would not change your behaviour? But if the answer would change your behaviour, I can only be a help to you by saying that you have already made the decision — you need a God."[1]

Do you understand what he is saying in this last sentence? With this remarkable answer, Bertolt Brecht has answered the question. He wants to say: the only basis for believing in God is that you need a God.

If you do not need God, you just leave the question unanswered. But if you need God, that is, if a belief in God would change your behavior, just go on and create one after your own image. This is in fact what he is saying. Make a God that will fit your need. Why not!

This is a fair description of the deep cynicism of the European unbeliever. Faith in God is the product of a human need. There are some outstanding needs, and some people can only be helped through faith in God. Okay, move on — believe in God if it helps you. I gave my discussion the title "Is Christianity an Ideology?" because this is exactly what Bertolt Brecht is saying. When religion becomes nothing but an instrument to achieve a practical goal — the fulfillment of my needs — then it is an ideology. Every ideology uses all kinds of metaphysical statements and moral rules to help people to achieve a practical goal.

I recently read a book by Dr. Normal Vincent Peale, *The Power of Positive Thinking*. This book starts with the story of a businessman who came to Dr. Peale for help. After listening to all his complaints of stress and inferiority, Dr. Peale did only one thing: he took a pencil and, like a doctor, he took a little piece of paper to write down the prescription. He said: "This is the medicine. Just take it regularly each day and you will be completely cured."[2]

When the man looked at this little piece of paper, he read a Scripture verse written by hand, Philippians 4:13: "I can do all things through Christ, who strengthens me." Dr. Peale adds that, as the businessman was not familiar with these words of Scripture, he made him repeat them three times, and then said: "Take in these words each time you go to work, each time that you feel nervous, or tired, or inferior." And so he sent him away. Some months later, the businessman came back and said: "It worked. It is marvelous. I can do my work in a confident spirit and I feel completely cured." There are hundreds of examples like this in Dr. Peale's book. In time of need, say Romans 12:2 three times. Begin the day with Luke 17:21, and you will see miracles. You always find the same exclamation at the end: It is great! It worked! It helped me a lot!

Without denying that the gospel is a powerful message, and that it is the foundation for the day, I nevertheless want to question this mentality. What would this lead to if we do not talk about the truth of something, but only about the effect it has on my life? Suddenly, whether it is true or not isn't important anymore, but only whether it works.

If this is the mentality among Christians, we may be caught in a trap without realizing it. We have fallen prey to the atheist's criticism of Christianity that it is an ideology.

What is an Ideology?

In the word *ideology* you have three levels. First, the central word is *idea*, the second word is *ideal*, and then you come to *ideology*. Now the word *idea* originally comes from the philosophy of Plato, the old Greek philosopher. Plato constructed a world of ideas which he saw as the true world. The real world, which is in contrast to this world, he saw as a world of shadow. He felt, and here he certainly showed his deep wisdom, that this world cannot be the real world. There must be something else. Thus, he constructed the world of ideas — beyond this world — with the help of the good aspects of this world.

Now that's the world of ideas: the idea of goodness and of love, of beauty and of righteousness. The idea becomes an *ideal* when it is applied to our world. An idea hangs in the air — it has no power, it is just an idea — but as soon as you say: "Wait a minute, this idea must be realized here and now" — you make your idea into an ideal.

Here is an example: Two businessmen are in danger of bankruptcy and one of them gets an idea: "Suppose we could gain a market for our products in China today; we would then overcome all our problems." They decide to try. The moment they realize this idea it becomes an ideal. Without this idea and the ideal, the business would have collapsed. Ideals are the dreams of mankind. Faced with a hard and bitter existence, with imminent death, many times victims of a cruel society, people have dreamed — dreamed their dreams about another world, a better world, a perfect world. As soon as they applied these dreams to their own world, they became ideals. Ideals are tremendously powerful. In fact, if you compare the history of mankind to an engine, the ideals are the petrol. Without the petrol, the engine would not work. All politicians, businessmen, even technicians and artists (and later on the Marxists would say "and theologians"), are led on by ideals more than they themselves realize.

Now we come to the third level, and I can explain to you what an ideology is, because an ideology is an *ideal* made absolute. As soon as someone makes his practical ideal his last and final purpose of life, for which he sacrifices everything, he is creating an ideology. This word *ideology* was used for the first time by scholars in France and they used it as a label for the third branch of their arts. The arts may be divided into three groups.

1. Logic
2. Grammar
3. Ideology

For *ideology*, the Greeks used the word *rhetoric*. That was the situation in 18th century France.

Until that time it was a "cool" and objective word for the study of ideas in the human mind, but during the French Revolution this changed. At the time of the French Revolution the revolutionaries said science should be used in the service of the practical goal of destroying the Empire of the French King and of building up the new democratic republic. From that time on, the use of the word *ideology* was as we know it today.

Now I come to a definition of this word as a system of metaphysical and moral truths that, in fact, is created and composed to serve a highly practical goal. This definition is from the German scientist Ernest von Topitz.[3]

I will give another example: the two businessmen again. Their problem is clear. Their business was in danger of bankruptcy. Their idea was good. China is a big country with lots of people who need our products, and so their ideal was: Okay, let's create a market. Then they fall into the trap of ideology. At the moment they start to sell their product, they start an advertising campaign in which they tell the Chinese people that this is God's most beloved country and therefore has the most healthy products in the world. Why is this an example of building up an ideology? Because suddenly they use a statement of truth: "This is God's most beloved country" (That's a statement of truth — it pretends to have truth.) to serve a practical goal.

So still the definition is: an ideology is a system of thought that pretends to come with truth and absolute ideals but which unconsciously serves a preconceived practical goal. To use a picture for this; imagine that the preconceived practical goal is a locomotive engine. Ethics and morality, truth and religion become nothing but wagons that must serve and be drawn by and follow the locomotive. They function as a means to achieve that practical goal. I said morality and practical truth are transformed to serve a practical goal. All those aspects of morality and truth that do not serve the practical goal are forgotten, and even the atmosphere of the truth and morals are changed to fit the train. They get a slightly different flavor, another smell.

Here, I always use the example of the difference between a cup of coffee and a glass of cola: there is almost no substantial difference. It is in both cases 99 percent water (H_2O — ask the scientist). The difference that the little amount of coffee makes to the water is essential, as is the little bit of the other substance that gives cola its taste.

In the same way, truth within and without the framework of an ideology is almost completely the same. Nevertheless, in taste and in smell and in flavor they are absolutely different. I will give a last example.

When Dr. Peale — the man I mentioned at the beginning of my lecture — gave the businessman the quotation from Philippians 4:13, he gave the man the *truth* in exactly the same way as Paul wrote it down. Ninety-nine point nine hundred and ninety-nine percent of the truth in Paul's mouth or in the mouth of this businessman is the same. But, nevertheless, there is a fundamental difference (I would almost say an absolute difference) between Paul and the businessman, or, maybe, I should say between Paul and Peale who advised the businessman, because in Paul's mouth it is the truth of God which he wrote down, even if it never helps you. He didn't write it to help you, he wrote it because it was true. But Peale gave Philippians 4:13 to the businessman because it could help him. Now you understand how subtle the accent is? He used the truth to serve a practical goal — mental health. The businessman took it in as a pill, to serve that practical goal and to receive personal strength. Here you see one example of an ideological misuse of Christianity and of the truth.

Who Said Christianity is an Ideology?

Indeed, many of the scholars who came from the French school of ideologists have come to the conclusion that Christianity is an ideology. The first one who stated this more explicitly was the German philosopher Feuerbach. Feuerbach was a philosopher of the 19th century, who lived between 1804 and 1872. His name means "fire creek." Marx said no-one could enter the 20th century if he had not gone through this "fire creek." He meant Feuerbach, because Feuerbach is the master of the atheist's criticism of Christianity which has worked its way down to today's man on the street. Feuerbach said:

There is a deep chasm — a deep split — between man as he is and man as he should become. Man in every period of history has dreamed about what he could be in his perfect state. His ideas about himself became ideals: how can I become the man I want to be?[4]

On this question Feuerbach concluded Christianity gives an answer. It is, "by faith in God." So we, as imperfect man, can become perfect, the man we want to be, by faith in God. He concluded that Christianity is an ideology because the whole truth about God and heaven and the new birth is an invention of the human mind to achieve a preconceived practical goal — the happiness of man.

For this purpose, man invented the idea of God, who had all the qualities that man himself failed to have. He started to believe in a God who is holy, loving, righteous, eternal — an ideal image of man himself.

And now he created this faith in God as a way of salvation to become the man he wanted to be. Now that is, in a very brief form, Feuerbach's criticism of Christianity. He did not say this literally, but Marx and, especially, Lenin (the whole Marxist explanation of Christianity) said it. Karl

Marx added: "It is an ideology that is especially helpful to the ruling class as the rulers in the bourgeois society use it to keep the working-class quiet."[5]

Marx holds to the same principle, the same basic view of man. Man is alienated from himself. He observed the deep alienation of the working man who had to work six or seven days a week and sometimes for sixteen hours a day. He saw the deep alienation that this wrought between man as he was and as he wanted to be. Then he went to the church, and the only message that he heard was about Heaven — and how you could become the man God wanted you to be later on in Heaven if you were obedient to Him here. The truth was preached in order to keep the working class quiet. Therefore, he called Christianity an ideology.

This is a difficult quotation from Karl Marx, but it is needed to understand the way in which Marx interprets Christianity. He says: "It is not the consciousness of men that shapes their being, but just the other way around, it is their being — and especially their social situation that shapes their consciousness."[6]

Do you understand what he is saying? Every system of truth and God and absolutes does not come from God and enter the mind of man to influence society. It is just the opposite. It is the society in which the man lives that influences man's mind and that creates faith in God. Therefore, in Marx's way of thinking, this conclusion is inevitable: there is no absolute truth, there is only the flow of history in which ideologies rise up and break down like the waves of the sea.

But, in Marx's case, it did not lead him to melancholy or despair because, he said, it depends how we build up our ideology. Marx was not an enemy of ideology, he just said you must choose the right one. If you have chosen the right ideology, then work on that, because that can change mankind. Choose the ideology that best achieves your goal — that is the happiness of man and the freedom of man — then follow it. He said that Christianity has been helpful, too, in the past, but it is not helpful anymore, because it has become the instrument of the ruling class. To liberate the working class, who should be liberated, we need a better ideology. To liberate the working man is the whole object of the Marxist system of thinking. So Marx, and later on, Lenin, publicly agreed that the Marxist-Leninist way of thinking is an ideology. They had no objection to admitting this. But because they did not see it as an insult to call their whole way of thinking an ideology, they expect that Christians will have the same reaction, that we, too, will not feel insulted when they say that, of course, Christians have their own ideology. You must understand that this is the mentality that you meet.

Now I will give some examples of ideological thinking. The Marxist-Leninist thinking is an ideology. Their ideology is that mankind should become free. The means of production and the product of man's work should be his own; he should be able to control it himself. Now that is the practical goal: the empire of freedom which is the locomotive engine draws the whole thinking of Marxism. Therefore, it is an ideology.

In the last World War we had an ideology (because of Hitler's view on race and blood) that the German race, being the most perfect race, should dominate the world. That is also an ideology, and everything of truth and beauty and religion in Hitler's thinking had to serve the achievement of that practical goal. These two examples make clear that as soon as a Marxist thinks about Christianity, he thinks along the same lines. So Christianity has a practical goal, and all the truths that are in the Bible and that are beautiful and that are about God are basically there to achieve this practical goal.

So, the answer to the second question: "Who said Christianity is an ideology?" is that the Marxists are saying it.

What is the Christian Reply?

This is the third and most important point. Should we give in, in a discussion? Should we give in and agree because we acknowledge the fact that there are many practical goals we want to achieve as Christians — beautiful goals like that of Dr. Peale's? Mental health and harmony is a beautiful goal. There are other Christians who have other beautiful goals, such as fighting for a righteous world — that's a beautiful and very important goal. To have a real care for those who are oppressed or poor — that is a profound and Christian goal. To defend our country against the enemy is a profound and important goal. Other Christians say the evangelization of the world before the year 2000 is an honorable goal . . . and so on. Isn't it true that faith in Christ can function as a tool to achieve these goals? We are almost tempted to say "yes." Nevertheless, we should see it as a real temptation today to say "yes," for as soon as you have acknowledged that Christianity is an ideology, you have agreed that faith in God is only useful and valid as long as it helps you to reach your goal. That's what you have done.

As soon as we say this, we have lost the battle in our own age. The battle today is not the level of ideas and ideals — there are many ideas and ideals that we have in common with non-Christians. The whole difference is that we should never have put God and his promises and the reality of God in the second place to serve this practical goal.

Here, I want to move deeper. This is what happens when, or if, we do.

We then use God for our own purposes, and immediately our ideals — sometimes honorable ideals — become idols. Even the most beautiful ideal — righteousness, a world filled with righteousness, a righteous society — peace in the world — or personal mental harmony — whatever it is, as soon as we use the Bible, scripture verses, hymn singing, faith in God, to reach this goal, then our ideal becomes an idol and we fall into the trap of an ideology. We put something or someone, even the most beautiful thing we can imagine, in the place of the Lord Himself.

Christianity is weak today, because that is exactly what we have done. As Christians we have made all kinds of ideologies. Non-Christians observe this, and, having sharp eyes, they analyze Christians and say that Christianity is an ideology — look at him and look at them!

I will give three examples myself. The first one I have already mentioned, but I want to put it more sharply.

1. When people use scripture texts as medical prescriptions to feel fine, when we go to a church meeting, a prayer meeting, hymn singing and so on as instruments to achieve practical goals such as feeling at ease, or mental health, personal energy, a cure of the personality, as soon as we do this we use the Christian truth as an ideology. A non-Christian will be right when he tells us so. He does not see any difference between transcendental meditation and Christianity or even Marxism. It is just the ideology you choose. Of course, practical goals differ, but the fundamental structure of all these movements is the same. It is a human invention to reach the practical goal that I have set myself.

Many people compare these movements, these different ideologies, and prefer a more up-to-date one to Christianity. I think that this is why Holland lost fourteen percent of the people who believed in a personal God in such a short time. They lost them not to atheism but to other ideologies — more recent ones — because Christianity was rotten in itself.

I will add two more examples of the misuse of Christianity, though I could mention many more.

2. Let us think for a moment of Christianity and economics. When the Bible is used to attack or support the prevailing economic system, we should be very careful, *not* because the Bible does not speak clearly about the use of money and unrighteous economic structures — it does — but because we are all men, and we have the tendency to put our practical aims first. In order to keep our own economic power, we use the Bible to prove that our position is right.

This happened when many Christians defended the economic structures that were formulated by Adam Smith, the father of the free market system. His basic position was that our society would function in the best way if each citizen acted on the basis of a well-considered self-interest — then the whole of society would flourish. Marx said exactly the opposite. He said that the individual would only be happy if the society was filled with justice. Now, I would say that we should be very careful in defending one or the other with Bible verses, because we are immediately in danger of making Christianity an ideology.

3. A third ideological use of Christianity can be observed in politics. In South Africa today many Christians defend the separation of the races with the help of their Christian principles. They say, for instance, that the Bible teaches us to love our neighbor like ourselves. We also have the commandment to love ourselves; therefore, we are called upon to establish the independent existence of the African people. So today many Christians defend discrimination between the races with Bible verses from Genesis or Proverbs. In this whole issue the danger of making Christianity an ideology is very great. When we make the preconceived goal of the survival of our country or the survival of our race, or our church — when we make that the final goal that all truth and morality must serve, we make Christianity an ideology.

In a subtle way, like water in coffee or cola, the truth changes — not in content but in color and smell. Thus, the God of all mankind becomes the God of our race and the God of our Nation. The God of all humanity becomes the God of our church, and the absolute love to our neighbor becomes unconsciously love to our brother. The concept of righteousness suddenly narrowed down to keeping up the existing order. In this way the truth and the beauty are lost. Immediately when we do this, a caricature of Christianity comes into existence.

After having considered these three examples, you can see ideological trends in Christianity — the misuse of Christianity. What is wrong with this? Why do I still maintain that Christianity is not an ideology? It is not, and I will explain why.

I defined ideology as a system of thought about truth and morality which unconsciously or unwillingly must serve a preconceived practical goal.

When you study this definition closely, you will discover that this preconceived practical goal, let us say the ideal you want to realize, receives a position higher than God. It receives a position higher than the truth and the absolutes. All things — God, truth and absolutes — must work together, must contribute to realize the goal. This means that the practical goal becomes your one and true absolute. Suddenly the ideal becomes your idol. This is the heart of each ideology. Each ideology, however beautiful it is, should be rejected by the Christian because it made the human ideal into an idol. This is the main reason why no Christian should join any party or movement that is inspired by an ideology.

This is very clear in Hitler's case. He made his practical goal, the rise of a great German Empire under his leadership, his final god. Today we recognize this clearly. The same holds true for the independence of the white race in South Africa or even for the final practical goal of Marxism — a mankind that is equal and free, not divided into classes. Even the beautiful goal which is first and foremost in your mind — what you want to do as people together or, as a church together, the most beautiful practical goal that you dream about — when you put it first, it becomes your God and everything then must serve that goal. Before we know what is happening, ideologies can grow within Christianity and choke it like weeds in a garden. Whether we need to find psychic harmony, or peace or mental strength, or whether we are fond of our own economic system, or our own nation and its greatness, unconsciously and before we know where we are, we have turned them into our God. The true God, the God of Israel, the father of Jesus Christ, is only used to serve that God.

Now we come to the heart of the matter: the true God will never accept that position. The God of the Bible wants to be loved for what He is Himself, because of what He is in Himself. The first commandment says that we should love God first and we should never accept any goal, however beautiful it may be, before God. "Thou shalt have no other gods before me." (Deuteronomy 5:7, NIV) This is the first commandment, and it answers the question: "Is Christianity an ideology?" No, it is not, on the basis of the first commandment.

There is a situation in one of the Gospels (John 6) when Jesus fed the crowd of five thousand people. When they came back the next day, He said: (verse 26)

> "Truly, truly, I say to you, you seek me, not because you saw signs, but because you ate your fill of the loaves. Do not labor for the food which perishes, but for the food which endures to eternal life, which the Son of man will give to you." When they answered, "Give us this bread," He said to them, "I am the bread of live." (RSV)

This passage does not teach us that food was unimportant. Nor was freedom, and we can go on — nor was peace, justice, mental health unimportant. In fact, Jesus had given it to them day after day. He worked from morning till night for all these practical goals to really bless the people. What he wanted was that the people, because of these marvelous gifts, would accept His love and the love of His Father. He wanted them to receive all these beautiful gifts that He gave them as windows that gave them the right outlook on God. This is what He wanted.

When the people came back, His message to them was that they had looked for the gifts but had forgotten the Giver. Now that is the tragedy of each ideology. In a way it is like a dog. When you give a dog a piece of bread, it runs away without looking back at the giver. And that is the root of each ideology.

The Lord wants to be loved in spite of His gifts. He wants to be loved for what He is in Himself. You are seeking the gifts, He said to the crowd, but not the Giver. You are seeking salvation, we could say to many people today, but do you also seek the Saviour? You could say that they looked for His hand, but not His heart. That is the greatest sin of all ideologies even when the practical goal you want to achieve is great and good and God-given. It changes into an idol as soon as you cut it off from the Lord Himself, when you no longer enjoy the Lord your God as the real thing and final goal.

Two examples from the Scriptures may illustrate this position, one from the Old and one from the New Testament.

1. In the Old Testament we read a good example. In 1 Samuel 4 the people of Israel were threatened by the Philistines. They penetrated into Israel and threatened to capture Jerusalem. In the Old Testament the Philistines are a symbol of those who hate God. So what do you expect? Of course Israel should oppose them and beat them, a good and very practical goal. So they did, but without real prayer. They just took their weapons, organized their army, and went to the battle.

But halfway, when they were losing, they took the Ark, which was for them the reality of God in Israel. They used the Ark for the achievement of their goal, which in itself was a righteous goal. In doing this, they subordinated the Lord Himself to their own practical goal. Now as soon as this happened the Lord taught them a lesson. He just let the Ark be captured and they lost the battle. In this way the Lord taught them never to subordinate His revelation to their own practical goals.

2. The second example is from the New Testament in Acts 19:13-19. We read that some sons of a Jewish priest Sceva watched Paul and admired his power and the miracles he performed. He was performing miracles in the name of Jesus. They saw that it was a beautiful thing and so what did they do? They imitated Paul's methods and did the same things in the name of Jesus. They did very many beautiful things. They did what all Christians do when they misuse the truth in an ideological way. They wanted the miracles and the power for themselves so they used the name of Jesus. But what happened? We read in Acts 19:13-19 that the demonic spirit that they wanted to cast out of the other person jumped on them and ripped their clothes off. They had to leave the house naked. This illustrates the ironical

end of an ideological misuse of the truth in the New Testament.

So, both the Old Testament and the New Testament make it clear to us that the Christian faith is not an ideology. God is God and not an idol. We serve God not because of the riches that He gives us but as a good in itself. The Christian faith is God-centered and not man-centered. Of course, it does not deny that man is blessed when he makes God his true King, as a flower is blessed when it opens up for the sun. Man is blessed when he makes God his true King and the center of his life, but the order can never be turned around. That is the whole point.

Abraham Kuyper, the Dutch theologian, once gave a lecture in which he summarized the teaching of Protestant Christianity. He lectured in America around 1900, and he said something at the end of these lectures which I want to quote:

> The starting point in every true religion is God and not Man. God alone is the goal, the point of departure and the point of arrival. He is the fountain from which the waters flow, and at the same time the ocean to which they all finally return. The pith and kernel of all true religion is the prayer of Christ, "Hallowed by Thy Name, Thy Kingdom come, Thy will be done."[7]

I think of the first commandment, which we talked about, and the first thing for which Christ taught us to pray. "Thy Name be hallowed." They are the only, the final, blow against all ideologies, which are all basically idolatries.

The only way to be freed from idolatries is to make the only true God your last and final integration point.

DISCUSSION QUESTIONS

1. What is an ideology? Explain a couple of examples.

2. The idea of an ideology sidesteps the question of truth, but uses experiences to justify the ideology. How have Christians projected a ideological Christianity?

3. Much Christian evangelism attempts to win converts by offering the advantages — the elements of human happiness — of belief. Is this an example of ideology? What would non-ideological evangelism be like?

4. How does the use of truth to serve another goal affect the truth?

5. How has Feuerbach's critique of Christianity affected individuals' views of Christianity?

6. Why did Marx view Christianity as he did? What is an appropriate response to him?

7. How can ideals become idols?

8. How can we understand and respond to ideologies inside or outside the church?

9. What did Abraham Kuyper believe was the center of all true religion?

10. Do you place conditions on your devotion to God, conditions that require God to make your life happier in exchange for your worship and obedience? How is this bargaining a violation of the First Commandment?

"We cannot answer the question: 'Are all religions
the same?' if we have not first verbalized the answer
to the question: 'What is the
heart of Christianity?'"

The Reality of God, Part III: Is Christianity a Religion?

Wim Rietkerk

Years ago, one of the Beatles, George Harrison, produced a song which
has become well-known throughout the world, with the title "My Sweet
Lord." The refrain that comes back again and again is:

> I really want to know you
> I really want to see you, Lord
> But it takes so long.

I heard George Harrison's song years ago. Later, when I was a teacher in a
secondary school we had a Christmas devotion. We gave the young people
an opportunity to make up their own liturgy. One of the first songs on the
program was George Harrison's song "My Sweet Lord." Now if you listen
to him, at first you certainly get the impression that it is a modern Christian hymn. Suddenly, as you listen to the chorus, you realize what he is
doing. He starts off with 'Halleluja.' Suddenly the words in the background change to Hari Krishna, Krishna, Krishna and Hari Rama, Hari
Vishnu and all the other Indian gods. In this subtle way he suddenly communicates a different message — and that is, basically aren't Krishna and
Christ the same? Now that leads me to the question that you will face
everywhere today. This question comes to the heart of the matter — do all
religions have the same content?

Mass communications has opened a closed society to a world community in which we get to know Moslems and Buddhists, and they all seem to be respectable people.

When the period of colonization ended, the feeling of superiority that the white race had over other races disappeared — or at least we hope so. At the same time, it took away the superiority of the white man's religion — Christianity. In the meantime, all our Christian countries are being influenced by what we call secularization, so that the Christian faith has become empty on the inside. Today we can compare many churches with a hollow tree! There have been theologians (for instance the German, Bonhoeffer) who have prophesied that we in the West will move into a non-religious era. Now this prophecy certainly has not been fulfilled because a remarkable thing happened. During the last ten years, while theologians predicted a non-religious era, suddenly we could even speak of a religious revival. The former President of the World Council of Churches observed that many people — more than we could ever have expected — are interested in religion. It is certainly true for the United States. Many young people today are involved in transcendental meditation and yoga. We see that Jehovah's Witnesses are making many disciples. The Mormons, too, are doing good business, as are the Bahais and the Moonies and whatever other groups there are. More and more people are interested in cults.

First, and this is the point that I want to talk about — this whole interest in "religion" is almost always accompanied by one powerful suggestion. George Harrison verbalized it in his song "My Sweet Lord" and that is: Basically aren't all the religions the same? Can't they be compared with all the rivers in the world? They are all different, but at the end they will flow in the direction of the same ocean, into which they discharge their water.

Secondly, isn't it hypocritical to take Christianity out of the realm of religions and to set it apart as the one true religion? Isn't it a sign of narrow-mindedness — the narrow-mindedness of people who never recognize anyone else in the world — a sign of intolerance? Or even a remnant of colonialism?

What is the Historical Root of the Problem?

When it comes to the heart of the matter, aren't all religions the same? That is the problem. In answering the question I want to move back a little bit in history and ask who posed this question for the first time? What kind of mentality produced it? What are the roots of this problem?

This George Harrison-type feeling may look quite new or advanced, but it isn't. The question "Aren't all religions basically the same?" was introduced into our culture out of the minds of the philosophers of the Enlightenment during the 18th century. Now you are probably expecting me to talk about Feuerbach — it was not Feuerbach, but Lessing. Lessing lived between 1729 and 1781 in Germany. He was a theologian who wrote a play on this question called "Nathan the Wise," published in 1779.

The main theme of this play is to be found in the story of the three rings at the end of the second act, where Sultan Saladin, one of the main characters, who is — of course — a Moslem, asks Nathan the Wise, a Jew, which of the three chief religions — the Jewish belief, Islam or Christianity — he considers to be the best. Nathan answers the question by telling the Sultan the following story in the form of a parable, as Jews do:

In days long past there lived in the East a man who possessed a very precious ring with a splendid opal, and this ring had a special virtue. The person who wore the ring was in favor with God and men. It stands to reason that in his last will and testament this man enjoined his descendants never to part with this ring. On his death-bed, he left it to his favorite son.

In the succeeding generations the ring happened to be in the possession of a father who loved his three sons in an equal measure. During his life he had promised the ring to each of his three sons, but none of them knew that his two brothers had been given the same promise. When this father felt that his end was drawing near, and that he was duty bound to give his sons the promised ring, he tried to avoid difficulties by ordering a goldsmith to make two other rings exactly like the original ring. When the work had been finished nobody — not even the father — could make out which of these rings was the original, the true one. The father then gave each of his sons one of these rings; in each case the other two sons did not know about this gift.

When the father had died, each of his three sons claimed that he possessed the true ring, and nobody could say which of them was right. "Similarly," Nathan says, "we cannot make out which is the true religion."

Saladin reacted by saying, "Well, you are joking. I think that the three religions you mentioned just now can be distinguished in matters of dress, of food and of drink."

"But not essentially," Nathan pointed out, "not in fundamental matters. Are they not all based on records and on oral tradition? And each of us believes what his parents told him, or puts his trust in other people who proved their faith by deeds of love.

"Why should I consider my ancestors less trustworthy than you do yours? And the same holds good for Christians, don't you think so?" Saladin granted that Nathan was right, and he did not know what to say next. Nathan continued his story by saying that the three sons asked a judge to decide upon their problems. Each of the sons swore that he had received his ring from his father himself, and that he was rather more inclined to distrust his two brothers than his father.

"And what about the judge?" Saladin asked. "I wonder what he is going to say."

Nathan then told him that the judge summed up the case by stating: "Only your father would be able to tell us which of you, his three sons, is right, or the ring itself will have to give evidence . . . but, wait a minute. You told me that the wearer of the true ring will be in favor with God and men, and full of love becaue the ring possesses a magic power. This enables us to settle the matter. The ring which lacks this power is spurious. My judgment is as follows: For the time being, accept matters as they are. As your ring was given you by your father, take it to be the genuine ring. And let each of you exert himself to the utmost to prove that his ring is genuine by love, by benevolence, by tolerance, by spiritual sacrifice to God. If thus the virtue of your stone becomes apparent among your descendants, I will summon you again before this judgment seat after a thousand years have passed. You can go now!"

This is the story of the three rings, and what did Lessing want to convey by it? Two things: first, he brought in a tremendous relativity. No one knows who possesses the true ring. He did not deny the truth was there, but he said no one can know it. That is again typical of the culture of the Enlightenment. The whole mentality that came out of this period, as we have already stressed, resulted in the loss of truth, or, more particularly, the attitude "if it is truth, you can't know it." Second, at the same time he painted a very clear picture of what the heart of all religions is. The heart of all religions, as communicated by the judge at the end of the story, said Lessing, was "God will reward an honest man, a virtuous man, by giving him the crown of immortality at the end of his life on earth, if he has lived a virtuous life." This is what Lessing himself felt to be the heart of the matter. Just like Kant and Goethe, his contemporaries, Lessing thought that the substance of Christianity consists of three ideas: God, virtue and immortality.[1]

He found the same substance in Islam and in all other religions. "Therefore," he said, "let us not ask the question 'Which of the religions is the true one?' because every religion is basically good. But 'wear your ring,' try to find favor with God and men. Let Jewish people profess their Jewish religion, Moslems, the Islam, Hindus, Hinduism, and Christians, Christianity. Let everyone practice virtue, and by doing this we will be loved by God and men."

Now the basic problem arises: Is this description by Lessing of the heart of all religions a definition in which true Christians recognize themselves? Here is the real problem.

He describes the substance of all religions: God rewarding an honest, virtuous man by giving him immortality. Is that the heart of all religions? Is that the heart of Christianity? I think it tells us a lot about Lessing and a lot about the thinkers of the Enlightenment, who thought it to be the center of all religion. The problem is that it is not the heart of Christianity. I will touch on the basic problem in Lessing's position and the position of all those people who say today "Aren't all religions the same?"

As soon as someone says, "All religions are the same," you should reply with a counter question. "So you say, but can you tell me what is that sameness? What is, then, the reality that all religions have in common?" Immediately you are immersed in the problem. Try it. No two persons give the same answer.

Lessing, when answering this question, said: The center of all religions is God, virtue and immortality. There is a God; live a virtuous life, and you will receive as a reward, immortality.

But the problem is this is not the heart of Christianity! You could say that it is the heart of Jewish legalism. I think it is the religion of the Pharisees in the New Testament. It is the religion that Jesus rejected and opposed. "Okay," you could say, "Lessing made the wrong decision. Perhaps he is an old-fashioned scholar. Today we have sharper guys, and maybe we will find better answers." I tried to find out what the people working in this field have said regarding what religions have in common. I have studied a lot of them, and I will give some examples.

First, the well-known scholar, Rudolf Otto, said: The center of all religions is awe for the mysterious.[2] Schleiermacher, another theologian of the last century, said: The heart of all religions is a sense of dependence on an all-embracing power.[3] Very well known in this field today is the writer Herman Hesse. He felt the center of all religions was finally the experience of oneness with the totality of being.

Other thinkers have other answers. For instance, today there are a lot of thinkers on the level of the Dutch theologian Kuitert who said: Each real religion is an attempt to provide man with a system of orientation according to how he wants to change the world. Religion is a map that must help man to find his practical goal. Clearly he has been influenced by Marxism in this definition. These are some examples. I could give more, but when you study them you come to the sudden awareness that no two are giving the same answer and you are left confused.

Whoever you ask to give a description of the center of all religions comes up with a different answer. When people succeed in finding an answer that is true for all, they produce such a general statement that you feel that it does not express anything at all. Of course, you could come up with the general statement that all religions deal with man in his relationship to the absolute or something like that. When the statement is so general, you realize that it expresses nothing at all. This means that the ideal of the Enlightenment is attempting to create a reasonable religion and to control reality with the mind of man, has failed. Man is attempting to control God with his mind yet again — but, as always, he has failed.

I think again and again of the well-known expression of old bachelors who, knowing that they were unable to have a long-term relationship with any woman, philosophized in their bachelors' club saying: "You know all women are the same, anyhow!" You wonder whether they really know women! As long as you do not know them, you can hold to the statement that they are all the same. The whole situation changes when you really get to know one.

This is leading me to the second point. What is the center of Christianity if we do not recognize ourselves in any of the definitions? Now I must describe the center of my faith. When I compare my faith with their definitions, then I must say that the definition of my faith is not included. It is now up to me to explain the center of our Christian faith. It's much harder to verbalize than you would have thought — but let's try.

We cannot answer the question: "Are all religions the same?" if we have not first verbalized the answer to the question: "What is the heart of Christianity?" Once we have formulated our answer, we can then make a comparison and see if other religions have the same answer.

What is the Center of the Christian Faith?

So now we come to the second point: "What is the center of the Christian faith?" Is it a fascinating view of God? Is it a very highly developed morality? Ethics? Is it the emphasis on the uniqueness of man? I think that each of these questions contains some truth — but they do not touch the heart of the matter.

1. The heart of Christianity can be found in one word. We meet this word on almost every page of the New Testament. The word is the name by which Christians are known — Evangelicals. "Evangel" = gospel = good news. We touch the heart of Christianity in this word.

Christianity is not built on the teaching of a prophet like Mohammed. Nor do we think of Moses in quite the same way as the Jews do. It is not built on deep meditation, like Buddhism, or a fascinating philosophy like anthroposophy. It is built on a message, good news, evangel, or the Greek for gospel. The apostles were neither prophets or philosophers. They were messengers, heralds.

All these New Testament words, *gospel, evangel, message*, refer to terminology which was, in the time of the New Testament, secular. The word *evangel* immediately makes us think of the pulpit, but in that time the word *evangel* was a secular word — like the words *The Evening News*. However, in New Testament times there was no radio or television. They had other means of communicating the news. How did they communicate the news? They did this by sending messengers or heralds. These messengers were tremendously important, particularly in time of war. We should for a moment try to understand the background of this word and what it really meant. Let us imagine that we are living in that time in a little city in the Roman Empire and that we know that the Barbarians have invaded the country. We would also know that the Emperor has come with his army to fight them. You can imagine that we would have stationed our observer on the wall to watch the fields; we would want to know the outcome of the battle. He would be watching for the herald. Then he sees the herald coming on a horse. A number of the citizens of the city meet together in the market place, and the herald comes in on his horse. You can imagine the tension. They would be anxious for the news. If the herald said, "We have lost," then they would know that the Barbarians would be coming and they would probably die. The opposite would be apparent, too. If he said, "We have won the battle," they would know that their life would be restored.

Here is the social and political background of the word *evangel*. Suppose that the messenger comes in and shouts, "We have won the battle!" You can imagine the effect this has on the crowd. This is the true content of the word *evangel*. That is exactly what the apostles were doing when they went out. They didn't bring profound philosophy of moral teachers or meditating Buddhists or something like that. They were messengers. Christianity is not primarily "good views" but "good news." I want to make this point very clear.

This is the heart of the matter: It is good news about a victory that someone else has wrought in space, time and history, on which my life here and now completely depends. That is Christianity.

This is how the Bible looks at our human existence. Think of the picture of an empire under the dominion of intruders, invaders, alien powers, under the leadership of the King of Darkness. Each man, wherever he lives or whoever he is, is under the control of these powers of darkness. The Bible calls it sin and death. The Emperor has not left us alone — he himself has waged the war and won the battle against the intruder. He has won. That is the meaning of the work of Christ on Calvary.

This victory is proclaimed by messengers, by heralds. In the heart of Christianity is this message — something happened there and then that

completely changed my whole existence here and now. We are now no
longer slaves of sin and death, but we are free through Christ. We may
pass it on to one another as good news. The battle is won, the enemy has
lost, you are free from the bonds of sin and death through Jesus Christ.
That is the heart of Christianity.

2. From this center flows a completely different teaching on the way of
salvation. I would like to make another point here. All religions outside
Christianity teach us a way of salvation — how we can be saved. All of
them say: You have to do this, and this and this and then, maybe, at the
end you will have eternal life. It is man climbing up the ladder to God from
below. The Jews have to observe the law; it is a characteristic of the Old
Testament, but that is what they teach. To the Moslems, obedience to the
five religious duties brings you to God. The Buddhists teach you the eight-
fold path. It is always man climbing up to God from below. The Christian
good news turns the ladder around, turns the way of salvation around. It
is no longer "by a long way" — think of that song of George Harrison's. It
always touches me when I hear that song — the touch of sincerity in it and
also this one sentence "but it takes so long." In Christianity it does not take
so long, but it is the joyful messge of how God by a long and painful process has reached us. The center of the Bible is John 3:16: "For God so loved
the world that He sent us His Son."

This victory has been wrought outside me without my help — far away
from me on the edge of the Empire, you could say. Not in Rome or Athens,
but on a hill outside Jerusalem, there the victory has been won — and there
the message that has changed my life originated. I do not need to do
anything to share in this salvation. That is the most beautiful part of Christianity. I just simply let it be true for me. Under the Christian message no
one needs to do anything — just simply accept that it has been done for him
and raise the empty hands of faith. That is the heart of Christianity.

Now this summarizes the second point I want to make here. The first
one was unique proclamation and the second is the unique way of salvation. It is salvation through grace and by faith alone. It is also expressed in
the heart of the Reformation — justification by grace alone.

3. Now for my third point. This leads automatically to a completely different concept of God. The God of the Bible is not the impersonal all-embracing energy that people worship in the East — infinite, but impersonal.
The God of the Bible is, as we understand from this good news, a very personal God, our King and Emperor, who did not want to lose us when the
intruder attacked but came and worked out the victory for us. The God of
the Bible is not the severe judge of the Jews, who just wants obedience, and
then gives love. He loves first and then asks obedience. It is not the im-

movable, all ruling, all determining Allah of the Muslims — but a God full of compassion and committed to His children and willing to change His plans for us. He gave up His son, His own life in a way, for us.

The whole concept of the personal infinite God of the Bible, the King who won the victory for us, just flows forward from the proclamation of the good news. Now those are the three points I wanted to make regarding the center of Christianity:

1. unique proclamation
2. unique way of salvation
3. unique disclosure of God

Of course, this is all centered in the person of Christ.

Dr. Friso Melzer, a well-known German missionary, once held a public debate in India with a Hindu, and they discussed the theme of this evening: Are all religions the same? Whatever Dr. Melzer said, it was always answered with an agreement and the statement, "Teachings like that are also present in Hinduism." In the end he got upset and said bluntly, "But what about Jesus Christ?" For the first time the Hindu said, "Yes, you are right. We do not have Him."[4]

Now that leads to the central point, for the whole teaching of Christianity flows like a river in a different stream and in another direction from Him as a person. The center of Christianity is in fact, a person, and not a meditation of philosophy or morality. I like this story from a Dutchman, A. Prost, who traveled through India. He said that once he went into a house of a Hindu and saw two pictures. In one picture he saw Krishna caressing and making love to his Radha, his beloved, who is hanging in a swing, searching for lust.

In the other picture, he saw Jesus on the cross of Calvary dying in agony and love for our salvation. Underneath both of the two pictures, someone cynically wrote the sentence:

Both are Hanging.

The missionary said, "I never saw so clearly the chasm between Krishna on one side and Christ on the other side."

Why did I take so much time to concentrate on the center of Christianity? Because I think that we now can start to give an answer to the question: Are all religions the same? All the characteristics of Christianity hang together with this central message of the Bible.

I would even dare to defend the statement that because this is in a way a secular message, it was not meant to be a deep, religious thought. It was an historic secular message that the disciples spread about something that really happened there in Jerusalem. As this is the heart of Christianity, it makes it very hard to believe that Christianity is a religion. It was

never meant to be a religion. Imagine that someone comes to the Falk-
land Islands at the moment. I am one of the inhabitants of the Islands and
have locked my family into our house because we have been invaded by
the Argentine enemy. Someone comes to my home and gives me the message that the British Troops have landed and we are free again. Imagine
what would happen if, when I get the message, I take a book and write in
golden letters in it. I have made a cult of it. Now this would be ridiculous. In the same way, something happened there and then to deliver you
from those things that threaten human existence. In the same way, it was
never meant that the message be written in golden letters in a book and a
cult be made of it. It should be accepted the whole world over. It should
create real joy and we should act upon it from now on in a new life under
the one true king. That is Christianity.

Now I know that I have simplified it a little. Of course the messengers
of good news need the help of written proclamation and it is good to
hand the message to the next generation. Of course the new King must be
worshipped. All kinds of religious attitudes and behavior centers around
worship and liturgy, and that is good, but essentially in coming down to
the heart of the matter, Christianity is not a religion at all. It is just good
news about the real world in which we live — about God's work of salvation in space, time and history — about God really being there.

When I look back over the other religions I ask the question: How
should a Christian, on the basis of his unique knowledge of God, evaluate the other religions? How should I look at the other religions?

Are all the other religions just idolatrous, meaningless lies — just the
product of the corruptness of man — nothingness? There have been
times when Christians took that position. I can quote from the early
church. A man called Tertullian said, "What has Athens in common with
Jerusalem? Nothing!"[5] Do you see what he is doing? It means that there is
only Christianity — the rest is lies, nothing but lies. Is that the valid position?

To answer this question rightly we have to turn to the Bible itself. The
first remarkable discovery that you make in the Bible is the emphasis of
the Bible on the world-wide general revelation of God the Creator, who
is the God of Israel and the Father of Jesus Christ. The whole Bible emphasizes the fact that he is not just the God of one nation or one group of
people, but that as it says in Romans 1:20: "Ever since the creation of the
world his invisible nature, namely, his eternal power and deity, has been
clearly perceived in the things that have been made." (RSV)

This is true universally. Think of Psalm 19. Paul can even say in Acts
14:15, 16, 17, to pagan people: "We also are men, of like nature with

you, and bring you good news, [there you have the key word again] that
you should turn from these vain things to a living God who made the
heaven and the earth and the sea and all that is in them." Then he adds:
"In past generations he allowed all the nations to walk in their own ways;
yet he did not leave himself without witness, for he did good and gave
you from Heaven rains and fruitful seasons, satisfying your hearts with
food and gladness." (RSV)

That is the point: "He did not leave himself without a witness." Did
God give them the saving knowledge of the good news right from
Heaven? Is that the center of Christianity? No! Otherwise Paul should
not have been there. He brought them the message of a God of whom
they had some awareness by other means. They already had an awareness in nature: the voice in their inner conscience and remarkable events
that gave them an awareness of His presence.

Paul is talking in Acts 17:23 to the Greeks. When he preached the Gospel to them he started to say: "The God whom you unknowingly serve I
proclaim to you."

Yes, the Bible is indeed saying that they have repressed this knowledge
of God, but no one can deny that the real knowledge was there. The non-
Christian religions are the human answer to this general revelation of
God. That is my definition, with emphasis on all aspects of this definition. There is truth underneath. When the Chinese religions observe a
unity in the Creation, a oneness between the microcosm and macrocosm,
which receives its expression in the book *Aging*, they have then found
truth — truth about the creative power of God that maybe we have lost.

When Indians express the need of silence and wordlessness before the
tremendous mystery of God, they have grasped something of God that
we, because of our great familiarity, have lost. If they already, with their
suppressed knowledge of God, have that awe, how much more should
we?

When Africans express a sense of awareness of an unseen world
around them, of spirits and powers, they are closer to the truth than a
secularized modern man. But all the moments of truth in their religions
do not hide the fact that there is no saving knowledge, no good news.
Their religions remain fully a human answer with all the ambiguity —
man's greatness on one side and man's wickedness on the other side.

It has become a totality of expressions, of feelings and cults where descendants of Adam and Eve have tried to evade the God to whom they
did not really want to turn back.

What always strikes me reading the Bible is this: there are many people
who knew God outside the circle of the covenant. You could think in the

Old Testament of Melchizedek, of Job, (Job was a man outside the Covenant) of Abimelech, of Jethro, of Nebuchadnezzar. The Lord said to Paul in Acts 18 before he preached the gospel in that city: "I have many people in this city." I conclude from this that God the Creator has a history with each man in any culture and in any nation. We should not make quick statements about how God condemns people we ourselves hardly know. Sometimes that is the church's mentality concerning Christianity.

The God of the Bible is the God of the Universe, of the whole of His creation and He is at work — more than we realize or are aware of. There are great mysteries behind God's dealing with the nations. The saving knowledge of God comes only through the good tidings. Let's make that very clear. A suppressed knowledge of the Lord makes it possible to sometimes say to people: "I proclaim to you the God whom you unknowingly serve."

DISCUSSION QUESTIONS

1. What was George Harrison trying to say with his song "My Sweet Lord?"

2. Are we advocating "narrow-mindedness" when we speak of Christianity as the truth, different from all religions?

3. Since both Christianity and Bahai speak of God, virtue, and immortality, why distinguish these "religions" over secondary points of doctrine?

4. What makes Christianity different from all religions?

5. How is God different from the images portrayed in religions?

6. What is the proper response to the claims of religions?

7. Like the heralds of old who announced the tidings of battle, Christian heralds tell of a momentous victory. Who won? Who lost? Where was the battle?

8. Why is it important that Christianity's message is centered around an historic event?

"He (modern man) is restlessly at work . . . to
have his desires satisfied right here in
this very moment."

The Culture of
Narcissism:
Loving Ourselves

Wim Rietkerk

We are all deeply influenced by the culture that surrounds us. This is true
for non-Christians and Christians together. Dr. Schaeffer used an example
to illustrate this: the example of the formless London fog. This fog was
sometimes so dense, because of all the smoking chimneys in that city that it
penetrated the houses of the inhabitants of the city, even when they kept
their doors closed.

This is exactly like our situation: our culture is our environment and it
shapes our personalities even when we do not want it to and keep our
doors closed. On the other side: if we would really be able to close ourselves off from the surrounding culture we would become sterile and we
would not be able to communicate the truth to our fellow-man.

In short we could say: our social environment is one of the manifesta-
tions of our collective fallen human race. It has "humanness" and "fallenness." to be a live Christian means to be able to relate to our culture in a
way that shows a critical distance on one side and a warm sense of responsibility and participation on the other side. It means to live in our culture
attached and *detached* at the same time. Or to put this in Biblical words:
we are called to be *in* this world, not *of* this world. (John 17:11, 16)

The culture in the West is moving fast and rapidly changing. Each
decade has a different face. The sixties are different from the seventies and
the seventies are different from the eighties. Now you all know that our

culture in the eighties has been characterized as the culture of *narcissism*. Why *narcissism*? What does this word mean?

In the first place, this word comes from the old Greek mythology. Narcissus is the main character in one of these old Greek myths. He was a young handsome man, and he was loved not only by the people but also by the gods. This went so far that the gods wanted him to marry one of the children of Hera, the wife of Zeus. Her name was Echo and her only problem was that she could not talk in a normal human way. The only thing she could do was to repeat the last words of the sentence that somebody spoke to her. For the rest, she was also a beautiful girl, a nymph. Once upon a time Narcissus met Echo in the woods. He thought, "Wow, that is a beautiful girl," and started to talk to her. But what happened? Of each question he asked her, she only repeated the last words. You can imagine how quickly this became boring and irritating. To make a long story short, in spite of the fact that they did fall in love with one another, their relationship broke up. Narcissus rejected her . . . but this caused the anger of the gods who were on her side and who felt insulted. In their anger they punished Narcissus with self-love. They made him fall in love with himself and so he was lying the whole day on the edge of a pond that mirrored his own face.

One day he embraced his own reflection in the water and drowned. The gods felt sorry about that and made a flower grow on the place where he drowned: a daffodil, a narcissus, called after the man that so tragically died — a consolation prize.

The second background of the word narcissism is to be found in the psychology of Freud. Freud used it as a description of that early stage in childhood in which the baby seems to be completely self-sufficient. It does not yet relate to an outer world, and is most overwhelmed by it. So it takes its refuge in its own inner self — sometimes with the help of day dreams and the comfort of its thumb.

When a mature man, because of harsh outer circumstances falls back into this mentality, psychiatrists speak of narcissism, which can be a severe psychological illness, in which the patient is completely withdrawn from the outer world and in a sick way preoccupied with himself and his own well-being. This is not just a normal self-love, egoism. It is a sick self-love that always is accompanied by feelings of failure, of inability to relate to others, and even of self-hate. "Deep inside me I have the feeling that no one is there," is a quotation from one of these patients.

Why has our culture been called narcissistic? The man who did it was Christopher Lasch in his book about the eighties which he gave the name, *The Culture of Narcissism*. He said,

The sixties were the decade of political conflict; in the seventies, however, many former radicals embraced the therapeutic sensibility and went to the spiritual supermarket of the West Coast, where they found Gestalt-therapy, biogenetics, rolfing, jogging, modern dance, meditation, acupuncture and zen-therapy; but today, in the eighties we have come so far that we recognize ourselves in the mirror of the statement of Jerry Rubin, "I have learned now to love myself enough so that I do not need another to make me happy."[1]

This he called narcissism today is the lack of reality in all our relationships, the waning of the sense of the historical time and the sensitivity for images. On all these points I will give you a wider explanation.

Many people complain about the lack of reality in their relationships, at home, in the church or in society. They function in many relationships, but they feel very unsatisfied. "It looks like a big machine," someone said. Every one operates in this machine like a little wheel, sometimes very smoothly, but is that what I am meant to be?

There is a waning of the sense of historical time. Americans seem to wish to forget not only the sixties, the riots, the new left, the disruptions on college campuses, Vietnam, Watergate and Nixon, but their entire collective past. In the Bible the past is something like a treasury from which we take new energy, but modern man has lost the past. He is restlessly at work to have his desires satisfied right here in this very moment. To give another quotation from the book of Lasch: ". . . modern man is pastless futureless man, born anew at every instant."[2]

The third characteristic is modern man's sensitivity for images. Most people in our society are not respected for what they are but for what they look like. Even the president is elected not on the basis of what he can do, but on the basis of the image he gives of himself and his abilities. The high-ranking managers today in society have found ways to sell themselves as capable personalities, and even the school system is based more on the image that the students give of their knowledge than a firm and solid knowledge itself. Our whole society is dependent on images. We do not love sport, but we love to look at others doing sport; we are unable to experience evil and joy, sin and sadness in our own lives, so we look at *Dallas* and have the experience through images on the T.V. I could give more examples.

All three of these characteristics have one thing in common: a lack of reality. You could say it also in other words: we have become onlookers, spectators. Richard Holloway wrote "We live in a peeping-Tom society in the West today. We are all voyeurs. We want stimulus without relationship. We want curiosity satisfied without commitment."[3] Peeping Tom was a voyeur in the narrow sexual sense, but in a wider sense he is a person that is unable to sustain or afraid of sustaining real contact with another. He does not want to get involved, because involvement is arduous and might bring failure. And so a new type of citizen is born: uninvolved, passive, unsurprised, and deeply bored, purged of expectation and impervious to mystery.

Today it is very common to explain this mentality of the people in the eighties in a sociological and psychological way. The best example of this attempt is the book mentioned earlier by Christopher Lasch. He combines these two methods of interpretation. On one side he explains it with the help of Freud, even using the word *narcissism*. What are the reasons for the psychological illness of narcissism? Generally this is caused by negligence, absence or bad treatment by the mother. Now taking over the basic assumption of Marx that man is a sociological being and that because of this he can be made or broken by society, his big mother, Lasch believes that the roots of narcissism today can be found in a society that makes tremendous promises but cannot fulfill them. The subtitle of his book is: *American Life in an Age of Diminishing Expectations*. Lasch gives some very good examples of the decline of family life, the bureaucracy in our society and, even more pointed, the fact that for a long time people have believed in Utopia, the growth of an economy and/or social security that would provide happiness for everybody. The collapse of these ideals has caused confusion, and disappointment and hate and, at the end, apathy.

As Christians we can agree with many of the observations of Lasch, but his observations certainly do not provide us with answers that give a true understanding. As we read Lasch we keep asking: okay, that is the development that took place, but why did it happen? Why could society not really fulfill the deep desire for happiness in man, and why did an energetic society break down into apathy?

Neither psychology nor society can really help us to find answers to these deeper-lying questions. In order to find them, we need to turn back to God's revelation. There is one example in the history of salvation that is really illuminating when we apply it to the history of our western civilization, and that is the example of the first King of Israel: King Saul.

The history of King Saul is like a mirror for western man. At first Saul raised Messianic hope among the Israelites. He was a beautiful man: "There was not a man among the people of Israel more handsome than he," we read in 1 Samuel 9:2. (RSV) At the end, however, an evil Spirit of God came upon him and he fell into the attitude of modern man: narcissism. This shows in the way he related to David: as long as David was an innocent boy playing the lyre when Saul was depressed, there was no problem, but from the day that he heard the people on the street singing "Saul has slain his thousands, but David his ten thousands," (we read) he hated David. He was concerned only about his own self-image and became more and more depressed. Outward glamour, but an inner void. Like Narcissus, he ends in suicide.

This history of Saul is very illuminating for the history of western culture. I could find you many quotations from people in Europe in the 18th century or from the Founding Fathers of the USA that talk about the high expectations that we could have about our future. Sometimes they used literally the words messianic expectations: we are called to be the new Israel, and science and technology should provide us with the means to create a new world. Has it come true? No, it has not; Lasch is right when he observes that. But he does not know why. We do, when we turn back to the Scriptures and see when Saul went wrong. At first, he really fought the good fight — in 1 Samuel 11 he delivered the citizens of Jabesh — but he is not glorying in himself. "today the Lord has wrought deliverance in Israel," (vs. 13, RSV) is his final word. But slowly we see a change in Saul, and it breaks through most clearly in the history of the fight against the Amalekites in Chapter 15. Once he had defeated them, because the Lord wanted him to do so and because He gave him the power for victory, Saul gloried in himself and went to Carmel, and there he built up a monument for himself. (1 Samuel 15:12, RSV) Then the prophet Samuel was sent to Saul with the message, "The Lord has torn the kingdom of Israel from you this day." (vs. 28, RSV) From that day on, Saul changed into a self-centered, sometimes bored, sometimes angry man, deeply insecure, sometimes very sentimental, but unable to relate any longer to his general and even his own son, Jonathan. He was caught in the circle of self-love and self-hatred at the same time. This, history reveals clearly as the turning point. The turning point in Saul's life was the very moment that he put himself in the center of the universe where he built himself a monument, instead of saying: Today the Lord has wrought deliverance.

Now this is exactly what has happened in our western culture — in a subtle way in Europe at the beginning of the 19th century and in the USA a bit later. The leading thinkers and politicians started to say: Man is autonomous — we can handle things by our own reason. And, at first, in a deistic way people said: We have to live as if God is not there — *et si deus non daretur* (in Latin) and the whole flow of our culture was polluted. A hundred years later, the leading philosopher in Germany, Ludwig Feuerbach, wanted written on his grave: *homo homini deus* (Man is the only god for man.). From that day, an atheism has penetrated our western culture.

There are some details in the history of Saul that have moved me very much. I would not deny that there is something tragic in the personal life of Saul — but the prophet does not talk with him on that basis. Samuel holds Saul fully responsible: "obedience is better than sacrifices and monuments," says Samuel to Saul.

In Greece and its mythology there is only tragedy, and Freud takes it over when he talks about modern man as Narcissus. Narcissus is a tragic figure; he can not help it that he is a victim of the gods and that his little failure is punished so severely. In the Bible it is different. Samuel held Saul responsible and called him to repentence, because he knew that the God of Israel is a God of mercy who is always willing to give his people a new chance.

It is amazing that the only moments that Saul received deliverance from his evil moods were the moments that he listened to the music of David, the true King! As David played, "Saul was refreshed." (1 Samuel 16:23) Is that not beautiful? As Saul listened to the sound of music from David's psalms, he experienced relief and got better.

Finally, the history of Saul and Samuel ends in 1 Samuel 15 by saying: "And Samuel did not see Saul again until the day of his death, but Samuel grieved over Saul." No cool judgment nor real farewell until the final day Samuel grieved over Saul. That means he had a deep compassion for this man he loved so much.

This all tells us a lot about the way we should relate to people that are drowned in Narcissism. *Compassion, responsibility,* and *playing* the lyre with the music of the Son of David are the three key words.

This leads me finally to the more practical part of this discussion. How do we do this: playing the lyre for our fellowman as David did for Saul? Or, to put it in the other words: What answers do we give when we deal with narcissism? Is each form of self-love wrong? What is honesty and reality in our relationships? Is it unavoidable to wear a mask? Should not Christians, especially, hide their weaknesses? What standards are we all called to live upon? The answers to these questions should make up the music we need to play for the Sauls today!

When I start to answer these questions I first want to make a fundamental remark, and that is: we as Christians do not make our own music. Our music is, and should be, the music of the Son of David. We should not stand up in our society and say to the people: Look at us! Look how we are relating to one another! Look to us and you will be delivered from your narcissism. Quite the contrary: we should help people to listen to the music of the Son of David, and it is *His* music that should be performed through our lives and words.

I think this is not just an introductory remark. It is the first and the basic rule when we want to stand up against narcissism. It is in itself already the first blow against narcissism — when we live in humility and obedience a God-centered life. Remember where Saul went wrong. It was in this at first invisible shift from God-centeredness to ego-centeredness. Why was David a man after God's heart? Because, in spite of all his failures and sins, he always had the Lord in the center of the universe. What was the heart of Jesus' personality and work? We read this in John 5:44 in his rebuke to the leaders of Israel: "How can you believe, who receive glory from one another and do not seek the glory that comes from the only God?" (RSV) and, when the first man confessed his faith in Him as the Messiah (Peter in Matthew 16:16), Jesus answered "Blessed are you Simon Bar-Jona, for flesh and blood has not revealed this to you, but my Father who is in heaven." (RSV) You see what he is doing? He does not say: now finally, I have some success — a print on my work, but He is saying: that is a gift from my Father in heaven. This is what I meant by saying that the first rule today is: we should not make our own music but this music of the Son of David.

Self-love is the main characteristic of man in the end-time. Think of Paul's words in 2 Timothy 3:1, 2: "But understand this, that in the last days there will come times of stress. For . . . " (RSV) and then he gives a sketch of the character of the men of the end-time. The first characteristic of these men is: they will be lovers of self, *autofilioi* in Greek; they will fall in love with themselves. (cf. 2 Peter 2:14) There is the first battle for a Christian against narcissism: being God-centered instead of self-centered.

Now a question arises here: Is there in the Christian life no place for self-love? Should we fight narcissism with altruism? I think it is very important to come to the right understanding of ourselves on this point. Too many times Christians have played a kind of music with their lives that was far from lovely. I think now of the Puritan attitude of the rejection of the body, and the emphasis on the denial of ourselves. Many times this attitude has been based on the word of Jesus: if any man should come after me, let him deny himself. We all know how this has led to a mentality that is very poor in the way people relate to themselves. Some Christians are known for their unwillingness to take their feelings seriously. They suppress their own sensuality, they are unable to enjoy their own bodies and emotions and capacities. Ranald Macaulay and Jerram Barrs wrote a book on this subject, called *Being Human*.[4] This whole mentality is not Biblical at all — it is more Platonic than Christian. When Christ said we have to deny ourselves, He never meant we have to negate ourselves. Just the opposite: it is because we are so precious and carry a treasure within us of beauty and richness that we should avoid the greatest danger that is possible, and that is to use it in the wrong direction for self-glorification instead of enjoying it as a gift and a talent from the Lord. To put it in one short sentence: we should enjoy each part of our body and our emotional life and our intellect as a gift from God. I quote the Bible: Rejoice, O young man, in your youth, and let your heart cheer you in the days of your youth; walk in the ways of your heart and the sight of your eyes . . . remove vexation from your mind. and put away pain from your body; . . . But know that for all these things God will bring you into judgment." (Ecclesiastes 11:9, 10, RSV) Within the structure of the covenant relationship with God there is a tremendous place for self-joy and self-growth!

Are there limits? What are the limits of a Christian "self-love"? Indeed: a Christian does not defend the position that everything that comes up in his physical or emotional life is pure and beautiful. We are part of a fallen mankind. There is much dirt and evil in our personalities. How do we relate to our own weaknesses?

I would like to answer that in three categories, physically, psychologically, and morally. Physically, I think the main emphasis would be acceptance where I discover my physical weaknesses: lack of energy, a weak nervous system, inherited imbalance, temperament, et cetera. I think we should learn to accept that we live in a fallen world. This acceptance is the basis of Christ's having accepted us, and creates room for growth. In learning to live with their weaknesses, many times people have discovered that their weaknesses have become their strengths.

On the level of my psychological life, I would like to use the word *fight*. We always have to fight our personal psychological weaknesses. I think now of the striving Paul describes in Romans 7. It should not be like that, but the reality is that it is always there during our whole life: or fight against our negative identity, coming up in jealousy, or pride, or self-defense, or inferiority feelings, et cetera. "For I do not do the good I want, but the evil I do not want is what I do." (Romans 7:19, RSV) The only way to fight is to *be in Christ*, to fall back always again in saying to the Lord: Thank you that I am already justified and sanctified and holy in you. Help me now lord to make Your music with my life . . .

Finally, on the moral level, the Lord has brought our self-love under commandment. He has not said: Thou shalt not love yourself, but He has said: Thou shalt love your neighbor as yourself. In this way He has made clear that He does not want us to fight self-love — but to use it. Look how much you love yourself, just as a fact. Go, then, and love your neighbor as much as you do yourself. If we do this, we will discover that our self-love will be free from narcissism because narcissism cuts the relationship with our fellowman.

Finally, I want to end with a quote from Pascal's Pensees: "We are not satisfied with the life we have in ourselves and our own being. We want to lead an imaginary life in the eyes of others and so we try to make an impression."[5]

> We recognize here narcissism, the desire to lead an imaginary life in the eyes of others. Pascal continues by taking these two apart, our imaginary being and our real being and saying: We strive constantly to embellish and preserve our imaginary being, and to neglect the real one. And if we are calm, or generous, or loyal, we are anxious to have it known so that we can attach these virtues (that belong to our real being) to our other existence (that we lead in the eyes of others); we even prefer to detach them from our real self so as to unite them with other. (Yea) we would cheerfully be cowards if that would acquire us a reputation for bravery. How clear a sign of nullity of our own being that we are not satisfied with one without the other and often exchange one for the other.[6]

After this quotation, I hope I can make clear how important it is that we build our self-love and self-acceptance on the rock of Christ. It is through Jesus Christ that we learn to be real in our relationships with ourselves. He accepts me on the basis of this work as I really am, my real being, and therefore I do not need to escape any longer in that imaginery being.

Furthermore, He has taught us what it means to have a real relationship with our fellowman. It means to look behind the mask of the imaginary being and sometimes even to pull it down (John 4; Luke 19: 1-10). It means always to make a separation between the pearl and the mud. Jesus looked to people as pearls in the mud and taught us to love the pearl and to hate the mud!

Finally, really relating to people means a willingness to identify myself with them — in the way Jesus identified Himself as the Son of God with us. In this way we will really grow in our personalities and the real growth of our personalities will be growth in identity. When we follow these basic principles in daily life, we are not promised a successful life or an easy life, but certainly we will experience reality. We will see reality in relating to ourselves and in relating to others that will break through the power of narcissism today. But always remember, this can only be done when the music we perform is the music of the Son of David!

DISCUSSION QUESTIONS

1. Why is it important to think about the common values and standards our culture operates on?

2. What is narcissism?

3. How does the world make promises it doesn't keep? How does this affect individuals?

4. What "images" influence your ideas about the world?

5. What was the turning point in Saul's life? What message does Saul's life give us today?

6. Why is religious escapism called platonic? What is the Christian answer to platonic tendencies?

7. Aren't Christians urged to love themselves? How is genuine self-love different from narcissism?

8. What are the psychological adversaries we are called to fight?

9. How does a relationship with Christ help us to be real with ourselves? With others?

Edith Schaeffer

Edith, the wife of Dr. Francis Schaeffer, was the co-founder of the L'Abri Fellowship in Switzerland. She has traveled widely and spoken in both the United States and Europe. In addition to her involvement with L'Abri, she has also written several books including *Hidden Art, Affliction, A Way of Seeing, L'Abri,* and *The Tapestry,* a history of the "life and times" of Francis and herself. Most recently, Edith finished *Lifelines* on the Ten Commandments from which this chapter has been taken.

Her future work includes a book and a Christian educational film series on common sense Christian living.

"After we have become God's children,
something is meant to be different about us, and that something
is meant to be shown by actions and deeds
in line with the truth."

The Sixth
Commandment*
Edith Schaeffer

I was sitting in a dentist's chair at the University of Pennsylvania's Dental School's practical clinic. Young dentists were getting their quota of fillings and specific kinds of dental work done. My student dentist was using my teeth to get his hammered gold fillings ticked off his list of requirements; so I had the only two hammered gold fillings I was ever to have done, right then! They are still intact by the way, and that was forty-four years ago; so the headache that came from the tap, tap, tap, was worth it! We were in Fran's second year in seminary, and Priscilla was on the way. I'll never forget the excitement of the moment, when in that dentist chair surrounded by fifty other people sitting in chairs getting dental work done inexpensively, suddenly I felt another faint tap, this time in my abdomen! I held my breath in secret excitement. My very first feeling of a life within me . . . somebody I didn't know yet had made me aware that "Heshe" (our name for the baby whose gender we didn't know yet) was making movements I could feel.

Life! What a mystery! Tiny cells, tiny chromosomes, multiplying to make a person so full of talents and personality that now after knowing

*From *Lifelines* by Edith Schaeffer, 1981/82. Used by permission of CROSSWAY BOOKS, Westchester, Illinois 60153.

Prisca for forty-four years I am still getting to know her. Consider the mar-
vel of personality and whole persons made up of so many factors, human
beings with a potential of existing forever, and of diverse creative skills only hindered by the fall. How can you describe life? How can I? We know
only that little bit that we discover in our short years of living since we first
made that movement our own mothers felt. How can we really know what
life means in full until we have our new bodies which will be hindered no
longer, and which will not die. It is the constant presence of death that
spoils the understanding of life! It was not meant to be so.

What a tragedy that the fall took place, and that death came as a result.
I wonder how long it took Adam and Eve to understand exactly what physical death meant. They experienced separation from God — in spiritual
death — as soon as they left the garden, never to know that walking and
talking face to face again. Their separation from each other and their
strains and stresses as a married couple, and the strains and stresses that
came with their children, were experienced constantly as days and months
and years went on. But death? The real understanding of death, the
separation of body from spirit, did not come for years, and then only as
they experienced total separation from Abel, but not yet the experience of
their own death.

The first death was the result of a killing, a direct murder in anger. It
must have come as a shock to Cain, as well as to Adam and Eve. A human
being's body, not breathing, not speaking, growing cold, was something
no one had seen before. Understanding must have come slowly and
agonizingly, and the realization must have come back in terrible shock
waves. In a way every person's experience of death in the family or death
taking place among a circle of friends is the same unbelievable shock. Yet,
there must have been a very realistic need to discover how final death was
when it was the first time it had ever taken place.

The human race has turned away from God so thoroughly that at the
time of Noah an opportunity for them was given for a period of years,
during which Noah built the ark, to discover what God was saying to
them, and to turn to Him in belief. They had an opportunity to demonstrate that belief by coming into the ark with Noah before the flood came.
However, the jeering and violent unbelief was so complete that no one but
Noah's family paid any attention to the warning that a flood would cover
the earth, and the population was wiped out. Only Noah was left, and
those with him in the ark.

It was after the flood was over, after Noah had offered the prescribed
sacrifices to God, that He made the beautiful promise never again to destroy the whole human race at once:

"Never again will I curse the ground because of man, even though the inclination of his heart is evil from childhood. And never again will I destroy all living creatures, as I have done.

As long as the earth endures,
seedtime and harvest,
cold and heat,
summer and winter,
day and night
will never cease." (Genesis 8:21, 22)

In the midst of making this promise, this covenant, with the first gorgeous rainbow sealing the promise, God spoke strongly concerning the responsibility each person had for the life of his fellow men.

"And from each man, too, I will demand an accounting for the life of his fellow man.
Whoever sheds the blood of a man,
by man shall his blood be shed;
for in the image of God
has God made man.
As for you, be fruitful and increase in number; multiply on the earth and increase upon it."
(Genesis 9:5-7)

This very first command to not kill, with the penalty of death for a death to demonstrate the preciousness of life, was given in the context of the command to have babies, who would be of course these human beings increasing in number, made in the image of God, precious to Him, having value in history.

Not only was the command given to be fruitful and multiply, but so often the picture of utter emptiness is spoken of as barren, as with a "barren womb," in many places in the Bible. In the Bible, birth is used to picture the entrance into the family of the living God, the company of believers forever. Birth is a beginning that is meant to have a continuity with life of a certain length on earth, and the new birth indicates a spiritual birth into everlasting life.

The body one has when the forty-six chromosomes have multiplied and grown for nine months within one's mother and then have become ready to live outside is so precious that when death entered the world through the fall, God had already planned the marvelous forming of the body of Jesus within Mary for nine months so that He could live, and die, and rise again to open the way for our resurrection and eternal life in our bodies. It was the excruciatingly important matter of our having our bodies for all eternity — changed, but the same bodies raised again — which made Christ's resurrection as the firstfruit so important. His resurrected body was the firstfruit, ours will be among the fruit to follow. All our bodies will be like his resurrected body.

Are the forty-six chromosomes leading to the whole person important? How marvelous is the work of God in creating human beings who could reproduce, who could have children from their physical oneness, children who would have eternal life one day, but who would also become adults and form new families, form the next generation.

Children are a gift of the Lord, the Bible tells us over and over again, and to treat the priceless gift of their lives entrusted into our hands lightly or carelessly is horrible to contemplate. If human beings are held accountable for the life of their fellowmen, being held accountable for the life of one of these precious gifts is staggering!

Come to Psalm 127:3-5.

Lo, children are a heritage of the Lord: and the fruit of the womb is his reward. As arrows are in the hand of a mighty man; so are children of the youth. Happy is the man that hath his quiver full of them: they shall not be ashamed, but they shall speak with the enemies in the gate. (KJV)

Think of priceless inventions such as telephones, cameras, typewriters, and sewing machines, and the difference they make in life. It is impossible to compare these with God's invention of human beings, made in His image to think and act and feel, to have ideas and choose, to be creative and love and communicate — and to reproduce. Each human being has potential for being involved in bringing a new being into existence. How awful to treat a new human being as a kind of counterfeit piece of matter that isn't of any value at all. But even more, how terrible it is to forget that God the Creator has said that children are an inheritance, and a reward of His, given as a good gift.

Blessed is every one that feareth the Lord; that walketh in his ways. For thou shalt eat the labor of thine hands: happy shalt thou be, and it shall be well with thee. Thy wife shall be as a fruitful vine by the sides of thine house; thy children like olive plants round about thy table. Behold, that thus shall the man be blessed that feareth the Lord. . . . Yea, thou shalt see thy children's children, and peace upon Israel. (Psalm 128:1-4, 6, KJV)

This picture the Psalmist gives to be sung with fervent voices and to be as a "hit song" upon the lips of the Israelites, and ours, is one evidence of a fulfilled life showing forth the answer to the question Who am I? I am one involved with life, life in the form of generations, caring for each other, bound together in a day-by-day communication, seeing each other, exchanging ideas in conversation, handing down traditions, but most importantly, making truth known to the next generation. Physical life is a precious commodity. Out of it comes the sweetness of the Beethoven Piano Trios, with a violin, cello, and piano bringing forth gorgeous waterfalls of music flowing not only over the ears of the listener, but through the whole "sounding" board of the physical system — made by God to respond to music as well as to hear it! In today's society, it is likely Beethoven would have been aborted. Our society does nothing to protect even the normal unborn life, and he had a succession of abnormal older brothers and sisters and unlikely family genes. In order for me to be hearing this music at this moment, not only did Beethoven have to be born, but Edison had to be born too, to start the whole thing of the phonograph, so that the Beaux Arts Trio can sit in New York and perfectly throw their talents and personalities into performing Beethoven trios nonstop for pressed records to bring them to — how many? Physical life — the mystery of the genes bringing forth another generation, God's "blessing," we are told. Human life is not something easily obtained. It is strong, but frail, and so easily taken away.

God who created human life — who knows what myriad capacities physical life has — is the only One who has absolute laws which continue to be the basis for physical life. He alone knows the total capacity of what He has made.

His law, His Ten Commandments, are worth finding out about, meditating upon, talking about, and attempting to put into practice. We need to listen to Him speaking to Noah. We need to stand beside Noah in all the freshness of the world after the flood, in the light of the rainbow, and hear the command that warns first of all that there is to be an accounting. There will be an account to settle up for every human being. One factor that will enter into the accounting is the seriousness of murder: anyone who commits murder must pay the cost with his own life. Coupled with that serious warning is the command to have children, making the begetting of life the opposite command to the cutting off of a life.

The close coupling of these two orders given by God to Noah as the civilization started afresh certainly points up the horror of accepting the murder of the innocent unborn people as is done in abortion. Of course, as people multiplied and again turned from God to false gods and idols of their own imaginations, the killing of babies soon came to be a part of their false worship. But for those who remained faithful to the true God, babies, from the moment of conception, were counted as a priceless gift.

As we come to the sixth commandment, standing to hear Moses read it immediately after his reading the commandment which had to do with the primary relationship of honoring father and mother, we need to understand it in succession, in context. People so very often isolate the commandments and begin to argue in the context where they want to place them without listening to God's Word and letting it speak.

Remember, the commandments as given in Exodus 20 start with "And God spoke all these words: . . ." Then comes the sixth: "You shall not murder."

Since unborn babies are the youngest in the human family, the youngest human beings who are alive, it is really logical to think of them first. No one can be murdered if he or she is not alive. To kill anyone, to stop the heart from beating, to stop the blood from circulating, the person has to be alive. It would be impossible to murder someone who was not alive. We need to think about the beginning of life, as well as the potential of life (such as in musicians), to have a background to talk about murdering. The murder of an unborn baby is the murder of a potential Beethoven or a potential member of the Beaux Arts Trio, as well as a potential farmer, baker, or candlestick maker. Each one is meant to be woven together with others to fulfill their needs and potentialities and to enable others to have a place in the community of human beings.

Idealistic? No, this is what was meant to be — always remembering that we live in an abnormal world, a spoiled world, and things are not as they were meant to be. Nevertheless we have a pattern, a standard, a set of commandments which are to help us get back on the solid rock of reality instead of sliding around in a bog of mud that leads to a patch of quicksand. Human beings hanging out their shingles to let it be known that their chosen job is to help kill babies before they are born is simply *not* what human beings were made to do in order to have a satisfying, rich and full life. To have the killing of unknown Beethovens and Helen Kellers as one's career and creative work is like having the tearing down of art museums as one's fulfillment of a yearning for beauty! We will always be affected by the pattern of "the scarecrow." If we have a career of breaking one of the Ten Commandments, we begin to be like Punks inside.

Aborting life, snuffing out tiny, growing people, murdering boys and girls of all nationalities, burning and destroying perfect little hearts, fingers and toes, brains and ears, vocal chords and wee feet, all just weeks away from being able to be washed, clothed, fed, cuddled, and affected for a lifetime by a warm and loving welcome into the world — what a career!

There are those who counsel people who are sad, broken, fearful, unhappy, full of guilt, without a base for life, seeking some sort of fulfillment and freedom by telling them, "Just kill your little baby, the grandchild of your parents and the cousin of your brother's children, just kill it, and go on without remembering what happened. Forget it, and be free to go on and enjoy your own body without that growing tumor inside of you. Be free to enjoy life alone, without ever hearing your own child's voice or seeing whether her eyes are blue or brown, her hair curly or straight, her talents for ballet or violin, her mind mathematical or philosophical. Forget it — you won't wake up in the night crying; that's just a lot of old wives' tales.

To give that kind of false counsel is to be sliding into the lies Satan would have people believe about themselves and becoming the mouthpiece for them. "You aren't really a mother. You won't feel like a mother. That was just a piece of tissue, something like marmalade in you. It's just like having a splinter taken out." What false counseling! What an example of the blind leading the blind! Each person who counsels someone to kill, to murder, the relative inside her own body is violating the sixth commandment, but also violating the fifth. We are to care for our relatives, or we are worse than infidels, and we are not to murder. So in an abortion two commandments are broken at once, two specifically.

In the tenth Psalm one can feel the strength of emotion we should have for the innocent girls or young women being given wrong or wicked advice, as well as for the innocent babies who if they could sing would sing, "Mama, Mama, Mama, don't believe their lies. Please let me look into your eyes. Mama, Mama, Mama, don't leave me" (From "Too Young to Die," by Dallas Graham).

> In his arrogance the wicked man hunts down the weak,
>   who are caught in the schemes he devises.
> He boasts of the cravings of his heart,
>   he blesses the greedy and reviles the Lord. . . .
> He says to himself, "Nothing will shake me;
>   I'll always be happy and never have trouble."
> His mouth is full of curses and lies and threats;
>   trouble and evil are under his tongue.
> He lies in wait near the villages;
>   from ambush he murders the innocent,
>   watching in secret for his victims.
> He lies in wait like a lion in cover;
>   he lies in wait to catch the helpless. . . .
> He says to himself, "God has forgotten;
>   he covers his face and never sees."
>
> (Psalm 10:2, 3, 6-9, 11)

What a picture of today — not just the violence of terrorists hiding in every kind of ambush to surprise victims in their own homes or places of business, but a picture of the pouncing on the unborn and dragging them out of hiding to be destroyed before they can ever ask, Who am I? and How can I be fulfilled? And what is more, so many, many times the mother is not given a chance to find out the answers either.

The anguished cry — "Oh, I wish I hadn't! Why didn't someone *tell* me I'd feel like this? No one explained to me that I'd dream of babies and wake up crying. No one told me I'd feel so empty" — is a cry that ought to be recorded for the people who are promising freedom — freedom physically, intellectually, morally, emotionally, psychologically and spiritually. Freedom for the whole person? And what about the one who gave the other half of the forty-six chromosomes . . . the father, the other parent of the dead child? The destruction has wiped out his own son or daughter before he could feel his arms around his neck or hear him ask a question. A generation wiped out. The blessing God had promised now never to be experienced.

Human beings have been made by God to have family relationships. In today's abnormal world many are cut off from this joy because of the spoiledness and sin that has come in to separate people. But to murder the next generation is to add guilt to loneliness as the years go on. The sin of murder and of not caring at all about one's relatives brings with it a penetrating effect in this life which needs to be dealt with.

Jeremiah speaks to the Israelites, but also to those who call themselves Christians today and feel that they are really the people of God. It is a word of warning from God.

This is the word that came to Jeremiah from the Lord: "Stand at the gate of the Lord's house and there proclaim this message: 'Hear the word of the Lord, all you people of Judah who come through these gates to worship the Lord. This is what the Lord Almighty, the God of Israel says: Reform your ways and your actions, and I will let you live in this place. Do not trust in deceptive words and say, "This is the temple of the Lord, the temple of the Lord, the temple of the Lord!" If you really change your ways and your actions and deal with each other justly, if you do not oppress the alien, the fatherless or the widow and do not shed innocent blood in this place, and if you do not follow other gods to your harm, then I will let you live in this place, in the land I gave your forefathers for ever and ever. But look, you are trusting in deceptive words that are worthless.

"'Will you steal and murder, commit adultery and perjury, burn incense to Baal and follow other gods you have not known, and then come and stand before me in this house, which bears my Name, and say, "we are safe" — safe to do all these detestable things? Has this house, which bears my Name, become a den of robbers to you? But I have been watching! declares the Lord.'" (Jeremiah 7:1-11)

Those who call themselves God's people, whether Protestants or

Catholics or Jews, whether evangelicals or liberals, whether charismatics or those who have a rigid form of worship — are all in danger of "trusting in deceptive words," in danger of saying words which are devoid of meaning, because of actions making it clear that the words are only a kind of outside paint job, covering up detestable things inside. Just saying "this is God's house," "this is a worship service," "praise the Lord," "we are praising God," "bless my soul," and other phrases of worship does nothing. God listens only if the Word of God is really believed and honored and lived by. Go back and read the list again as God enumerates the things that are detestable to Him. He sees into the lies and actions, as well as into the minds and hearts, of each congregation of people saying, "We are safe because we are saying the right words." The list is frightening because we all can find ourselves described.

As we think of the sixth commandment now, that murder is forbidden, we see around us today the shedding of innocent blood in abortion, at every stage of life *before* birth, in allowing babies to starve to death *after* they are born if there is something wrong which the doctor thinks would make life "not worth living." The door is also open to euthanasia, the killing of the mentally ill, senile, or just old, for growing numbers of reasons, including economic reasons.

So very many religious people, including many who profess to be believing Christians who want to live by the Bible, think that they are not bound by God's severe word concerning murder when they shrug their shoulders about abortion, infanticide, and euthanasia. They act as if it ts something Christians, believers, can differ about, like music, or what kind of a bell the church is going to have.

Another lie is the evaluation of human life as having to come up to a certain measurable standard to be "life worth living." If we were to compare the best person alive today with what human beings would be like had there been no fall, what "normal" was like without any imperfections, not one person would have a "quality of life worthy to be lived." Thank God He has told us that we have a purpose now, even though the creation has been devastated and we are so spoiled. And thank God He has told us that one day we shall all be restored, and our new bodies will be our experience of reality — forever. Then we will know what perfection is like. The waiting period, as we live now, is to be an important one, as well as a busy one, whatever our handicaps are. Murder is not the way to care for each other's problems and afflictions!

Recently in an English seminar for *Whatever Happened to the Human Race?* a doctor stood up in the audience and told of how her own little girl was born with spinal bifida and of how she and her husband (also a

doctor) read on her chart that she was to be given no care, no medica-
tion, and no food by mouth. She was being starved to death on the decision of some doctor or doctors that her life was not worthy to be lived.
This couple kidnapped their own baby and took her home from that hospital, cared for her, gave her antibiotics when she was ill, loved and fed
her, did all they could without the operation which had been refused
them by social medicine. The little girl still needs that operation, but at
two is beautiful in spite of being paralyzed from the waist down, is very
bright and talkative, and a joy to her parents as well as a happy child.

What else can allowing a baby to starve to death, to become dehydrat-
ed because of the removal of all liquid, be called except murder? And
who is guilty? As Christians, are we concerned and asking the Lord what
He would have us do in this moment of history as standards swiftly slide
from an absolute base to a relative one, changing with all the winds of
opinion blowing from every side?

Suicide is another kind of murder — the murder of oneself rather than
of another person. Of course, sudden mental breakdown, a demented
mind, temporary insanity, can cause such swift action that time to reconsider is lost. God knows the heart, and He also knows all forms of illness
and breakdown in the mind and emotions that can take place. God
knows our strains and stresses and weakness. He tells of the varying
weaknesses of His children and warns us to care for the weaker brother.
People who are easily hit by temptation often are hit by diversity of
temptation, and the stronger should help the weaker, whatever the
weakness may be. Care must be taken not to push anyone into a place of
temptation.

Certainly the whole movement of writing books and telling people
how to commit suicide rather than going on with old age or cancer or
whatever is something that must be fought by Christians. We are responsible for letting it be known that suicide is murder — and that the sixth
commandment has not been canceled out. It is still one of God's absolutes. We are responsible to let it be known that there is no such thing as
"sin with dignity"!

We each are tempted in different areas. Isaiah 5:20-23 describes a
diversity of areas in which we need to confess horrible deeds to the Lord
and ask for help not to do them again.

> Woe to those who call evil good
>   and good evil,
> who put darkness for light
>   and light for darkness,

who put bitter for sweet
  and sweet for bitter.
Woe to those who are wise in their own eyes
  and clever in their own sight.
Woe to those who are heroes at drinking wine
  and champions at mixing drinks,
who acquit the guilty for a bribe,
  but deny justice to the innocent.

In many countries where statistics number so and so many Christians, there is only a tiny minority who ever come out of the woodwork to make clear that they recognize that what is being done in their countries, their states, their cities or villages, their small communities, or even their churches or assemblies is directly contrary to the Word of God. It is even contrary to the basic Ten Commandments He gave to show people how to live.

For a believer who claims to be in God's family, either to help people to murder without it hurting their consciences, or to shrug one's shoulders and say, "It doesn't matter; we can differ on these subjects," is to be placing oneself in the Judge's chair and remaking the laws upon which to base the judgement.

So often human beings feel they are better than God. When they cannot understand all that God has commanded, they draw up another set of rules, and feel pious about it too, thinking their rules are not only better, but more compassionate and full of love. What twisted love! What twisted compassion! What lack of trust!

Long, long before Moses stood reading the Ten Commandments, God had made clear to the family of Noah as they began a new period of history that because people are made in the image of God and have such importance, when anyone murders another person, then the murderer is to die. Capital punishment was ordered by God to make clear the preciousness of life. The emphasis is direct and complete: the murderer is to die in the place of the murdered one, to show the sinfulness of the sin of snuffing out human life. The reason is, "for in the image of God has God made man." That was reason enough.

When we come to the time of Moses, the clear command, "You shall not murder," was explicitly widened in what came right after that. For instance in Exodus 21, the next chapter, explanations are given as to punishments for breaking this commandment. "Anyone who strikes a man and kills him shall surely be put to death." It is made clear that if this is done unintentionally, then there is a great difference, and he may flee to a place of refuge.

Note carefully: it took a death for a death when Christ died for us. The penalty for the worst sins was death. We have committed the worst sins in one way and another. And death *has* paid the price! Until we see that, we can't understand the total meaning of the death of Christ. It was capital punishment. Really so. But as the Son of God, the Lamb of God, the Savior, the Messiah, the King of kings, He could die in the place of so many! He, as infinite, could take the place of so very many finite ones. The only infinite One is God. Jesus as the I AM made it clear He could die in the place of all who would believe and bow and accept what He was doing for them, as well as making it clear He would rise again, and demonstrate that those for whom He died could also have the glorious hope of resurrection.

Can't you see, capital punishment is what the death of Jesus is all about. It is for us He died! He took that punishment. He didn't say with a shrug, "It's all right. Go ahead and sin by breaking all the command-ments. It's all right. Just live peaceful lives and turn your backs on what others do. When wickedness increases, just shut your eyes." No, Jesus said:

"Do not think I have come to abolish the Law or the Prophets; I have not come to abolish them but to fulfill them. I tell you the truth, until heaven and earth disappear, not the smallest letter, not the least stroke of a pen, will by any means disappear from the Law until everything is accomplished. Anyone who breaks one of the least of these commandments and teaches others to do the same will be called least in the kingdom of heaven, but whoever practices and teaches these commands will be called great in the kingdom of heaven. For I tell you that unless your righteousness surpasses that of the Pharisees and the teachers of the law, you will certainly not enter the kingdom of heaven." (Matthew 5:17-20)

This immediately precedes the very next words Jesus said as He was sitting on a mountainside teaching the people who were crowded there, with a diversity of open or shut minds, listening.

"You have heard it said to the people long ago, 'Do not murder, and anyone who mur-ders will be subject to judgement.' [Note here that Jesus puts the two things together, murder and the capital punishment for that act.] But I tell you that anyone who is angry with his brother will be subject to judgement. [What judgement? Jesus is comparing anger which is strong enough to kill in one's mind, to murder. We can commit murder in our heads when we are angry. This Jesus says is worthy of the strong judgement for a committed murder — not by another human being, but by God.]

"Again, anyone who says to his brother, 'Raca,' is answerable to the Sanhedrin. ["Raca" is an Aramaic term of contempt, and the Sanhedrin had a penalty for using it.] But anyone who says, "You fool!" will be in danger of the fire of hell."

What is Jesus saying? He is communicating clearly that the kind of anger that is within us when we say "you fool" is the kind of anger that is murder in our thoughts. He is saying that civil law may have its punishments, but that God's law when broken puts people in danger of hell. God will not look the other way. Breaking His law is serious.

We need to go back and cry with the disciples when Jesus spoke of how impossible it would be for a rich man to turn away from his great material possessions to put God first. We need to cry, "Who then *can* be saved? If our thoughts are akin to murder, and hell is the 'capital punishment' for such sin, who then *can* be saved?"

The answer is that with man it is impossible, but with God all things are possible. God has provided the substitute, the capital punishment which only Jesus could take in our place. The punishment has already been taken. It can accrue to us if we believe God as He tells us this amazing provision has been made for us and accept it. Fantastic love! Amazing grace! Stunning compassion! But at what a cost!

In 1 John 3, John is talking about love being a mark of the Christian and that which should make believers different from unbelievers. Among all that is given in this chapter, this particularly fits in right here:

> Do not be like Cain, who belonged to the evil one and murdered his brother. And why did he murder him? Because his own actions were evil and his brother's were righteous. Do not be surprised, my brothers, if the world hates you. We know that we have passed from death to life, because we love our brothers. [An evidence we can see in ourselves after we have accepted Christ as Savior is the evidence of a growing love that comes for others in the same family!] Anyone who does not love remains in death. Anyone who hates his brother is a murderer, and you know that no murderer has eternal life in him. This is how we know what love is: Jesus Christ laid down his life for us. And we ought to lay down our lives for our brothers. If anyone has material possessions and sees his brother in need but has no pity on him, how can the love of God be in him? Dear children, let us not love with words or tongue but with actions and in truth. (vv. 12-18)

True, we cannot keep the commandments well enough to earn our salvation. True, forgiveness is given on the basis of the perfect life of Christ and His death in our place, His taking the capital punishment that belonged to us. But after we have become God's children, something is meant to be different about us, and that something is meant to be shown by actions and deeds in line with the truth. In our growing Christian lives we should be coming closer to keeping the commandments of God, by the help of the Holy Spirit. We should also be helping others to know what they consist of and how important they are. Surely, to encourage murder is not a part of the Christian life.

Then, just as we are about to reconsider our own lives and thoughts and actions, and to thank God that our situation is not hopeless, but that He has given hope, and a solution for each of us personally, suddenly one jumps up and says, "Hey, what about war?"

What about war?

First, the Bible is clear that the same God who commanded, "You shall not murder" also told His Old Testament people that they were to wage war. The people they fought were nations which had come to a place of a fullness of wickedness that demanded immediate judgement. At the time of Noah, God used the flood to judge those who had so completely turned away from him into wickedness. At the time of Sodom and Gomorrah, God destroyed the cities because the wickedness was total. In the battles which God commanded His people to wage, they were being used as His instrument of judgement when those about them had come to a fullness of wickedness. Prophecy in the New Testament makes clear that judgement is ahead. One day there will be a final battle before true and lasting peace will be ushered in. That final battle is described in the book of Revelation.

No one who takes the Bible as the authority from God can say that war has always been a breaking of the commandment "You shall not murder."

Christians have differed through the centuries as to whether there should be any war during the time between Christ's death and the last battle. We are told to turn the other cheek personally, but whether this extends to the national level is something Christians can differ on. In a fallen world there is a problem involving nations. The State is called upon to bring forth justice in a world that requires police forces to do this in each nation. This inward protection of each country extends to the borders. And the protection takes a variety of forms.

Within a country, and at the border of countries, there is continually a question of responsibility, and the facing of the question, Am I my brother's keeper? When a Christian sees a brutal man abusing a small child, and that man will not listen to reason, at some point the Christian with compassion and love for his neighbor, in this case the child, must do what he would if the child were his own and intervene with force.

Since the time of the Old Testament we have not had God commanding an individual war for judgement, nor His choosing a nation to represent Him. In a fallen world there can be all kinds of rationalization and manipulation, especially in a day of mass communication. However, there are cases where there is no other way to stop horrible injustices, mass murder, oppression, including torture, aggression and all the rest, except by war. We are far enough away from the war with Hitler's Germany now to judge it with some objectivity. Realizing what was happening there, one could ask how Christian love could possibly do nothing when we are told that "love always protects," "love never fails." If a nation such as the United States could intervene, how could it stand by and watch without attempting to help those crying out for help? Of course, no one can have the kind of certainty that the Old Testament people had when God specifically commanded them to go to war and laid out the strategy as with Gideon, but in a fallen world such a situation as Hitler's Germany calls forth strenuous action.

If we had been the ones in power in the countries which could help, and we knew in detail all that was going on in Hitler's Germany, could we have sunned ourselves in peaceful gardens and fields, on beaches or in mountain resorts, sending messages to those in Germany such as "Stand fast against the atrocities even at the cost of your lives" while we continued to enjoy our personal peace? Would we not have to intervene with force when all other means had failed?

War is complicated, and so is a police force, because people are complicated and sinful, and there are so many kinds of mixed motives as well as individually sinful acts. However, recognizing the complications does not change the fact that there comes a time for nations, as well as for the police force and for individuals, to intervene on the behalf of people who are being harmed, as well as for judgement.

This does not mean there will not be tears, nor does it mean that individual Christians do not have to face a decision about whether or not they can support any particular war. Naturally, as with all other situations in this spoiled world since the fall, there is no perfect nation and no perfect soldier. But Christians need to decide whether they can support the war they face. If not, they must be willing to say no, even at great personal cost. However, there will continue to be situations in a fallen world where such judgement and intervention will be needed, right up to the time when Christ Himself returns with justice to judge and fight the final battle.

Is it an easy decision to make? No. Never. And the reason why is always the same! The world is made up of imperfect people. However, in war, theoretically at least, those against whom the war is fought are those who have done something as a nation that is overwhelmingly wicked and who are continuing to do that which needs to be stopped. Other solutions failing, the extremity of war is demanded. In this kind of situation, war becomes its own kind of capital punishment on a larger scale. It is not simply a punishment; it is also a means of stopping an individual or nation from continuing in a "fullness of wickedness."

The One in whose image people were made, who says life is so precious that no human being is to murder another one without paying for that act with his own life, is one day going to put an end to all the wickedness which will have "filled the cup to overflowing" with the final battle. Satan, the liar who brought death and murder into the creation of God to devastate it, will be vanquished, and the victory will be complete.

I saw heaven standing open and there before me was a white horse, whose rider is called Faithful and True. With justice he judges and makes war. His eyes are like blazing fire, and on his head are many crowns. He has a name written on him that no one but he himself knows. He is dressed in a robe dipped in blood, and his name is the Word of God. The armies of heaven were following him, riding on white horses and dressed in fine linen, white and clean. Out of his mouth comes a sharp sword with which to strike down the nations. "He will rule them with an iron scepter." He treads the winepress of the fury of the wrath of God Almighty. On his robe and on his thigh he has this name written: KING OF KINGS AND LORD OF LORDS. (Revelation 19:11-16)

Yes, an end is coming to murder, an end is coming to killing. Listen to 1 Corinthians 15:24-26. This comes right after we have been told that as in Adam all die, so in Christ all will be made alive; "Then the end will come, when he hands over the kingdom of God the Father after he has destroyed all dominion, authority and power. For he must reign until he has put all his enemies under his feet. The last enemy to be destroyed is death."

Then in Revelation 21:4 we are given a glimpse of the new heaven and the new earth, where the promise is given: "He will wipe every tear from our eyes. There will be no more death or mourning or crying or pain, for the old order of things has passed away."

DISCUSSION QUESTIONS

1. Why did the fall result in death? How should we view death? Why?

2. Why are humans valuable? How should this effect the way we relate to one another?

3. In considering children, the Bible consistently says that they are gifts and are to be highly valued. In light of these truths, what should our responsibility be in protecting them?

4. What graphic picture does Edith give of abortion? How does this contrast with today's understanding of abortion?

5. Explain what happened at the seminar in England. If you were in the situation described, what would you have done?

6. How does Christ's death fulfill the law for us?

7. Why should we take "strenuous action" against evil? How does our view of this commandment affect this?

8. Why could a war be considered justified?

Francis Schaeffer

Time magazine once called Francis Schaeffer "a missionary to the intellectuals." He has had a great influence in making Biblical Christianity a reasonable alternative to complete secularism for many thinking people. His books include titles such as *Escape from Reason, The God Who is There, True Spirituality* and most recently, *A Christian Manifesto.*

Dr. Schaeffer has collaborated with his son in writing and producing several film series: "How Should We Then Live?", which explains the history of ideas from Roman civilization until the present; "Whatever Happened to the Human Race?", a series exposing the loss of human rights today, including the right to life, due to the emerging dominance of the humanistic world view; and most recently, "Reclaiming the World," which deals with major issues confronting Christians in today's world.

Francis and his wife Edith give leadership to the international study and religious community, L'Abri, located in Switzerland. This grew out of the Schaeffer's opening of their home to young people who were traveling throughout Europe. Schaeffer dialoged with these people, listening to their ideas and challenging them on the basis of their presuppositions. Through the years, Dr. Schaeffer has sought to show how Christianity is the only philosophical system which fits the truth of the world. Today there are L'Abri centers in Switzerland, Great Britain and the United States.

"Christianity is not just a series of truths but *Truth* — Truth about all of reality. And the holding to that Truth intellectually . . . brings forth not only certain personal results, but also governmental and legal results."

The Abolition of Truth and Morality*

Francis Schaeffer

The basic problem of the Christians in this country in the last eighty years or so, in regard to society and in regard to government, is that they have seen things in bits and pieces instead of totals.

They have very gradually become disturbed over permissiveness, pornography, the public schools, the breakdown of the family, and finally abortion. But they have not seen this as a totality — each thing being a part, a symptom, of a much larger problem. They have failed to see that all of this has come about due to a shift in world view — that is, through a fundamental change in the overall way people think and view the world and life as a whole. This shift has been *away from* a world view that was at least vaguely Christian in people's memory (even if they were not individually Christian) *toward* something completely different — toward a world view based upon the idea that the final reality is impersonal matter or energy shaped into its present form by impersonal chance. They have not seen that this world view has taken the place of the one that had previously dominated Northern European culture, including the United States, which was at least Christian in memory, even if the individuals were not individually Christian.

---

*From *The Christian Manifesto* by Francis Schaeffer, 1981/82. Used by permission of CROSSWAY BOOKS, Westchester, Illinois 60153.

These two world views stand as totals in complete antithesis to each other in content and also in their natural results — including sociological and governmental results, and specifically including law.

It is not that these two world views are different only in how they understand the nature of reality and existence. They also inevitably produce totally different results. The operative word here is *inevitably*. It is not just that they happen to bring forth different results, but it is absolutely *inevitable* that they will bring forth different results.

Why have the Christians been so slow to understand this? There are various reasons but the central one is a defective view of Christianity. This has its roots in the Pietist movement under the leadership of P. J. Spener in the seventeenth century. Pietism began as a healthy protest against formalism and a too abstract Christianity. But it had a deficient, "platonic" spirituality. It was platonic in the sense that Pietism made a sharp division between the "spiritual" and the "material" world — giving little, or no, importance to the "material" world. The totality of human existence was not afforded a proper place. In particular it neglected the intellectual dimension of Christianity.

Christianity and spirituality were shut up to a small, isolated part of life. The totality of reality was ignored by the pietistic thinking. Let me quickly say that in one sense Christians should be pietists in that Christianity is not just a set of doctrines, even the right doctrines. *Every* doctrine is in some way to have an effect upon our lives. But the poor side of Pietism and its resulting platonic outlook has really been a tragedy not only in many people's individual lives, but in our total culture.

True spirituality covers all of reality. There are things the Bible tells us as absolutes which are sinful — which do not conform to the character of God. But aside from these the Lordship of Christ covers *all* of life and *all* of life equally. It is not only that true spirituality covers all of life equally, but it covers all parts of the spectrum of life equally. In this sense there is nothing concerning reality that is not spiritual.

Related to this, it seems to me, is the fact that many Christians do not mean what I mean when I say Christianity is true, or Truth. They are Christians and they believe in, let us say, the truth of creation, the truth of the virgin birth, the truth of Christ's miracles, Christ's substitutionary death, and His coming again. But they stop there with these and other individual truths.

When I say Christianity is true I mean it is true to total reality — the total of what is, beginning with the central reality, the objective existence of the personal-infinite God. Christianity is not just a series of truths but *Truth* — Truth about all of reality. And the holding to that Truth intellectually — and then in some poor way living upon that Truth, the Truth of what is — brings forth not only certain personal results, but also governmental and legal results.

Now let's go over to the other side — to those who hold the materialistic final reality concept. They saw the complete and total difference between the two positions more quickly than Christians. There were the Huxleys, George Bernard Shaw (1856-1950), and many others who understood a long time ago that there are two total concepts of reality and that it was one total reality against the other and not just a set of isolated and separated difference. The *Humanist Manifesto I*,[1] published in 1933, showed with crystal clarity their comprehension of the totality of what is involved. It was to our shame that Julian (1887-1975) and Aldous Huxley (1894-1963), and the others like them, understood much earlier than Christians that these two world views are two total concepts of reality standing in antithesis to each other. We should be utterly ashamed that this is the fact.

They understood not only that there were two totally different concepts but that they would bring forth two totally different conclusions, both for individuals and for society. What we must understand is that the two world views really do bring forth with inevitable certainty not only personal differences, but also total differences in regard to society, government, and law.

There is no way to mix these two total world views. They are separate entities that cannot be synthesized. Yet we must say that liberal theology, the very essence of it from its beginning, is an attempt to mix the two. Liberal theology tried to bring forth a mixture soon after the Enlightenment and has tried to synthesize these two views right up to our own day. But in each case when the chips are down these liberal theologians have always come down, as naturally as a ship coming into home port, on the side of the nonreligious humanist. They do this with certainty because what their liberal theology really is is humanism expressed in theological terms instead of philosophic or other terms.

An example of this coming down naturally on the side of the nonreligious humanists is the article by Charles Hartshorne in the January 21, 1981, issue of *The Christian Century*, pages 42-45. Its title is, "Concerning Abortion, an Attempt at a Rational View." He begins by equating the fact that the human fetus is alive with the fact that mosquitoes and bacteria are also alive. That is, he begins by assuming that human life is not unique. He then continues by saying that *even after the baby is born* it is not fully human until its social relations develop (though he says the infant does have some primitive social relations an unborn fetus does not have). His conclusion is, "Nevertheless, I have little sympathy with the idea that infanticide is just another form of murder. Persons who are already functionally persons in the full sense have more important rights even than infants." He then, logically, takes the next step: "Does this distinction apply to the killing of a hopelessly senile person or one in a permanent coma? For me it does." No atheistic humanist could say it with greater clarity. It is significant at this point to note that many of the denominations controlled by liberal theology have come out, publicly and strongly, in favor of abortion.

Dr. Martin E. Marty is one of the respected, theologically liberal spokesmen. He is an associate editor of *The Christian Century* and Fairfax M. Cone distinguished service professor at the University of Chicago divinity school. He is often quoted in the secular press as the spokesman for "mainstream" Christianity. In a *Christian Century* article in the January 7-14, 1981, issue (pages 13-17 with an addition on page 31), he has an article entitled: "Dear Republicans: A Letter on Humanisms." In it he brilliantly confuses the terms "being human," humanism, the humanities and being "in love with humanity." Why does he do this? As a historian he knows the distinctions of those words, but when one is done with these pages the poor reader who knows no better is left with the eradication of the total distinction between the Christian position and the humanist one. I admire the cleverness of the article, but I regret that in it Dr. Marty has come down on the nonreligious humanist side, by confusing the issues so totally.

It would be well at this point to stress that we should not confuse the very different things which Dr. Marty did confuse. *Humanitarianism* is being kind and helpful to people, treating people humanly. The *humanities* are the studies of literature, art, music, etc. — those things which are the products of human creativity. *Humanism* is the placing of Man at the center of all things and making him the measure of all things.

Thus, Christians should be the most humanitarian of all people. And Christians certainly should be interested in the humanities as the product of human creativity, made possible because people are uniquely made in the image of the great Creator. In this sense of being interested in the humanities it would be proper to speak of a Christian humanist. This is especially so in the past usage of that term. This would then mean that such a Christian is interested (as we all should be) in the product of people's creativity. In this sense, for example, Calvin could be called a Christian humanist because he knew the works of the Roman writer Seneca so very well.[2] John Milton and many other Christian poets could also be so called because of their knowledge not only of their own day but also of antiquity.

But in contrast to being humanitarian and being interested in the humanities Christians should be inalterably opposed to the false and destructive humanism, which is false to the Bible and equally false to what Man is.

Along with this we must keep distinct the "humanist world view" of which we have been speaking and such a thing as the "Humanist Society," which produced the *Humanist Manifestos I and II* (1933 and 1973). The Humanist Society is made up of a relatively small group of people (some of whom, however, have been influential — John Dewey, Sir Julian Huxley, Jacques Monod, B. F. Skinner, etc.). By way of contrast, the humanist world view includes many thousands of adherents and today controls the consensus in society, much of the media, much of what is taught in our schools, and much of the arbitrary law being produced by the various departments of government.

The term humanism used in this wider, more prevalent way means Man beginning from himself, with no knowledge except what he himself can discover and no standards outside of himself. In this view Man is the measure of all things, as the Enlightenment expressed it.

Nowhere have the divergent results of the two total concepts of reality, the Judeo-Christian and the humanist world view, been more open to observation than in government and law.

We of Northern Europe (and we must remember that the United States, Canada, Australia, New Zealand and so on are extensions of Northern Europe) take our *form-freedom balance* in government for granted as though it were natural. There is form in acknowledging the obligations in society, and there is freedom in acknowledging the rights of the individual. We have form, we have freedom; there is freedom, there is form. There is a balance here which we have come to take as natural in the world. It is not natural in the world. We are utterly foolish if we look at the long span of history and read the daily newspapers giving today's history and do not understand that the form-freedom balance in government which we have had in Northern Europe since the Reformation and in the countries extended from it is unique in the world, past and present.

That is not to say that no one wrestled with these questions before the Reformation nor that no one produced anything worthwhile. One can think, for example, of the Conciliar Movement in the late medieval church and the early medieval parliaments.[3] Especially one must consider the ancient English Common Law. And in relation to that Common Law (and all English Law) there is Henry DeBracton. I will mention more about him in a moment.

Those who hold the material-energy, chance concept of reality, whether they are Marxist or non-Marxist, not only do not know the truth of the final reality, God, they do not know who Man is. Their concept of Man is what Man is not, just as their concept of the final reality is what final reality is not. Since their concept of Man is mistaken, their concept of society and of law is mistaken, and they have no sufficient base for either society or law.

They have reduced Man to even less than his natural finiteness by seeing him only as a complex arrangement of molecules, made complex by blind chance. Instead of seeing him as something great who is significant even in his sinning, they see Man in his essence only as an intrinsically competitive animal, that has no other basic operating principle than natural selection brought about by the strongest, the fittest, ending on top. And they see Man as acting in this way both individually and collectively as society.

Even on the basis of Man's finiteness having people swear in court *in the name of humanity*, as some have advocated, saying something like, "We pledge our honor before all mankind"[4] would be insufficient enough. But reduced to the materialistic view of Man, it is even less. Although many nice words may be used, in reality law constituted on this basis can only mean brute force.

In this setting Jeremy Bentham's (1748-1842) Utilitarianism can be and must be all that law means. And this must inevitably lead to the conclusion of Oliver Wendell Holmes Jr. (1841-1935): "The life of the law has not been logic: it has been experience."[5] That is, there is *no* basis for law except Man's limited, finite experience. And especially with the Darwinian, survival-of-the-fittest concept of Man (which Holmes held) that must, and will, lead to Holmes' final conclusion: law is "the majority vote of that nation that could lick all others."[6]

The problem always was, and is, What is an adequate base for law? What is adequate so that the human aspiration for freedom can exist without anarchy, and yet provides a form that will not become arbitrary tyranny?

In contrast to the materialistic concept, Man in reality is made in the image of God and has real humanness. This humanness has produced varying degrees of success in government, bringing forth governments that were more than only the dominance of brute force.

And those in the stream of the Judeo-Christian world view have had something more. The influence of the Judeo-Christian world view can be perhaps most readily observed in Henry DeBracton's influence on British Law. An English judge living in the thirteenth century, he wrote *De Legibus et Consuetudinibus* (c. 1250).

Bracton, in the stream of the Judeo-Chdistian world view, said:

And that he [the King] ought to be under the law appears clearly in the analogy of Jesus Christ, whose vice-regent on earth he is, for though many ways were open to Him for his ineffable redemption of the human race, the true mercy of God chose this most powerful way to destroy the devil's work, he would not use the power of brute force but the reason of justice.[7][8]

In other words, God in His sheer power could have crushed Satan in his revolt by the use of that sufficient power. But because of God's character, justice came before the use of power alone. Therefore Christ died that justice, rooted in what God is, would be the solution. Bracton codified this: Christ's example, because of who He is, is our standard, our rule, our measure. Therefore power is not first, but justice is first in society and law. The prince may have the power to control and to rule, but he does not have the right to do so without justice. This was the basis of English Common Law. The Magna Charta (1215) was written within thirty-five years (or less) of Bracton's *De Legibus* and in the midst of the same universal thinking in England at that time.

The Reformation (300 years after Bracton) refined and clarified this further. It got rid of the encrustations that had been added to the Judeo-Christian world view and clarified the point of authority — with authority resting in the Scripture rather than church *and* Scripture, or state *and* Scripture. This not only had meaning in regard to doctrine but clarified the base for law.

That base was God's written Law, back through the New Testament to Moses' written Law; and the content and authority of that written Law is rooted back to Him who is the final reality. Thus, neither church nor state was equal to, let alone above, that Law. The base for law is not divided, and no one has the right to place anything, including king, state or church, above the content of God's Law.

What the Reformation did was to return most clearly and consistently to the origins, to the final reality, God; but equally to the reality of Man — not only Man's personal needs (such as salvation), but also Man's social needs.

What we have had for four hundred years, produced from this clarity, is unique in contrast to the situation that has existed in the world in forms of government. Some of you have been taught that the Greek city states had our concepts of government. It simply is not true.[9] All one has to do is read Plato's *Republic* to have this come across with tremendous force.

When the men of our State Department, especially after World War II, went all over the world trying to implant our form-freedom balance in government downward on cultures whose philosophy and religion would never have produced it, it has, in almost every case, ended in some form of totalitarianism or authoritarianism.

The humanists push for "freedom," but having no Christian consensus to contain it, that "freedom" leads to chaos or to slavery under the state (or under an elite). Humanism, with its lack of *any* final base for values or law, always leads to chaos. It then naturally leads to some form of authoritarianism to control the chaos. Having produced the sickness, humanism gives more of the same kind of medicine for a cure. With its mistaken concept of final reality, it has no intrinsic reason to be interested in the individual, the human being. Its natural interest is the two collectives: the state and society.

DISCUSSION QUESTIONS

1. In relation to society, what has the Christians' major mistake been? What effect has this had?

2. What is pietism and what effect has this had on today's Christian movement?

3. What is true spirituality? Explain.

4. What does it mean that Christianity is true?

5. What is humanism? Explain its effect on our society.

6. How does a world view (Christian or Humanist) effect our society and its legal systems?

7. What is the "form — freedom" balance in government? How does it work? What are the two conflicting concepts of law in today's society?

8. Why is it important that authority rest in scripture alone? If law is based on Biblical truth how does this effect those in powerful positions?

9. What responsibility do we have as Christians to Biblically evaluate society and government?

Barry Seagren

Barry Seagren was born in Pittsburgh. Trained as a physicist at Haverford College near Philadelphia, he was employed as an aerospace engineer, where he did theoretical studies related to the Saturn program.

During that year, Barry, a nominal churchgoer, stumbled into a Bible-believing church for the first time and heard the Gospel. He became a Christian that year and the course of his life changed. Although his intention had always been to go to graduate school in his field, he decided to enroll for a year of informal studies at Covenant Seminary. One year became four. In 1969, Barry graduated magna cum laude with a Masters of Divinity. While at Covenant, Barry received the Homiletics (writing and delivering sermons) Award.

During his seminary years at Covenant, Barry became familiar with Dr. Schaeffer and had the chance to study at Swiss L'Abri one summer. After completing his degree, he and his wife, Veronica, returned to the Swiss L'Abri as workers, where they remained for the following ten years. In 1979 they came to Southborough, Massachusetts and helped found the U.S. L'Abri. The Seagrens have three children.

". . . we could sit around and share our ideas and feelings about who or what God is. What would we learn from that? Something about each other's feelings and ideas, not a thing about God."

Who Is God?
Barry Seagren

The Knowability of God

Is this a reasonable question? Many would say "no." We cannot know anything about God. That is totally beyond our scope. God is totally other. To many people, even to raise the question is either totally naive or hopelessly arrogant. Theology cannot be the study of God. At most, it is the study of people's *ideas* about God. We must understand that, from a certain point of view, they are right. Left to our own devices, we would be fools to even address this question. God is not open to our examination. There is no way to investigate this issue, no possibility of doing research on this topic. There is no way to puncture the heavens and examine God. One possibility is that we could sit around and share our ideas and feelings about who or what God is. What would we learn from that? Something about each other's feelings and ideas, not a thing about God.

There is another possibility. We could look at nature, the world around us. Whatever a person creates is a reflection of his nature, an expression of who he is. Thus, if indeed there is a God who created the world, by looking at that world we could learn something about the one who created it. This seems promising, and, indeed, a person should be able to understand something of God's sheer existence and his enormous power simply because he lives in God's universe. Yet there are two problems associated with this. First, there is a very minimal amount of knowledge available.

No real content, just the general impression of the existence and power of a God. Secondly, the message we get from nature is often ambiguous. Consider the Swiss Alps. It is hard to stand in the Alps and not be moved to awe and worship. Yet for those who have lived for generations in the tiny alpine villages, the mountains are ominous, looming over them, cutting them off from the rest of the world, making their farming an exceedingly difficult enterprise. The religion of such people is apt to be one of superstition and fear. Thus, there is a certain amount of knowledge to be gained from nature. We are inexcusable if we ignore it. That is the message of Romans 1. It should send us off on our search. Yet it cannot really provide the answers. Any substantial knowledge of God eludes us. The questions seems unanswerable. The subject is totally closed to us.

We must realize that it is not only this question, but all the really important questions that are closed to us. Who am I, who is man, how did it all begin, what is the meaning of life, what has gone so dreadfully wrong, why are we all losers, is there any solution, what happens after death, how will it all end? These are totally beyond our scope. The questions are too big, we are too small. The old illustration of the blind men trying to describe an elephant is apt. One felt the ear and said the elephant was like a leaf; another felt the trunk and said it was like a snake; the third felt the leg and concluded that an elephant was like a tree. The problem was that their observations were so partial as to be totally misleading and useless. This is where we stand in trying to address the fundamental questions of life. We see such a small slice of the pie that we really cannot draw any valid conclusions. Many have understood this and have become cynics and skeptics. They are right in the sense that, left to ourselves, we must respond to the basic questions with total silence.

There is only one other possibility. That is a word from outside the finitude and relativity of our human situation. God, if He is there, could disclose himself. He who is God and who created all things could speak and explain it to us. He could reveal to us the things we need to know. He could describe Himself to us in language we could understand. He could give us the information which is not available in any other way. This is precisely the claim of the Bible. It is God's communication to us in human language. That claim is made in many places, perhaps most clearly in 2 Timothy 3:16, where we are told that all scripture is inspired by God. The word *inspired* has its etymological sense: God breathed. In scripture the breath of God is often an image for God's immediate creative agency, as in Genesis 2. Here the meaning is the same. The assertion is that scripture is the product of the creative breath of God. He is the ultimate author. This is why the Bible is so important. It gives us the only real possibility of knowledge. Without it we are totally in the dark, left to speculate fruitlessly on the major questions of life with no way even to begin to tackle the big issues. We must understand very clearly that if the Bible is God's true, authoritative, written word, then, and only then, can we have knowledge. And we can have knowledge not because we have been clever, but because God has been gracious and given us the information we need. *Unless God speaks, we cannot know.* This is the key to epistemology. If the Bible is just one more human religious book, we are in the dark. On the other hand, if the Bible is the written word of God — His communication to us — clear, truthful, and authoritative, only then can we have an answer to our question, Who is God?

The Existence of God

Surely the most basic and important point in discussing God is that He is there as opposed to not being there. He exists. Hebrews 11:6 stresses this: "anyone who comes to him must believe that He exists . . ."

Some would object that this is so basic that we do not even have to mention it. Some would urge us not to belabor the obvious and to get on to something more profitable, like what kind of God he is. Unhappily, in our day it is not at all belaboring the obvious to insist that we are talking about an objective being. I remember speaking with a theology student who was objecting to the use of antithesis: right versus wrong, true versus false. I responded that surely the great antithesis is that God is there as opposed to not being there. "No, you must not say that," he replied. He was not talking simply about the problem of knowing whether God exists. His was a more profound objection. He felt that reality is so ambiguous that to say either "God exists" or "God does not exist" was simplistic and inappropriate.

Most people would not be quite so blunt, but the same mentality exists widely today. To many people, God exists insofar as we believe he exists. The important thing is our faith. Whatever you believe, that is true for you. The really important thing is that you have a faith which gives meaning to your life. We have all heard this sort of talk often — it is really a matter of faith, everyone has a right to his own beliefs, to his own religion.

We must reject this mentality. We must emphasize that what we think or believe is not the issue. The issue is whether God is really there and what sort of God He is. What we believe or do not believe about Him is entirely secondary. Perhaps a couple of very simple illustrations will clarify. Everyone here has had to get here. Where you think the seminar is, where you believe it is, is not the issue. The issue is where it actually is. There is an objective world out there against which your beliefs are tested.

If your beliefs do not match reality, you simply will not get to the seminar. Of course a person has a right to his own beliefs, but he also has a right to get totally lost if his beliefs do not pass the test of the real world. To give another illustration, suppose a student is asked to name the first president of the U.S. "John Lennon," he answers brightly. "Wrong," says the teacher. "What do you mean?" objects the student, "That's my belief, I hold it sincerely and it means something in my life. I think everyone has a right to his own beliefs. Who are you to impose your religion on me? Who are you to say my faith is wrong?" What shall we do? He is right in the sense that we will not turn him over to the police. Yet we may turn him over to the psychiatrist. We will certainly fail him in history. Again, there is an objective world out there, and our beliefs, our convictions, must be measured against the real world.

This is elementary and obvious: a real world, a definite universe out there, a world which exists quite apart from my opinions. My opinions have to conform to it. We all accept this in virtually every area of life. Yet the extraordinary thing is that when we come to the really basic issues of life, there and only there, people shift gears. Suddenly a whole different approach appears. "It is true for you if you believe it. It is all a matter of faith. Everyone has a right to his own beliefs. I think all religions are true." When you examine them, these are extraordinary sentences which no sane person would dream of uttering in the classroom, the business world, or virtually any area of life. Yet when we come to the so-called "religious" area, this is what we hear.

What it represents is an entirely different notion of truth. Usually *truth* means words which correspond to reality and explain reality. Yet when one comes to the big questions, there is this shifting of gears. *True* comes to mean "meaningful for you," "significant in your life." It is an entirely different approach. We are asked to give up the old correspondence notion of truth and operate upon a notion of truth as significance. This sounds profound at first. Yet what it means is that religion by definition is something totally separate from normal reality, something totally subjective, something which exists solely within some nebulous realm of meaning or significance. We must reject this. We are not allowed to shift gears that way. We must stick to the normal notion of truth. Why? Simply because there is an objective world, a definite universe, and that includes what some would call the spiritual realities. It is better to call them simply the unseen part of reality. The "religious" realities, the big issues, may be less physical, yet they are no less real and definite. Hence, the normal notion of truth must apply. The big issues must not be segregated and treated in some totally different way.

I feel the word *religion* is part of the problem. That word is always the signal to shift gears. People will talk happily about virtually all areas and issues, and always within the normal notion of truth, yet when the basic issues of life are raised, suddenly these are labelled "religious" and we find ourselves in a totally different sort of discussion. If that word could be struck from the English language, we would be way ahead. We must often insist that we are not religious people and that we are not interested in religion. We are interested in truth, in reality, in the way things actually are, and we are Christians because we are convinced Christianity is the truth.

To return to the initial point, the existence of God, it is not at all belaboring the obvious to insist that we are talking about a God who is actually there as opposed to not being there and that He is a definite sort of God. This emphasis is most necessary in our day. This is the first and most basic point about God. We are not talking about religion, we are talking about truth, about reality. The God described in the Bible really exists. He is there, whether anyone thinks about Him, knows about Him, or believes in Him. Isaiah 40:18-23 makes this point strongly. We are not talking about the idol which one fashions out of silver, we are talking about the One who sits above the circle of the earth. In our day we usually do not make images of silver, but we certainly make mental images. Our insistence is that we are not talking about the image we have in minds, but about the One who is really there.

I am not claiming that I have "proved" God. That is quite outside the scope of this discussion. I am simply insisting that we treat the question of God as an objective question, not a matter of my faith, my feelings, what is meaningful to me, a religious issue. Rather, the One described in the Bible is either there or not there.

The Character of God

As we come to the character of God, the first thing which must be made explicit is that the God described in the Bible is personal. This means He is not just the ultimate reality, undifferentiated being, or even blind force. He is a person in the sense that He thinks, acts and feels. God has ideas and opinions; He has feelings and emotions; he makes choices; there are things He loves and things He rejects. In other words, He has a certain moral nature, a definite character. He is a person as we are persons.

This sets the God of the Bible apart from the gods of the East. In eastern thought, God is all, and all is God; He embraces all that is. The Bible insists that this is not true. To God, not all things are the same. It is not true that everything is a part of God, not true that there is a bit of God in everything and everybody. Rather, He is a definite, distinct, discrete person. When we say that God is infinite, we do not mean that He encompasses all things. Rather, we mean that He is without limit in His specific attributes. His power does not end, His justice does not stop, He knows all that can be known.

The fact that God is personal, and that to Him not all things are the same, is the basis, and the only basis, for true moral values. God is not all-encompassing, not undifferentiated being. Rather, He is a person with a definite character. That character becomes the moral absolute of the universe. Not everything is consistent with the character of God. That which is consistent is by definition good, that which is in contrast to the character of God is evil. God's moral nature is that absolute standard of right and wrong. Apart from this notion of a personal God with a definite moral nature, there is no real basis for right and wrong.

How then shall we describe the character, the nature of God? What is He like? There are many ways to approach this, but perhaps the best, because it is the most central in the Bible, is the twin attributes of holiness and love. God is holy, God is love — both totally and simultaneously.

Holiness is a difficult notion for us. In some circles it is almost a derogatory term. Think of the phrase "holier than thou." To us, a holy man is someone who sits in a monastery somewhere, smiles benignly and serves no earthly function whatsoever. The truth is that most of us would probably not like to be described as holy. Holy is a word in great need of rehabilitation. Yet, we must use it, as it is, perhaps, the most basic word the Bible uses to describe the character of God. The basic notion of holiness is separateness. Holiness is that characteristic of God that sets Him apart from his creation. We may think of it as having three facets. The first is majesty. God is high and lifted up, awesome, possessing a blinding holiness before which none can stand. He is aweful in the original meaning of that term. The second facet is righteousness. This is what we are apt to think of first when we hear the word *holy*. He is in no sense evil. He is perfect, entirely good, just, and righteous. The third facet is wrath. This is a very unwelcome concept to the modern mind. It does not mean that He has a hot temper. Rather, it refers to the fact that He cannot accept or tolerate evil. His standard is no less than His own perfection, and He must stand in opposition to anything which contradicts His own character. Again, the root idea of holiness is separateness. When we speak of the holiness of God, we are referring to that absolute transcendence, that blinding perfection and awesomeness before which no one can stand. We can say it very simply. God is not our "buddy," He is the holy God.

Many passages in the Bible speak of this:

Exodus 15:11: "Who among the gods is like you, O Lord? Who is like you — majestic in holiness, awesome in glory, working wonders?" (NIV)

Habbakuk 1:13: "Your eyes are too pure to look on evil; you cannot tolerate wrong." (NIV)

Isaiah 6:3-5: The call of Isaiah came through a vision of the holiness of God. Isaiah's reaction to seeing God was "let me out of here" — "Woe is me, for I am a man of unclean lips . . . and my eyes have seen the King, the Lord Almighty." (NIV)

Luke 5:8: Peter had the same reaction when he realized that Jesus was no less than God in the flesh. "Go away from me Lord, I am a sinful man." (NIV)

Love is a more familiar concept, something we are more comfortable with, and, thus, we need to say less about it. The Bible asserts in so many words that God is love. This is an equally basic and essential statement about God's nature. It refers to His care, His compassion, to the fact that He seeks our good and not our harm. It is His valuing, His esteeming of that which He has created. It is not at all a response to that which is lovely. Rather, love, especially God's love, is something which takes the initiative. God sets His love upon us, esteems and cares for us, despite the fact that we in our sinfulness are most unlovely. One of the best ways to appreciate the love of God is through the images the Bible gives us. God is like a mother hen brooding over her chicks; He is like a father who gives Himself totally for His children.

What needs to be stressed is that we need both these elements. If we have only holiness, we have a stern, distant, severe, unrelenting, harsh deity, one who is ready to pounce if we step out of line. Sadly, many people see God in this way. Sometimes it is because of their upbringing; other times it is due to bad teaching. It is wrong only because it is so incomplete, so one-sided. Without love, holiness degenerates into harshness. We can see the other side of the problem equally clearly. If we have only love, our view of God becomes a very sentimental one. Love degenerates into sentimentality. Again, many people see God in this way, the benign grandfather figure sitting comfortably in heaven, allowing everyone to bask in his unconditional approval. This is all too often the portrayal of Jesus a child gets in Sunday School — "gentle Jesus, meek and mild." This is surely the worst line ever written about Jesus because it is so one-sided. This Jesus is spineless and thoroughly unattractive. Without holiness, love degenerates into sloppy sentimentality. Consider the balanced way in which the Bible presents Jesus. He wept openly over Jerusalem because of His love for it and yet stormed into the temple in total moral outrage, overturned the tables of the money changers and drove them out with a whip. Unless we maintain simultaneously the holiness and the love of God, we have only a caricature of God, we do not have the true God as He presents Himself in the Bible.

This is a real dilemma. We cannot fully appreciate the wonder of the good news until we feel this dilemma. Holiness and love are both strongly taught in the Bible. We see them both as necessary to an accurate view of God. Yet it seems impossible to hold both together. God cannot reject me without making a mockery of His love.

The answer, of course, is in the cross of Jesus Christ. Here, holiness and love meet. Here is the supreme display of the character of God. We often see the cross as an expression of the love of God. It is important to see that the Bible presents it as equally a demonstration of His love and His holiness.

Romans 5:8: "God demonstrates his own love for us in this: While we were still sinners, Christ died for us." (NIV)
Romans 3:26: the cross was to demonstrate his justice

The first point is familiar, but perhaps the last point requires some elaboration. God has decreed that the penalty of sin is death. That is how a holy God must respond to that which violates His character. When sin is committed, the life of the sinner is forfeited. Yet, throughout history this did not happen. People sinned with impunity; nothing seemed to happen, the axe never fell. Sin often went unpunished. This passing over of sin raised a question concerning the righteousness of God. Is He the lenient judge, threatening but never carrying out? Suddenly the answer comes. The life of His son is given to pay the penalty of sin. Justice is served, and God's holiness is demonstrated and vindicated. The cross is a demonstration of the justice of God.

Thus, on the cross, justice and love meet. Out of His love God offers up His own son to satisfy the demands of His holiness. God's holiness is maintained; God's love is displayed. This is the absolute and central glory of the gospel. Here is how God can accept me without compromising His own character. Jesus paid my penalty. My sin is dealt with, not just overlooked. In this way, as Paul says, God is *just and the justifier*. This is one of the most profound and important statements in the entire Bible. In the cross, God is seen to be both holy and loving. His full character is displayed, and we are reconciled to Him.

DISCUSSION QUESTIONS

1. Why is nature inadequate to teach us about God?

2. What are the fundamental questions that demand answers which only God can supply? Why?

3. Why is the Bible important in knowing who God is?

4. When Barry said that God's existence is not a matter of religious belief, he suggests that our thinking does not condition God's personhood. Then why should we think about God's existence?

5. Does a person's sincerity in their belief justify that belief? Why?

6. People today mentally ascribe to the definition which says "truth is relative and subjective" yet they operate according to the conviction that "truth is absolute and objective." Explain this inconsistency and why it's wrong.

7. Why is God's absolute character necessary for there to be real morality?

8. How is God's love made clear in our daily lives? His holiness?

9. How is the cross the demonstration of the justice of God?

10. What kind of Christian outreach is suggested by the dual character of God (holiness and love)? Are certain evangelistic techniques in need of a clearer vision of the character of God?

"Only the Biblical teaching that man bears the image of God can give us a basis for the uniqueness of man . . . man's sensitivity, his love, his ability to think and communicate, his creativity."

Who is Man?
Barry Seagren

Who are we? There is much confusion, because people simply do not know. They do not know what distinguishes them from the animals or, worse yet, from machines. They see themselves as sophisticated apes or as biochemical machines. They feel threatened by ever more powerful and more "human" computers. This is not simply an academic question. It has huge implications for how we treat each other. If we do not know what makes us unique, how we differ, for example, from the animals, we will inevitably begin to treat each other as no different from the animals.

Created
The Bible gives quite a full answer to this question. The place to begin in developing it is with the creation of man as recorded in Genesis 1:26ff. At this point in the narrative we have come to the sixth of the creative days. All else is prepared, and the stage is set for the culmination and apex of God's creation, man. The importance of this moment is signaled in two ways. First of all, we read that, "let us." This is an elaboration of the simple fiat which has been used up to this point. There is a note of consultation and deliberation. Who is the "us"? This is not the plural of majesty. It can be shown that the Hebrews knew of this form but did not use it themselves. The only explanation is that we have here an intimation of plurality in the Godhead, something that remains obscure until the revelation of the

doctrine of the Trinity in the New Testament. The full Godhead is involved in the creation of man.

The second note of importance is the use of the word *create*, the Hebrew word *bara*. This is different from the common word for *do* or *make* and from the word for *form* or *fashion*. It is too much to say that *bara* by definition means create out of nothing. Yet it is a unique word. It is used of God alone; man cannot create in this sense. Furthermore, it always signals something radically new, something which does not just flow naturally from what came before, something which is the prerogative of God alone. The word is used only three places in the whole account. It is used in verse 1, the summary statement of God's calling the raw material universe into being out of nothing. It is used in verse 21, the first appearance of conscious life, and it is used here in verse 27 for the appearance of human life. It seems significant that these are the three places where naturalistic evolution faces discontinuities which it cannot account for. Evolution posits the gradual continuous development from lower forms to higher, everything flowing naturally from what came before. There is no room in such a view for discontinuities. Yet, in thinking of the origin of the world, we face three big discontinuities: How do we get something out of nothing to begin with? How do we derive conscious life from non-conscious life? and how do we understand the existence of human life, something radically different from all else in creation? It is precisely here, where evolution faces gaps it cannot explain, that the Genesis record pointedly uses the word *bara*. God, who alone can create, has done a new thing. With the creation of man, the word is used three times, as if to underscore yet again the uniqueness of man.

The key words used in describing the creation of man are the words *image* and *likeness*. *Image* simply means a material representation. It is often used of a statue or a carved figure. It is used in the New Testament to describe Caesar's image on a coin, the implication being that the coin which bears Caesar's image is to be rendered to Caesar and we who bear God's image are to be rendered to God. The word *likeness* means similarity, pattern, picture, or semblance. It is used by Ezekiel as he struggled to describe his vision — the likeness of living creatures, the likeness of men, the likeness of faces, the likeness of fire. Thus, the two terms are strongly overlapping. There is no real distinction between them. They reinforce each other. Used together, they emphasize that man is the exact image of God, the very likeness of God. He is not an unsuccessful portrait or approximation. Rather, he is a faithful representation, on the finite material level, of God Himself.

This is the defining essence of man. This first statement in the Bible concerning man is also the most fundamental one and the most important one. Man is a finite representation of the infinite God. The second commandment fits in here. We are forbidden to make any material representations of God. Why? The first reason, of course, is the temptation to idolatry. A second reason is that God has already given us a material representation of Himself, namely us, and that is the only one appropriate to express His nature. Anything we would attempt to make would be a caricature of God. Here is the significance of man. At this point he is different from anything else in creation. In that he bears the image of God, his relationship is upward to God, not downward to the remainder of creation. Man is still finite, yet there is no stronger link possible to God, no greater significance which could be given to him. At the same time, the statement that man bears the image of God is also the fundamental limitation on man. His meaning is always derivative. He is not self-existent; he is not autonomous. He is not great in himself; he is great in that he is a representation of God. His glory is a reflection of God's glory, as the moon's light is a reflection of the sun's. He has tremendous meaning, but always in relation to God, never in himself.

This view of man is the only possible alternative to the views which are current in our society. The first of these is that of Eastern mysticisms. These normally begin with the rejection of the creator-creature distinction and the assertion that reality is composed of basically one ingredient. That one ingredient is usually thought of in spiritual terms. To put it simply, God is all and all is God. Thus man, too, is a part of God, an overflow of the very being of God. This seems at first a heady and noble idea, a very high notion of man indeed. Yet this view ends by denying the reality and meaning of separate finite existence. Individuality must be an illusion, because all is one. The individual is simply the wave which seems to have an individual existence, but, upon closer inspection, is seen to be just a part of the ever-rolling sea. Thus, the assertion of the divinity of man ends with the denial of his individuality.

The second view current in our society is that of western materialisms. These, too, begin with the rejection of the creator-creature distinction and the assertion that reality is composed of basically one ingredient. The difference is that, in the West, that one ingredient is thought of in material terms. In this view, man is not basically different from the rocks and the plants and the animals. He may be more complex, but, in the end, he and they can be understood in purely material terms. Thus, there is no reason for treating him any differently. There is no basis for human values, human aspirations, anything which transcends the material. There have been many attempts to dress up this view, but they all ultimately fail. If one begins simply with matter, there is no way ever to go any higher, and man cannot be more than a complicated bio-chemical entity.

Only the Bible, beginning with the creator-creature distinction and the notion that man is created in the image of God, offers us an alternative to these views. In the same way, only the teaching that man is the image of God gives us a viable basis for the human sciences — psychology, sociology, and certain aspects of medicine. If these disciplines do not begin with the assertion that man bears the image of God, they will go quickly and seriously astray. The starting point is crucial; if these disciplines do not understand who man is, wrong and harmful results will surely follow. Only the Biblical teaching that man bears the image of God can give us a basis for the uniqueness of man and for all that is noble in the human race, man's sensitivity, his love, his ability to think and communicate, his creativity.

One note should be added here. Genesis 1:27 makes it clear that man means male and female. Male and female equally and jointly bear the image of God. At this point there is an absolute equality of the sexes. In no sense is one a lesser being. In Genesis 2 we find more detail concerning the roles and functions of the sexes, and, there, differences are drawn out. Yet here, at the fundamental level of creation, there is an equality. Man and woman together are image bearers of God.

A corollary of the fact that man bears the image of God is that he is given dominion over God's creation. (Genesis 1:26, 28-30). Man in God's image has primacy over God's creation. He is the vice regent, charged with the working of God's will, responsible to God for his stewardship. At this point the Biblical teaching is in great contrast to the ancient creation myths. Some of the myths presented the lesser gods as rebellious and complaining about having to look after the earth. To relieve them of their burden, man was created. He was simply a slave, a drone to allow the gods to have leisure. The Bible says quite the opposite. Work is in no sense a curse, though it later becomes so through the fall. Originally work has value, diginity, nobility. It is man's role as the vice regent of God, exercising his stewardship over God's world. After the fall, he begins to subdue the earth to his own ends and not to God's glory, and his dominion is soured. Then work, indeed, becomes toil; labor becomes drudgery. In the beginning it was not so. Man is not allowed to be idle. He is given a noble task: dominion. This is basis for the dignity of work. It is also our mandate for culture, science, industry, agriculture. Adam exercised his dominion immediately in tending the garden and in naming the animals. We continue to exercise it whenever we study and develop the world in which God has put us.

I have spent a good deal of time on the concept of image because it is so crucial. It is the basis for how we see ourselves and how we see our work. It is the basis for how we are to treat each other. We are constantly to keep in mind that the person we face bears the image of God. He is a finite representation of the infinite God. No higher value could possibly be given him, and we dare not treat him as any less. Christian or non-Christian, he has value, his thoughts have value, the work of his hands has value simply because he bears the image of God. We live in an age that increasingly does not know who man is. It is inevitable that it will increasingly fail to treat him properly. Oppression, exploitation, manipulation will become more and more justifiable. All this must happen once the proper view of man is lost. If we do not know why he differs from a stick or a stone, we will begin to treat him as a stick or a stone.

As Christians, we know who man is: he bears the image of God, and we must treat him as if he did in all the relationships of life. The tragedy is that there are too many examples in which Christians treat the non-Christian as something less than he really is. The non-Christian is seen as less than nothing. Sometimes this is justified by an appeal to the doctrine of total depravity, but this is certainly not the proper meaning of total depravity. Man is totally unable to stand before God on the basis of his own moral goodness, but he has not ceased to be a human being, made in God's image. Total depravity is a statement concerning his moral acceptability, not his human worth. We dare not act as though the non-Christian cannot love and cannot have moral sensitivity, social conscience, human compassion. We dare not spurn non-Christian art as valueless and non-Christian thought as devoid of insight. We must affirm the humanness, the dignity, the worth of the saved person, and at the same time lament that he, in all his human sensitivity, is lost and under the wrath of God. He is still the image bearer of God.

Fallen

When God finished His work of creation, He pronounced it all very good, and then God rested. This rest signified that He was indeed finished. The work was complete, perfect. He was satisfied. He did not botch the job. There was no tinkering left to do. The creation did not in any sense contain the seeds of its own destruction. The whole creation, and especially man, was exactly what God meant it to be. It all reflected the glory of the one who made it.

If all this is true, the question is, why am I such a mess? I think not simply of human sinfulness and human cruelty, but of the fact that each of us is such an emotional mess. We so easily make shipwreck of our lives and turn all our relationships into disaster. Finally, we are subject to decay and death. Every day brings us that much closer to the grave. What we see in ourselves and in our world seems to mock the statement that man is the image of God, that all was very good. Did God lie when he said it was all very good? If man as we see him now is the way God created him to be, we are forced to conclude that God is either malicious or incompetent. Dr. Schaeffer has often quoted the French poet Baudelaire, who looked upon the mess of this world and of the human race and concluded, "If there is a God, he is the devil." Is there any answer to Baudelaire?[1]

We must read on from the account of creation to Genesis 3 and the account of the fall. Adam and Eve, the first human pair, were placed in the Garden of Eden with only one condition upon them. They must not eat of the fruit of the tree of the knowledge of good and evil. If they did, they would die. There was nothing magical about the tree. The issue was obedience or disobedience to God. Adam and Eve, as people made in the image of God, had the ability to make real choices. Would they choose to affirm their position as creatures before God, or would they attempt to assert themselves in rebellion against their creator? Unhappily, they chose to disobey God.

This had four immediate and disastrous consequences. The first was alienation from God. Instead of delighting in His company as they had before, they hid from the Lord God among the trees of the garden. They were afraid of God. It has often been said that religion is a crutch for those who cannot face life. This episode teaches us that the opposite is far more true: atheism is a crutch for those who cannot face God. The second consequence was a loss of integrity. Notice the answer Adam gives when God calls for him: "I was afraid because I was naked, so I hid." This is a half truth at very best. It betrays an entire lack of courage, of honesty, of integrity. Adam, unable to face up to his misdeed, instead compounds it. We continue in so many ways to follow his bad example. The third consequence was a spoiling of relationships. When God created Eve as a partner for Adam, his reaction was one of joy. "This now is bone of my bones and flesh of my flesh." Now he repudiates her and attempts to shift the blame: "The woman you put here with me — she gave me the fruit." Instead of joyful union, there is suspicion and recrimination. The marriage battle has begun. The fourth consequence is a loss of dominion. God decrees that the ground will produce thorns and thistles. Life henceforth will be a struggle, and man will be a loser in his battle to subdue the earth. The final blow will be death itself.

We all find ourselves in precisely the same predicament. We are Adam's heirs. When Adam and Eve turned away from God, they not only brought all this upon themselves, they brought it upon the entire human race. God had indeed created a perfect world. It was their disobedience which brought sin and suffering and, finally, death itself to the human race. This is central to our understanding of evil and suffering, of the dark side of human nature, of why we are all such a mess. It was not originally this way. God did not create us this way. God's creation was good. It did not contain the seeds of its own destruction. God is not responsible for evil. This world, so full of sin and suffering, is not the result of a perverse and wicked God, nor of a weak god who was unsuccessful in his attempt to create. Rather, it became this way as a result of human rebellion against God. It could have been otherwise. There was no inevitability to the events of Genesis 3. Adam was under no compulsion. There was nothing in his nature which made his sin certain. He was a perfect man with complete ability to make a true choice. If he had made a different choice, we would live in a dramatically different world. Thus, the events of Genesis 3, as significant events in a true history, are the essential starting point for our understanding of the goodness of God and our understanding of evil and suffering. What we see now, in ourselves and in the world, is simply the wreckage of what God originally created — marred and twisted and broken by human rebellion. It was not always so, and it need not have happened this way. There has been a fall.

Sometimes we have the feeling we are not what we used to be. In an absolute historic sense this is true. We are abnormal people living in an abnormal world. As we look at man, we still see vestiges of his original glory. people are often wonderful. There is still a real nobility in the human race. Yet there is also so much cruelty, sinfulness, pettiness, emotional and psychological turmoil. We are broken people, moral and spiritual and emotional cripples. We are a shadow of our original selves. The world is polluted, and we are polluted. Sin, suffering, evil, calamity, injustice, will characterize this world until Christ returns. We as Christians are not exempt from this. Our sins are forgiven, we are on our way to heaven, yet now we, too, live in the midst of all the muck. We, too, are broken people in a broken world. This must be continually emphasized because all too often one runs across people who seek to evade it, who act as though becoming a Christian can make one immune to the struggles of this life. Consider some examples.

A while back I heard a young man who was traveling around speaking and singing in churches. He had a chorus which he repeated several times in the course of his message:

You're going to love your new life with the Lord
No more sighs, no more sorrows,
No more worries about tomorrow,
You're going to love your new life with the Lord.

Is this fair? Is this the impression we want to give a new convert? Of
course not. I learned later that what he sang was not even true for him as
he sang it. He and his wife were living in a small camper, traveling
around the country on virtually nothing, and at that time his wife could
not join him at the service because their young daughter was seriously ill
in the camper. Our "new life with the Lord" is not a life devoid of sighs
and sorrows.

One time in the Swiss L'abri we had a student who took very seriously the
popular teaching about giving thanks for all things, even the bad things. In
prayer meeting he would often thank God for all the mistakes he had made
that week, all the people he had hurt, all the sins he had committed. This
drove many of us to really think through what the passage about giving
thanks for all things really meant. His practice came very close to denying or
even sanctifying the evil and suffering in this world. We concluded that the
passage in question is properly expounded by those passages which talk
about giving thanks *in* all things, *i.e.* being thankful people, trusting God
and not giving way to bitterness and resentment even in the midst of difficult
situations. We never in the Bible find an example of someone giving thanks
for something wrong, some calamity, but we certainly find many examples
of those who were able to trust God in the midst of such situations.

I spoke of this once in a sermon, and a woman who was a dwarf came
up afterward and thanked me warmly for the message. She said that she
had always been told that she should be thankful to God that she was a
dwarf. This was the first time anyone had drawn the distinction between
being a thankful dwarf and being thankful for being a dwarf. The distinction is utterly crucial. Without it we are forced to turn a blind eye to the
fallenness of this world and of ourselves, or even to call evil good.

Another example is of the pregnant woman who believed that because
she had prayed over her baby and committed it to God, there is no possibility that the child could be abnormal. Where is there such a promise in
the Bible? Where are God's people granted immunity from the sorrows of
this life? The promise of God is strength in the midst of the battle; joy in
the midst of the sorrows. The promise is that "*when* (not if) you go
through the deep waters, I will be with you."

A final example is that when Dr. Schaeffer was stricken with cancer four
years ago, there were many people who were shaken by it. How could

such a thing happen to him, they wondered. Why would God allow this to befall such a godly man? Others, with the best of intentions, wrote that surely God meant to heal him. If he only had sufficient faith, if he would only claim the power of God, he would be healed. With such an attitude, what becomes of our doctrine of the fall? What about Paul's thorn in the flesh which was not removed though he asked three times? Other times, the attitude is conveyed, if not the words, that if only you were right with God, this would not have happened to you. This is not only theologically wrong in its virtual denial of the fall, but it is also cruel and thoughtless. Often the hard things of life come our way for no other reason than that we live as broken people in a broken world.

We must do justice to what we say we believe concerning the fall. Even as Christians, we live in a fallen world. There is the battle, the struggle, the agony of life. There are no easy answers to sin and suffering. To gloss over this is not only false, it is also unfair and unloving. We misrepresent the nature of this present world and of the Christian life and of the present estate of man. We set ourselves and others up for big disappointments.

Redeemed

We have seen what man was originally as he was created in the image of God. We have seen what he became when Adam and Eve brought sin, corruption, and suffering to the whole race through their disobedience. That original image was severely marred and defaced. Though we still bear the image of God, we are deeply scarred by the fall. We will look now at the question of redemption, the hope that the Bible holds out for a solution to our problems. We will see that redemption is essentially the recovery or the restoration of the image of God.

Consider first just the bare theoretical possibility of a solution, a change, a redemption. This depends totally upon the scheme of creation in the image of God and then a fall from that image which we have outlined. If man has always been as we find him now, then there would be no rational hope for a change. If we were to say that sin and corruption belong to the essence of man, that this is the way he has always been, then we would have to conclude that there is no rational hope of removing them short of annihilating man as man. However, if it is true that man has fallen from some original state, then we would have, in theory at least, the possibility of that fall being reversed. If there is now an abnormality, it is reasonable to think of that abnormality being removed. Now redemption would not mean the annihilation of man, but rather quite the opposite, the restoration of man, the recovery of the image of

God. Thus, it is precisely because of the Biblical teaching that man was originally the image of God but now that image has been marred, that redemption is a logical possibility. It is simply his being restored to what he once was.

It is important to see that the Bible presents redemption or salvation in just such terms. The notion of restoration to the image of God permeates the whole concept of redemption. Colossians 1:15 describes Christ as the image of the invisible God. Second Corinthians 4:4 describes Him as the image of God. Hebrews 1:3 describes Him as the exact representation of the being of God. Thus, Christ is what Adam was originally, the exact image of God with full dominion over God's creaton. In Him the image is not defaced, as it is in us, but rather, He is the express image of God. The being of God is accurately and fully represented in Christ. Jesus, of course, is more. He is not simply the image of God, but God in the flesh. Yet in His humanity, He is described as the image of God. In this sense, He is true humanity, man as man was intended to be. As we think of Jesus' humanity, we must not think of Him as a superman, but rather as a normal man. Jesus is the only normal person who has walked this earth since the fall. The rest of us are marred and broken remains of what we were intended to be.

Scripture further teaches that Christ, as the image of God, becomes the pattern of our restoration. In Romans 8:29 we learn that the goal of the Christian life is for us to be conformed to the likeness of God's Son. Here the same language of image and likeness appears again. Christ is our visible and tangible pattern as we strive to be restored to what we were created to be, namely the image of God. Redemption does not mean the annihilation of our natures, but rather the recovery of our true natures. The same thing is stated in 2 Corinthians 3:18. "we . . . are being transformed into his likeness with ever-increasing glory." (NIV) Salvation is a transformation into the likeness of Christ, who is in turn the exact likeness of God. We are further told in this passage that this is not a humanistic thing. Rather, it comes from the Lord, who is the Spirit.

The completion of 2 Corinthians 3:18 is found in 1 John 3:2. In 2 Corinthians we were told that, as we contemplate or behold the Lord's glory, *i.e.* the glory of God as revealed in Christ, we are gradually transformed into his likeness. In 1 John, that is brought to sudden completion. When we see Him face to face at His second coming, we shall be fully like Him. The transformation is brought to sudden perfection. First Corinthians 15:49 rounds out this picture. We have born the likeness of the earthly man, *i.e.* we are Adam's heirs and find ourselves in his predicament. The corruption he brought upon himself he passed on to us, his children. In our marred and broken state we bear the image of Adam far more than the original image of God. Yet, "we shall bear the likeness of the man from heaven." Christ is the second Adam, not a superman, but rather man as man was intended to be. God's purpose for us is that we shall bear that image. Again, salvation is basically the recovery of the image of God.

This has important implications for our view of ourselves as Christians and our view of the Christian life. We are seeking to recover the image of God. That means becoming normal people again. Our humanity is not to be smashed, but to be affirmed and renewed. Salvation has nothing to do with transcending normal human experience; rather, it is the recovery of normal human experience. Dr. Hans Rookmaaker used to say that Christ did not come to make us Christians, He came to make us human beings.

This is the key to our approach to the Christian life. It releases us from a view of spirituality in which the "spiritual" is exalted as something high, transcendent, apart from the normal, out of the ordinary, a spirituality separate from daily human experience. This "superspirituality" has many facets. What underlies them all is the derogatory term, "merely human," either said or implied. Often the mind is rejected as unspiritual. Normal life is despised as being low, unspiritual. The things of the intellect, the will, the emotions, are "merely human." They must be put aside in the interests of the "truly spiritual." The spiritual cannot break through while the human stands in the way. The quest for this sort of spirituality often involves a dependence on feelings and a thirsting for experiences, a reliance on various spiritual techniques to bring us near to God. I feel that many people have experienced a lot of frustration in trying to attain this sort of elusive, ill-defined, transcendent "spirituality."

Once we see that salvation is basically the recovery of the image of God, we are released from this futile quest for a super-spirituality and brought into something more human, more sane, more practically attainable, and ultimately more truly spiritual. Because spirituality is the recovery of the image of God, the affirmation of the human, it is an affirmation of every realm of human endeavor for which God has created us. It has something to do with my attitudes, my behavior, and my thought life. This sort of spirituality has a place for the arts, for culture, for creativity, because these were the things for which we were created in the first place. There is a place for the mind, the intellect, the rational because that is an aspect of the image of God. there is a place for human emotion, both the joys and the sorrows. There is a place for human choice and human effort. These are not impediments to spirituality; rather, they are the stuff of spirituality. There is a place for the family, for marriage, for children, for work, for the material world.

All those things which Adam and Eve were meant to enjoy are suddenly a part of the Christian life, of true spirituality. Our job is not being religious; our job is being human. All of life is religious; all of life is spiritual. All those areas in which we as image bearers of God and vice regents over His creation were meant to develop are suddenly areas of spirituality. As Christians we are to recover the image of God, to affirm our humanity, to pursue all the areas of truly human endeavor, and to pursue them in the power of the spirit and to the glory of God. Redemption, salvation, spirituality is as ordinary as this, and it is nothing less than this.

Who is man? He is the image bearer of God, knocked from that noble estate by the fall, and now, in Christ, seeking to recover his true humanity.

DISCUSSION QUESTIONS

1. In understanding man, why is it important to start at creation?

2. How does Eastern religion undermine true humanity?

3. How has the value of man been modified by the materialistic view prevalent in the West.

4. How are men and women equal? Have they been assigned the same or different tasks?

5. How does being made in God's image affect how we are to live?

6. How has the fall affected man (who we are and what we are to do)?

7. Are we to be thankful to the Lord *for* all things or *in* all things?

8. Our typical ideas about salvation are narrower than Barry's picture. What implications does this fuller picture carry for doing the work of God in the world?

9. How does being human relate to being spiritual?

10. What is a proper response to the hurtful elements of the world: cancer, dictators, dishonesty, wars, hunger?

11. Have you sought a sense of worth using the mindset of fallen creation (money, job, community prestige) or from within the truth of creation — redemption (child of God, steward of creation)? Explain.

"It is our attitudes and behavior which are of
greatest interest to God, not our feelings
and experiences."

Spirituality?
Barry Seagren

What Should We Expect?

All too often, certain attitudes in our culture have infected our views of spirituality. This has led to much frustration. People feel they are not growing as Christians, when often it is their expectations which are wrong. They feel they are not "spiritual" when in actuality they have a distorted concept of what spirituality is. Their concept has been influenced by the world. The main problem is the thirst for experiences. We live in a day when the mind is distrusted and one's feelings are seen as the "real" self. Be spontaneous, we are told. Act authentically. Do what feels right. Be true to your feelings. This comes out in Christian circles as the obsession with feeling the presence of God, feeling the leading of the Spirit, having a distinctly experiential relationship with God, experiencing the fullness of the Spirit. We must say at once that these things are indeed good, and we all wish we had a deeper experience of them. We certainly do not advocate a Christianity which is only cerebral, a dead orthodoxy. Yet, when these things are sought in and for themselves, it can lead to a spiritual hedonism, an attitude and mentality which is all too close to the secular reliance on feelings and quest for experiences.

The emphasis of the scripture is elsewhere, namely on Christian character. Spirituality is basically the recovery of the image of God, the recovery of our true humanity. It is our attitudes and behavior which are of greatest interest to God, not our feelings and experiences. Attitudes and behavior are the basic "stuff" of spirituality. The basic attitude we seek is one of trust; the basic behavior is one of obedience. The old gospel tune is right — "Trust and obey, for there's no other way." Those words may have been expounded superficially and trivialized, but in basic emphasis they are right. Attitudes and behavior: trust and obedience. This is spirituality. An emphasis on these things will free us from the frustrating quest for some elusive experience and will allow us to turn our attention to something we can profitably grapple with, something we can get our teeth into.

Let us elaborate on these two points. First of all, trust is simply a synonym for faith. For our day, *trust* is a far better word than the somewhat nebulous term *faith*. Faith is not simply assenting that certain things are true. Rather, it is putting my weight down upon them, specifically putting my weight down upon Jesus Christ, trusting in Him, relying upon Him. With great irony James says, "You believe that there is one God. Good! Even the demons believe that — and shudder." (James 2:19, NIV) His point is that faith is not just assent to certain propositions. It involves a further issue: what are you going to *do* about it? Will you begin to trust in Christ for your salvation, to rely upon Him, to put your confidence in Him alone? This is not just for salvation. We are to be people of faith in the whole of our lives, people who trust God in all the things of life. The Old Testament makes the same point. In the Psalms, again and again where we might expect to find the word *faith*, we find the word *trust*. God's people are supremely those who trust Him, not those who sense or experience Him. "O Lord of hosts, blessed is the man who trusts in thee (Psalm 84:12, RSV).

In James 2, where James discusses the relationship between faith and deeds, he gives two examples of those whose faith was a living and practical trust and not just a bare assent, Rahab and Abraham. Female and male, Gentile and Jew, sinner and saint, their common bond was that they stepped out in reliance upon the God whom they said was there. Rahab cut herself off from her own people and jeopardized her life by harboring the spies. Abraham demonstrated trust to the utmost, setting out to sacrifice his own son, being convinced that God was able, somehow, to fulfill his promise. These were definite times of stepping out in reliance upon God. They were courageous and venturesome acts which put into practice their trust in the God of Israel. They were things which from a worldly point of view were absolutely foolhardy. This raises the question of practical faith, living trust for each of us. Where are the moments of stepping out, of venturing forth, of putting our weight down on that which we say we believe? Perhaps these are not everyday matters. Certainly harboring spies and sacrificing sons were not everyday affairs for Rahab and Abraham. Nevertheless, the question requires an answer. What do we do that we would not do if we did not believe?

Obedience is the other aspect of spirituality. We are to be increasingly conformed to the image of God. Our character is to reflect His character. This is the way we were created. The fall has meant that we are all bent in the wrong way. Misbehavior comes naturally to us now, whereas good behavior requires great effort; it goes against the grain of our fallen natures. Yet it is precisely this which is a very important aspect of spirituality. Often we do not like to hear this. Behavior and obedience is dreary stuff indeed. We would much rather seek a spirituality which is more "spiritual" in the modern sense of the term. Yet the dreary topic of obedience, or the cultivation of Christian character, is precisely where the Bible puts its emphasis. Galatians 5:22-23 has always been an important passage to me. It tells us that "what the Spirit longs to produce in us is not experiences, not gifts, but character, behavior, obedience, conformity to the image of God." The fruits of the Spirit are precisely the aspects of Christian character. Second Peter 1:5-7 gives the same emphasis. How do we fill out our initial saving faith? With the various facets of Christian character — goodness, knowledge, self-control, perseverance, godliness, brotherly kindness, love.

Ephesians 4:22-24 gives the same message and begins to get into the "how" as well. We are to turn away from our misbehavior, to have our minds, that is our thinking and our attitudes, renewed and thereby to grow in righteousness and holiness. Colossians 3:5-10 puts it even more strongly. We are to put to death that which is wrong, i.e. to reject it in an uncompromising way. This is what Jesus means when He says, "If your eye offend you, pluck it out." He did not mean that the eye is the source of sin, but rather that we should take whatever measures are necessary to squeeze sin from our lives and to conform our behavior to the law and character of God. Perhaps a couple of illustrations will clarify. We would all like to adopt what I call the "pressure cooker theory of human nature." That is, we need to sin a bit once in a while, just as a pressure cooker needs to blow off steam occasionally. That relieves the pressure. It is downright unhealthy to be so totally uncompromising; we must not be fanatics. Unless we loosen up and blow off a bit of steam now and then, we are in danger of blowing up. That is what we would all like to believe, and what many of us practice. The Bible would give us a different view of human nature, what I call the "mice in the walls" model. I am sure we have all slept in an old house that had mice living in the walls, racing around all night long, making it very difficult to sleep. That is a far better model of the remnants of sin in human nature. It would be the height of foolishness to think that if we only give the mice a bit of food, indulge them a bit, they will be satisfied and leave us in peace. No, indeed. The only way forward is to be as uncompromising, as ruthless as possible, to starve them out, and the quicker, the better. So it is with the remnants of sin in our natures. To many this is again dreary stuff. It is written off with such derogatory terms as "repressive," "puritan," "legalistic." Yet, Biblically, we are called to conformity to the character of God, a scrupulous obedience, an uncompromising rejection of sin. This is the stuff of spirituality.

How Shall We Achieve It?

Again, attitudes and mentalities prevalent in our culture have seeped into our approach to the Christian life and have deeply influenced our answers to this question. One problem is the "instant everything" approach. We have fast foods, miracle diets, instant photo processing, easy credit, etcetera. This creeps into Christianity in the hope that one day we will be struck by lightening and from that time forward we will live on a different plane; we will suddenly be "spiritual." I feel that many are attracted to the charismatic movement feeling that this hope is held out in the "Baptism of the Spirit." I would hasten to add that most charismatic people would disavow this, stressing that the baptism by no means confers an instant spirituality. Whether part of the charismatic movement or not, most of us must acknowledge that we secretly harbor this hope. We find the Christian life hard going; trust and obedience are tedious disciplines. We wish we could just wake up one morning and suddenly find ourselves "spiritual." The Bible holds out no such hope; we have been seduced by our culture. The other way in which our culture seeps into our approach to the Christian life is in its emphasis on techniques. The bookstores are full of how-to-do-it manuals on everything from sex to career direction to car repair. The Christian bookstores are full of the same sort of thing — how to find your spiritual gift, how to pray, how to find the will of God, how to have a Christian home. We certainly do not want to reject an emphasis on practicality. Nevertheless, being a Christian is an individual and personal thing, not a mechanical one. Hence, it cannot be reduced to three easy steps. The Bible never gives us such things. The Bible gives us a framework of truth followed by exhortation to put that truth into action.

The statement which best summarizes the "how" of spirituality is in Romans 8:13. "If by the Spirit you put to death the misdeeds of the body, you will live." (NIV) What, then is the way of life? This statement gives us three important elements.

The first is that there is a "deeds of the body" which needs to be put to death. The problem is not external circumstances; the problem lies deep within us. Out of context, this statement could be taken to mean that the problem lies in the fact that we are physical beings, and therefore anything bodily or physical must be suppressed as a hindrance to spirituality. This motif may have been present in Greek thought, but it is certainly not Biblical. The Bible, supremely in its teaching on the resurrection, affirms the value of the physical world. Paul's statement in Romans is clarified by his statement in Colossians 3:5, where again we are told what is to be put to death. This time it is our earthly nature, which is said to include greed, certainly not a physical function. It is further elaborated in Galatians 5:19-21, a list of sins most of which could be committed by a disembodied spirit. This time the problem is rooted in our "flesh" or "sinful nature." The point is that we are corrupt within, even after our conversion. This corruption must be ruthlessly strangled and not allowed to gain control and dictate our lives. Real life, that is our growth in trust and obedience, is dependent upon putting the "flesh" to death. How shall we do it? The remainder of the statement gives us a tremendously balanced picture of the "how."

Is it by simply gritting our teeth and getting on with the job? Is the Christian life a will-dominated life in which the responsibility for growth lies fully and squarely in our laps? No, it is not. It is "by the *Spirit*" that we are to grow. It is this emphasis which keeps the Christian life from being just one more moralism or legalism. But what does "by the Spirit" mean? This is one of those things which is hard to get our hands on. Many have taken the phrase in a strongly mystical sense. There is certainly a mysticism to it in the sense that we cannot fully put it into words. Yet it is not mystical in the sense of being separated from anything that can be considered by the mind, anything content-ful. Perhaps it is explained best in Romans 8:5, where living by the Spirit is related to setting the mind on what the Spirit desires. We get the same emphasis by comparing Ephesians 5:18-20 with Colossians 3:16, 17. Ephesians and Colossians are parallel letters, probably written at the same time, and certainly these two passages are parallel. The point to notice is that, in the Colossians passage, the statement "be filled with the Spirit" is rendered "let the Word of God dwell in you richly." Again, the two concepts are strongly related. Living by the Spirit is not an empty mysticism, but is strongly related to filling the mind with the Word of God. Word and Spirit go hand in hand. Thus, we are led again to the primary role of the scripture. (See also Psalm 119:9 and John 17:17.) Living by the Spirit and living in the Word may be distinguishable, but they cannot be separated. They go together. The Word of God has a threefold function in our lives. First, it is a source of information, teaching, doctrine. Second, it is a means of communication with God, a means of guidance, encouragement, challenge, and rebuke. Third, and this is something most do not think of, it is an instrument of shaping or reshaping my mentality, my outlook on life. My mind is to be renewed and brought into ever closer correspondence with the mind of God through exposure to the scriptures. Thus the Christian life is not just moralism, a process of pulling up my socks and getting my act together. It is something that takes place "by the Spirit," and the work of the Spirit is closely related to the role of the written word.

On the other hand, is the Christian life a largely passive affair? Are trust and obedience produced only as I stand aside and let the Spirit get to work? One is often given this impression. The sooner I get out of the way, the sooner the Spirit can get on with the job. My thoughts, my actions, my feelings, my choices are "merely human;" they are an impediment to the "truly spiritual." This is the opposite extreme, and the Bible repudiates this just as strongly. Paul emphasizes that "YOU put to death . . ." This is the third crucial element in Romans 8:13. This call to action, to effort, is echoed throughout the Bible. In 2 Peter 1:5 we are admonished to "make every effort" to finish our faith. In Philippians 3:12-14 Paul speaks of "pressing on." In 1 Corinthians 9:24-27 he speaks of the Christian life as a race for which he trains and fights. In 1 Timothy 6:11-12 Timothy is told to "flee," "pursue," "fight," "take hold." This is the opposite of passivity, the opposite of a "let go and let God" mentality. Sanctification is my responsibility. It will not happen apart from my effort. We are human beings made in the image of God, and our choices and our actions count. Spirituality is not a process whereby I disappear and God becomes everything. No, spirituality is a recovery of the image of God, a recovery of my true humanity, a recovery of my individual identity as a significant person living before God. In the how of spirituality there is a strong "you do it." Trust and obedience will not come apart from my effort to trust God and my effort to conform my life to His standards.

Thus, as we consider spirituality, we are not promised instant success, nor are we given a blueprint. We are unique individuals who must struggle to grow in trust and obedience. Yet this passage, as much as any of the Bible, points us in the right direction, gives us the right mentality. There is a sinful nature which neither trusts nor obeys God and must be subdued. It is not just a matter of activity. Sanctification is a work of God. On the other hand, it is not just a matter of passivity. Sanctification is my responsibility. It is God's power and my effort simultaneously. *"By the Spirit you put to death the misdeeds of the body."*

DISCUSSION QUESTIONS

1. How do expectations affect our view of spirituality?

2. Can you summarize the goal of true spirituality? What difference does this make?

3. What does it mean to trust God? How does this affect our everyday life?

4. As we obey God more, what qualities should we expect to find emerging in our lives? Are these distinguishable for any spiritually mature person?

5. How does the "mice in the walls" theory lead us to a more active battle against sin?

6. How have Christians allowed themselves to be baptized in the "instant everything" way of living? How does this attitude affect us?

7. Is there a difference between living in the Spirit and living in the Word? Can we have one without the other?

8. Different periods of life involve us in different struggles to attain mastery over sin. Identify your struggle at this point in life. Where have you come from? What progress can you witness to?

9. What resources have you found most helpful in your spiritual growth? How can you be a resource in some way for others?

Notes

Jerram Barrs

Christianity True to the Way Things Are
[1] David Hume, *A Treatise of Human Nature*, ed. L. A. Selby-Bigge (Oxford: Clarendon Press, 1896), pp. 183-187.
[2] ibid.
[3] Bertrand Russell, *Why I Am Not A Christian* (New York: Simon and Schuster, 1957).
[4] See Perry London, *Modes and Morals of Psychotherapy* (New York: Holt, 1964), p. 169ff.
[5] D. Aikman, "Cambodia: An Experiment in Genocide," *TIME*, July 31, 1978, pp. 39-40.
[6] Bertrand Russell, *Why I Am Not A Christian.*

The Christian and Society
[1] See Jonathon King, *Waltzing Materialism* (New York: Harper & Row, 1978), p. 30.
[2] ibid., p. 20.
[3] Aleksander I. Solzhenitzyn, *A World Split Apart* (New York: Harper & Row, 1979), p. 17.
[4] ibid., p. 19, 21.
[5] ibid., p. 49.
[6] ibid., p. 49, 51.
[7] See Francis Schaeffer, *A Christian Manifesto* (Westchester, IL.: Crossway Books, 1981).

A Biblical Ethic
[1] Aleksander Solzhenitzyn, *A World Split Apart* (New York: Harper & Row, 1979), p. 47, 49.
[2] See John Cotton, Abstract of the Laws of New England, *Journal of Christian Reconciliation*, Vol. 5, Winter, 1978-79 (Durham, NC: Chalcedon, 1979).
[3] See Truman Capote, *In Cold Blood* (New York: Random House, 1966).

The Christian Mind
[1] See Jonathon King, *Waltzing Materialism* (New York: Harper & Row, 1978), p. 30.
[2] J. Gresham Machen, *Christian Faith in the Modern World* (London: Hodder and Stoughton, 1936), p. 70.

Male/Female Relationships
[1] Paul Jewett, *Man is Male and Female* (Grand Rapids: Eerdmans, 1975).

Dick Keyes

Image and Reality — Part One
1 Daniel Boorstin, *The Image* (New York: Atheneum, 1961).
2 Ben Stein, "Norman Lear vs. Moral Majority: The War to Clean Up TV," *Saturday Review*, Feb., 1981, p. 26.
3 Daniel Boorstin, *The Image*, pp. 15-16.
4 Erving Goffman, *The Presentation of Self in Everyday Life* (Garden City: Doubleday Anchor, 1959), pp. 4-5 cites William Sanson's novel, *A Contest of Ladies* (London: Hogarth, 1956), pp. 230-232.
5 ibid.
6 Jacqueline Thompson, *Image Impact* (New York: Ace Books, 1982).
7 E. Graydon Carter, "Reagan Assassination Attempt: A Story Made for TV," *TIME*, April 13, 1981, p. 108.
8 William A. Henry, III, "El Salvador: War as a Media Event," *TIME*, March 29, 1982, p. 74.
9 Steve Turner, "Exclusive Pictures," *Nice and Nasty* (London: Razor Books/Marshall, Morgan and Scott, LTD. 1980).
10 Lewis Lapham, "Gilding the News," *Harpers*, July, 1981, p. 39.
11 Jane Maas and Kenneth Roman, *How To Advertise* (New York: St. Martin's, 1976).
12 "Modeling the 80's Look," *TIME*, Feb. 9, 1981, p. 82.
13 William A. Henry, III, "A Free GOP Commercial," *Boston Globe*, July, 1980.
14 Clyde Haberman, "Convention Replay: When TV Runs Hot, Politics Boil Over," *New York Times*, July 20, 1980.
15 Daniel Boorstin, *The Image*, p. 46.

Image and Reality — Part Two
1 See Daniel Boorstin, *The Image* (New York: Atheneum, 1961), p. 46.
2 Ernest Becker, *Escape from Evil* (New York: Freepress, 1975), p. 164.
3 Kenneth Briggs, "Methodist in Search of a Coherent Identity, Acknowledge Crisis," *New York Times*, April 27, 1980.
4 Virginia Owens, *The Total Image* (Grand Rapids: Eerdman's, 1980), pp. 27-28.
5 ibid., pp. 28-29.
6 Steve Turner, "Creed," *Nice and Nasty* (London: Razor Books/Marshall, Morgan and Scott, LTD, 1980), p. 90.
7 Daniel Boorstin, *The Image*, p. 186.

The Meaning of Shame and Guilt
1 Jean-Paul Sarte, *Being and Nothingness* (New York: Citadel Press, 1964).

Ranald Macaulay

The Christian Mind
[1] Harry Blamires, *The Christian Mind* (Ann Arbor, MI: Servant, 1978), p. 3.
[2] Charles Malik, *The Two Tasks* (Westchester, IL.: Crossway, 1980), p. 33.
[3] See John Calvin, *Commentary on Genesis*, Vol. I (Edinborough: Calvin Translator's Society, 1844-1859).
[4] Richard Lovelace, *Dynamics of Spiritual Life* (Downers Grove, IL.: Inter-Varsity Press, 1980), preface, p. 19.
[5] Charles Malik, *The Two Tasks*.

Grace and Law
[1] Watchman Nee, *The Normal Christian Life* (Wheaton, IL.: Tyndale House, 1961), p. 154.

Being Human: The Nature of Spiritual Experience
[1] Gerald Cragg, *The Church and the Age of Reason* (New York: Penguin, 1961), p. 162.

Wim Rietkerk

Reality of God, Part One
Is God A Projection?
[1] Dave Millikan, *Sunburnt Soul* (Australia: Anzea, 1981), p. 82.
[2] Francis Schaeffer, *He Is There and He Is Not Silent* (Wheaton, IL.: Tyndale House, 1972), p. 37.
[3] See John Wisdom, *Logic and Language*, ed., A. G. Flew (Oxford: Blackwell, 1973), p. 192-193.
[4] Ludwig Feuerbach, *The Essence of Christianity* (New York: Harper & Row, 1957).
[5] ibid.
[6] ibid.
[7] ibid.
[8] ibid.
[9] See Sigmund Freud, *The Future of an Illusion*, ed., J. Strachey (New York: Norton, 1975).
[10] See Dr. Hans Rookmaaker, *Modern Art and Death of a Culture* (Downers Grove, IL.: Inter-Varsity Press, 1970).
[11] C. S. Lewis, "The Silver Chair," *Chronicles of Narnia*, Book 4 (New York: Macmillan, 1953).
[12] Ludwig Feuerbach, *The Essence of Christianity*.

[13] Francis Schaeffer, *The God Who Is There* (Downers Grove, IL.: Inter-Varsity Press, 1968).

Reality of God, Part Two:
Is Christianity An Ideology?
[1] Bertholt Brecht, *Kalendar-Geschicten* (Berlin: Gebruder Weiss, 1949), p. 128.
[2] See Norman Vincent Peale, *The Power of Positive Thinking* (New York: Prentice Hall, 1953).
[3] See Ernst von Topitz, *Ideology*, ed., Lanzan Meller (Germany, 1972), p. 53.
[4] Ludwig Feuerbach, *The Essence of Christianity* (New York: Harper & Row, 1957).
[5] Collected Works of Marx and Engle (New York: International, 1975).
[6] ibid.
[7] Abraham Kuyper, *Calvinism: Six Stone Lectures* (New York: F. H. Revell, 1899).

Reality of God, Part Three:
Is Christianity A Religion
[1] G. E. Lessing, *Nathan the Wise* (New York: Fredrick Unger, 1955), Vol. 1, p. 553.
[2] See Rudolf Otto, *Ideas of the Holy*, John W. Harvey, tr. (New York: Oxford Univ. Press, 1958).
[3] See Friedrich Schleiermacher, *The Christian Faith*, ed., H. R. Mackintosh and J. S. Stewart (Philadelphia: Fortress, 1977).
[4] See Dr. Friso Melzer, "Offensive," *Journals*, No. 4, 1979.
[5] See Tertullian, *Apologetics*.

The Culture of Narcissism
[1] Christopher Lasch, *The Culture of Narcissism: American Life in an Age of Diminishing Expectations* (New York: Norton, 1979), p. 14.
[2] ibid., p. 3.
[3] Richard Holloway, *Beyond Belief: The Christian Encounter with God* (Grand Rapids, MI: Eerdman's, 1981), p. 3.
[4] See Jerram Barrs and Ranald Macaulay, *Being Human* (Downers Grove, IL.: Inter-Varsity Press, 1978).
[5] See Pascal's *Pensees*, A. J. Krailsheimer, tr. (New York: Penguin, 1966), p. 270.
[6] ibid.

Francis Schaeffer

The Abolition of Truth and Morality

1 *Humanist Manifesto I* and *II* (New York: Prometheus Books, 1973).
2 This must not be confused with the humanistic elements which were developing slightly earlier in the Renaissance. Francis A. Schaeffer, *How Should We Then Live?* (Old Tappar, NJ: Fleming H. Revell Co., 1976), pp. 58-79.
3 See *How Should We Then Live?*, pp. 40 and 109.
4 See Will and Ariel Durant's book, *The Lessons of History* (New York: Simon and Schuster, 1968), pp. 84-86.
5 American Law Review, XIV, 1880, p. 233.
6 Harvard Law Review, XL, 1918.
7 Henry DeBracton, Translation of *De Legibus et Consuetudinibus* (Cambridge, Mass.: Harvard-Belknap, 1968).
8 See James L. Fisk, *The Law and Its Timeless Standard* (Washington: Lex Rex Institute).
9 See Will and Ariel Durant's *The Lessons of History*, pp. 70-75.

Barry Seagren

Who Is Man?

1 See Francis Schaeffer, *He Is There and He Is Not Silent* (Wheaton, IL.: Tyndale House, 1972), p. 27.